The Liberty Index

Mabel

Mabel, Mabel, a sweet full-size donkey. I pictured her wearing a straw hat. I had gone to pick up a llama and Mabel came, too. It took about five men to get her loaded. Her hooves were at least a foot long and curled up. She had a hard time loading because her hooves kept hitting on the bottom of the trailer and she would slip.

She was so scared. We backed down by the barn and closed the gate. It seemed as if Mabel was standing true to the saying "stubborn as a mule." We unloaded the llama, and she was not going to budge. We walked away from the trailer and knew she would get out when she was ready. I put the rest of the horses to bed for the night, and the curiosity got the best of her. She backed out and stood there looking at us. She had the wounds of an old beating on her. The hair hadn't grown back yet.

Well, mabel didn't know what grain was, or kindness. It took us two months to get her to walk into the barn on her own. I feel it was a man who had done the damage to her. When our farmhand would try to walk around her, she would cower and try to sit down. We doped her up to trim her feet and at first she was in a bit of discomfort but soon realized she could run and play. She paired off with our little mini-donkey, Eeyore. Playing and nibbling on each other. The vet came and gave her all of her spring shots. And to our surprise, Mabel is in foal. No, not to Eeyore's, she was too far along. She has been with us for about 6 months and is making progress. We can walk past her and she might stand there. She has the most pathetic cry when Eeyore is out of sight. We are awaiting her little package. Look for pictures posted in the cookbook.

Cakes, Cookies, Pies, Pastries & Candies

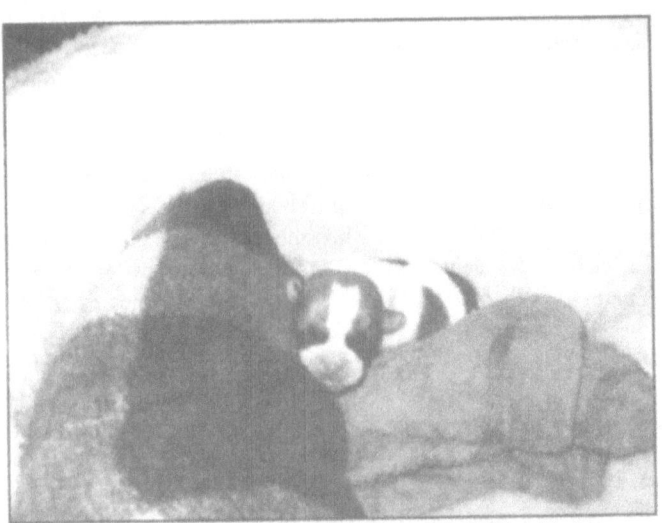

1 day old - Lil Man   fat & sassy   Mama died giving birth

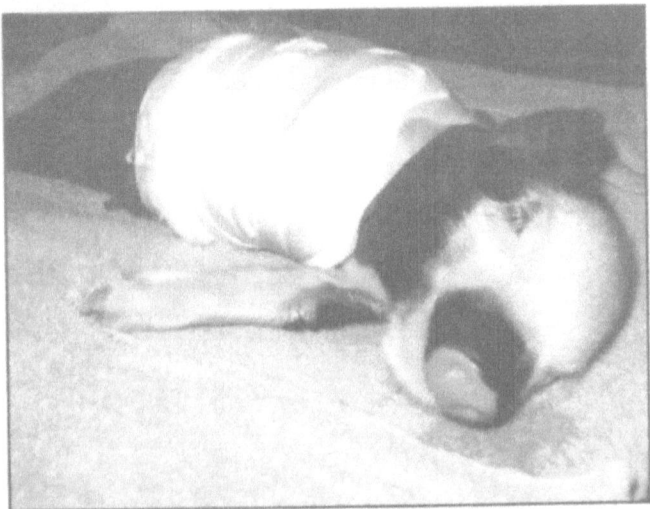

Newborn piglet mangled front leg we saved

About the Book

The author proposes an original idea concerning the «Liberty index». He suggests considering this particular side of «Liberty Index» on the «field» of the spare time of population, where realization of big and small freedoms takes place. He calculates Liberty Index based on the services of education, enlightenment and entertainment taking into account the economic relations: production, distribution, exchange and consumption.

From the Author

Today many people talk about human freedom, but until now we do not have an index which would show which have increases or decreases of people's freedoms.

What «specific material» should we use when carrying out our research on the subject of human freedom?

The freedom of the population is realized in their spare away work time. This situation should somehow be taken into account by the «Liberty Index».

I suggest we include segments of the spare time of millions of people, assimilated by «enlightenment services», «entertainment services» and «educational services» in the Liberty Index.

Every day we are involved in the services of enlightenment, entertainment, education. This circumstance should be taken into account in the «Liberty Index». This index can be represented in a three dimensional space.

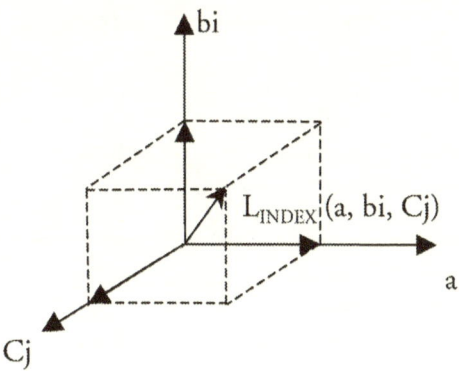

where

a—the vector of education services;

bi—the vector of enlightenment services;

Cj—the vector of entertainment services.

$$\text{Liberty}_{\text{INDEX}} = a + bi = Cj$$

I suggest we examine the services of education, enlightenment or entertainment taking into accounting the following four views of economic relations:

- production—p
- distribution—d
- exchange—e
- consumption—c

Production process	Distribution process	Exchange process	Consumption process
Economic estimates of education services—p_1	Economic estimates of education services—d_1	Economic estimates of education services—e_1	Economic estimates of education services—c_1
Economic estimates of enlightenment services—p_2	Economic estimates of enlightenment services—d_2	Economic estimates of enlightenment services—e_2	Economic estimates of enlightenment services—c_2
Economic estimates of entertainment services—p_3	Economic estimates of entertainment services—d_3	Economic estimates of entertainment services—e_3	Economic estimates of entertainment services—c_3

In the «Liberty Index» there should be a refraction of lives of the population, of one million, two million … ten million people in their spare time, away from work. Such an index would be general.

CHAPTER 1

The Three Dimensional Economic Estimates

The conceptions of a significant part of the population about the economic results of the intellectual sphere are formed on the basis of the publications of magazines («Forbes», «Times» etc.)

Everyone knows that the fortunes of Hollywood movie stars are estimated at hundreds of millions of dollars.

In this connection, the ordinary reader would ask—if movie stars earn such huge amounts of money what remains for those who are on the other side of the screen?

An analysis of economic literature shows that indicators—«the number of visitors», «the number of spectators», and «the number of listeners»—have not changed since the emergence and formation of the intellectual sphere.

Living in the 21st century, we should find out why in the intellectual sphere they use old showings which do not represent the economic results of the activity of its branches.

The first reason is that while calculating the results the intellectual sphere of economic estimations are added up to statistic showings—«the number of visitors».

It is impossible to put together these values because they are of a qualitatively different nature.

The aforementioned circumstance does not allow us to carry out a precise calculation of the results of the intellectual sphere.

The second reason is that they are placed simultaneously on the same axis of numbers:

- the cost of intellectual values (books, pictures, newspapers and magazines) vector «a»—and expenses connected with the creation of intellectual services—vector «b». At such consideration vectors—a and b—are partially overlapped (see graph).

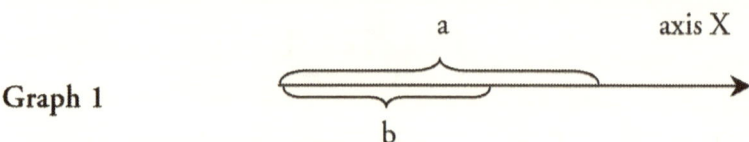

Graph 1

The said overlapping does not make it possible to work out a «family» of special economic estimations, criteria and indicators of the utilization of the resources of the intellectual sphere.

There is a way out of this situation. Intellectual values and intellectual services should be considered in a three dimensional space.

I suggest that we consider a solitary product of the labor of the intellectual sphere in a three-dimensional space. On axis «X» we should set intellectual values, on axis «Y»—expenses connected with the creation of intellectual services and on axis «Z»—a resource of the spare time of the population assimilated by intellectual services.

A graphic interpretation of a solitary product of the intellectual sphere would look like this:

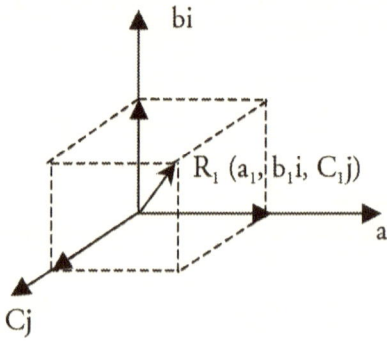

where

> a—cost estimation of intellectual values (in material form);
>
> bi—expenses connected with the creation of intellectual the services;
>
> Cj—cost estimation of a resource of the spare time of the population involved in the creation process of intellectual services.

If we proceed from the notion that the human resource during the spare time is an economic resource, it should be estimated. Then everything takes its proper place. The total vector R reveals the cost of an aggregate intellectual product:

$$R = a + bi + Cj$$

The position of vector R is changing, depending on the values of the vectors a, b and C.

If a film was both successful and profitable, the component Cj becomes longer, so does the vector R.

Actually, it is not a simple as it seems. The estimations on each of the axes are not frozen. They are not fixed. Everything is subject to changes. All these transformations influence the vector R. Sometimes it becomes longer, other times shorter.

The reader should not «be afraid» of the indicators—i and j. They are only used to show the fact that material intellectual values are set on the «X» axis, on «Y» axis expenses connected to intellectual services are set. The spare time of the population as a specific, economic resource is set on the third axis «Z».

Everything that happens on axes «X», «Y» and «Z» is easily conceived in a three-dimensional space. Judge for yourself: if there is no stream of visitors in museums, libraries, cinemas etc, then, of course, vector Cj will be absent—the vector which shows the cost estimation of the resource of the spare time of the population involved in the creation process of intellectual services. In this case we move from a three-dimensional space to a two-dimensional one:

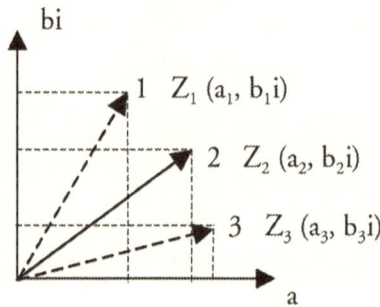

where

a—the cost estimation of intellectual values (in material form);

bi—the expenses connected to creation of intellectual service.

The examination of the aggregate intellectual sphere in a two-dimensional space is the case when «visitors», «cinema viewers» are absent in the general stream of resources.

What is the situation that came to be in the domain of the spare time of the population?

How should we use the spare time of the population?

I suggest we examine the problem of the spare time of the population taking into account the services of education, enlightenment and entertainment.

Mistakes in the Estimations of the Movement of the Services of Education, Enligntenment and Entertainment in Economic Space

In the branches of «education» there are the following streams of resources:

1) a stream of resources as means of labor—books, computers etc.—the stream estimated economically;

2) a stream of manpower—workers in the branches of «Education»—the stream estimated economically;

3) a stream of financial resources;

4) a stream of visitors is not considered an economic resource and is not estimated economically.

If old estimations in which some resources not taken into account are used, conclusions will be within the frames of these ideas. It is obvious.

In the branches of «enlightenment» there are the following streams of resources:

1) a stream of resources as means of labor and tools—work of art etc.—the stream estimated economically;

2) a stream of manpower—workers in the branches of «enlightenment»—the stream estimated economically;

3) a stream of financial resources;

4) a stream of visitors is not considered an economic resource and is not estimated economically.

The same situation happens in the «entertainment» branches. Here we have the following streams of resources:

1) a stream of resources as means of labor and tools—«entertainment»—the stream estimated economically;

2) a stream of manpower—workers in the branches of «entertainment»—the stream estimated economically;

3) a stream of financial resources;

4) a stream of visitors is not considered an economic resource and is not estimated economically.

It happened so in the economic theory that the «visitors» of museums, libraries and cinemas, television viewers, and radio listeners are considered as a statistic component of the general stream of resources.

Such kind of position in the theory leads to a deadlock.

We have to add up qualitatively different values.

$$\left| \begin{array}{c} \text{Cost estimation} \\ \text{of conventional} \\ \text{resources} \end{array} \right| + \left| \begin{array}{c} \text{Statistic index of the} \\ \text{«number of visitors» and} \\ \text{«number of listeners»} \end{array} \right| = \quad ?$$

It is impossible to carry out arithmetic operations with these components.

A stream of visitors is a special human resource, which acts as an «object of labor» in the intellectual sphere. And as an object of labor it should be estimated and included in the cost of intellectual services. If we economically estimate the stream of visitors of the intellectual sphere, it will allow us to combine conventional resources with unconventional ones. In fact, why not?

Intellectual services assimilate the human resource in spare time.

The assimilated part of the spare time of population should not be excluded while calculating the value of intellectual services.

The reader might think that we are somehow very far from the economic problems of the intellectual sphere of USA, Europe, Japan, China and India. On the contrary, we are more than close. We are right in the center of the problems of the intellectual sphere.

Without economic estimation of the human resource cost in the spare time of the population (assimilated by intellectual services), we will not be able to balance the accounts.

The number of visitors of the intellectual sphere is very large.

This stream is estimated in hundreds of billions of people. And if we do not economically estimate these multi-billion streams, if we do not take them into account.

Thus we do not do anything illogical: we take into account all the resources, which have «entered» the intellectual sphere.

The «Education», «Enlightenment» and «Entertainment» daily create a vast number of various intellectual services, such as:

- school services;
- college services;
- university services;
- library services;
- exhibition services;
- museum services;
- concert services;
- theatre services;
- circus services;
- Church services;
- cinema services;
- services of sports-entertainment character (attractions, aqua parks, DisneyLands);
- services of entertainment character (summer sports);
- services of entertainment character (winter sports);
- show services of football;
- show services of ice-hockey;

- show services of ball-hockey;
- show services of field hockey;
- show services of basketball;
- show services of volley-ball;
- show services of baseball;
- show services of rugby;
- show services of «Formula—1»;
- Radio services;
- TV services.

In the process of movement, the above services pass through four economic sectors:

Production → Distribution → Exchange → Consumption

At every stage of movement we shall have:
- economic estimates of «production» relations;
- economic estimates of «distribution» relations;
- economic estimates of «exchange» relations;
- economic estimates of «consumption» relations;

Now in these services do not include A_{STP} resource

However, on the way of movement there is a significant number of the problems of economic character:

- in the process of the production (creation) of «Education», «Enlightenment» and «Entertainment» services one of the resources joining them i.e. the stream of visitors A_{STP} is not taken into account;

- in the process of the distribution of «Education», «Enlightenment» and «Entertainment» services one of the resources joining them (i.e. the stream of visitors A_{STP}), is not taken into account;

- in the process of the exchange of «Education», «Enlightenment» and «Entertainment» services one of the resources joining them (i.e. the stream of visitors A_{STP}), is not taken into account;

- in the process of the consumption of «Education», «Enlightenment» and «Entertainment» services, one of the resources joining them (i.e. the stream of visitors A_{STP}), is not taken into account.

Now in these services do not include A_{STP} resource

At every stage of movement we shall have:

- economic estimates connected to the movement within each of these four relations;

	Economic estimates of production		Economic estimates of distribution		Economic estimates of consumption		Economic estimates of exchange
1	Economic estimates of the production of school services without A_{STP}	→	Economic estimates of the distribution of school services without A_{STP}	→	Economic estimates of the consumption of school services without A_{STP}	→	Economic estimates of the exchange of school services without A_{STP}
2	Economic estimates of the production of college services without A_{STP}	→	Economic estimates of the distribution of college services without A_{STP}	→	Economic estimates of the consumption of college services without A_{STP}	→	Economic estimates of the exchange of college services without A_{STP}
3	Economic estimates of the production of university services without A_{STP}	→	Economic estimates of the distribution of university services without A_{STP}	→	Economic estimates of the consumption of university services without A_{STP}	→	Economic estimates of the exchange of university services without A_{STP}
4	Economic estimates of the production of library services without A_{STP}	→	Economic estimates of the distribution of library services without A_{STP}	→	Economic estimates of the consumption of library services without A_{STP}	→	Economic estimates of the exchange of library services without A_{STP}
5	Economic estimates of the production of exhibition services without A_{STP}	→	Economic estimates of the distribution of exhibition services without A_{STP}	→	Economic estimates of the consumption of exhibition services without A_{STP}	→	Economic estimates of the exchange of exhibition services without A_{STP}

Economic estimates of production		Economic estimates of distribution		Economic estimates of consumption		Economic estimates of exchange
6	Economic estimates of the production of museum services without A_{STP}	$\rightarrow$ Economic estimates of the distribution of museum services without A_{STP}	$\rightarrow$	Economic estimates of the consumption of museum services without A_{STP}	$\rightarrow$	Economic estimates of the exchange of museum services without A_{STP}
7	Economic estimates of the production of concert services without A_{STP}	$\rightarrow$ Economic estimates of the distribution of concert services without A_{STP}	$\rightarrow$	Economic estimates of the consumption of concert services without A_{STP}	$\rightarrow$	Economic estimates of the exchange of concert services without A_{STP}
8	Economic estimates of the production of theatre services without A_{STP}	$\rightarrow$ Economic estimates of the distribution of theatre services without A_{STP}	$\rightarrow$	Economic estimates of the consumption of theatre services without A_{STP}	$\rightarrow$	Economic estimates of the exchange of theatre services without A_{STP}
9	Economic estimates of the production of circus services without A_{STP}	$\rightarrow$ Economic estimates of the distribution of circus services without A_{STP}	$\rightarrow$	Economic estimates of the consumption of circus services without A_{STP}	$\rightarrow$	Economic estimates of the exchange of circus services without A_{STP}
10	Economic estimates of the production of church services without A_{STP}	$\rightarrow$ Economic estimates of the distribution of church services without A_{STP}	$\rightarrow$	Economic estimates of the consumption of church services without A_{STP}	$\rightarrow$	Economic estimates of the exchange of church services without A_{STP}
11	Economic estimates of the production of cinema services without A_{STP}	$\rightarrow$ Economic estimates of the distribution of cinema services without A_{STP}	$\rightarrow$	Economic estimates of the consumption of cinema services without A_{STP}	$\rightarrow$	Economic estimates of the exchange of cinema services without A_{STP}

	Economic estimates of production		***Economic estimates of distribution***		***Economic estimates of consumption***		***Economic estimates of exchange***
12	Economic estimates of the production of the services of the sports-entertainment character (attractions, aqua parks, DisneyLands) without A_{STP}	→	Economic estimates of the distribution of the services of the sports-entertainment character (attractions, aqua parks, DisneyLands) without A_{STP}	→	Economic estimates of the consumption of the services of the sports-entertainment character (attractions, aqua parks, DisneyLands) without A_{STP}	→	Economic estimates of the exchange of the services of the sports-entertainment character (attractions, aqua parks, DisneyLands) without A_{STP}
13	Economic estimates of the production of the services of the entertainment character (summer sports) without A_{STP}	→	Economic estimates of the distribution of the services of the entertainment character (summer sports) without A_{STP}	→	Economic estimates of the consumption of the services of the entertainment character (summer sports) without A_{STP}	→	Economic estimates of the exchange of the services of the entertainment character (summer sports) without A_{STP}
14	Economic estimates of the production of the services of the entertainment character (winter sports) without A_{STP}	→	Economic estimates of the distribution of the services of the entertainment character (winter sports) without A_{STP}	→	Economic estimates of the consumption of the services of the entertainment character (winter sports) without A_{STP}	→	Economic estimates of the exchange of the services of the entertainment character (winter sports) without A_{STP}
15	Economic estimates of the production of the show services of football without A_{STP}	→	Economic estimates of the distribution of the show services of football without A_{STP}	→	Economic estimates of the consumption of the show services of football without A_{STP}	→	Economic estimates of the exchange of the show services of football without A_{STP}
16	Economic estimates of the production of the show services of ice-hockey without A_{STP}	→	Economic estimates of the distribution of the show services of ice-hockey without A_{STP}	→	Economic estimates of the consumption of the show services of ice-hockey without A_{STP}	→	Economic estimates of the exchange of the show services of ice-hockey without A_{STP}

Economic estimates of production		Economic estimates of distribution		Economic estimates of consumption		Economic estimates of exchange
17	Economic estimates of the production of the show services of ball-hockey without A_{STP}	$\rightarrow$	Economic estimates of the distribution of the show services of ball-hockey without A_{STP}	$\rightarrow$	Economic estimates of the consumption of the show services of ball-hockey without A_{STP}	$\rightarrow$	Economic estimates of the exchange of the show services of ball-hockey without A_{STP}
18	Economic estimates of the production of the show services of field hockey without A_{STP}	$\rightarrow$	Economic estimates of the distribution of the show services of field hockey without A_{STP}	$\rightarrow$	Economic estimates of the consumption of the show services of field hockey without A_{STP}	$\rightarrow$	Economic estimates of the exchange of the show services of field hockey without A_{STP}
19	Economic estimates of the production of the show services of basketball without A_{STP}	$\rightarrow$	Economic estimates of the distribution of the show services of basketball without A_{STP}	$\rightarrow$	Economic estimates of the consumption of the show services of basketball without A_{STP}	$\rightarrow$	Economic estimates of the exchange of the show services of basketball without A_{STP}
20	Economic estimates of the production of the show services of volley-ball without A_{STP}	$\rightarrow$	Economic estimates of the distribution of the show services of volley-ball without A_{STP}	$\rightarrow$	Economic estimates of the consumption of the show services of volley-ball without A_{STP}	$\rightarrow$	Economic estimates of the exchange of the show services of volley-ball without A_{STP}
21	Economic estimates of the production of the show services of baseball without A_{STP}	$\rightarrow$	Economic estimates of the distribution of the show services of baseball without A_{STP}	$\rightarrow$	Economic estimates of the consumption of the show services of baseball without A_{STP}	$\rightarrow$	Economic estimates of the exchange of the show services of baseball without A_{STP}
22	Economic estimates of the production of the show services of rugby without A_{STP}	$\rightarrow$	Economic estimates of the distribution of the show services of rugby without A_{STP}	$\rightarrow$	Economic estimates of the consumption of the show services of rugby without A_{STP}	$\rightarrow$	Economic estimates of the exchange of the show services of rugby without A_{STP}

Economic estimates of production		Economic estimates of distribution		Economic estimates of consumption		Economic estimates of exchange
23 Economic estimates of the production of the show services of «Formula—1» without A_{STP}	→	Economic estimates of the distribution of the show services of «Formula—1» without A_{STP}	→	Economic estimates of the consumption of the show services of «Formula—1» without A_{STP}	→	Economic estimates of the exchange of the show services of «Formula—1» without A_{STP}
24 Economic estimates of the production of the radio services without A_{STP}	→	Economic estimates of the distribution of the radio services without A_{STP}	→	Economic estimates of the consumption of the radio services without A_{STP}	→	Economic estimates of the exchange of the radio services without A_{STP}
25 Economic estimates of the production of TV services without A_{STP}	→	Economic estimates of the distribution of TV services without A_{STP}	→	Economic estimates of the consumption of TV services without A_{STP}	→	Economic estimates of the exchange of TV services without A_{STP}
Aggregate estimation of production	→	**Aggregate estimation of distribution**	→	**Aggregate estimation of exchange**	→	**Aggregate estimation of consumption**

In other terms, each of the estimates, each of the criteria, each of the indicators does not take into account the A_{STP}. Proceeding from the above, we can calculate the total number of logical mistakes:

Name of «Education», «Enlightenment» and «Entertainment» services		Quantity of forms of economic estimates in the context of economic relations		Types of economic estimates, criteria and indicators	
25	X	4	X	3	= 300

Calculations show that there is a whole number of economic problems with the «Education», «Enlightenment» and «Entertainment» spheres, left beyond the spectrum of examination.

Hence we see that the total number of errors amounts to hundreds. They are present in all the estimates, criteria and indications we apply.

While we simply add up the errors we forget that they do not act separately, but are systematic. That is why when we calculate the total negative result we should include the systematizing effect (or emergentment effect) as well.

It is necessary to point out that if the errors attributed to the economic theory are not eliminated, they aggravate the general economic situation. These mistakes recur year and year out. They do not disappear. For this reason the intellectual sphere is likely to be developing with significant distortions.

Conclusion: The economic theory of the intellectual sphere prompts that there is a paradox in the «logic»: the economic processes disregard time as a factor. It is confirmed by the parameters used in the intellectual sphere: «visitors», «cinema goers», etc. From this context the following questions arise:

1) How is it possible to investigate economic processes in the intellectual sphere without considering the duration of the visits to the establishments of Enlightenment, Education and Entertainment institutions, etc?

2) What effect do visitors, as a resource, to theatres, museums, churches, cinemas, schools, universities have on economic indicators?

I suggest we consider the economic processes of the intellectual sphere, which include temporary components. The flow of visitors to museums, libraries, shows enterprises, schools and universities as a resource involved in the process of creating intellectual services. In relation to this, the population's spare time is also a resource component of intellectual services. We have no reasons to exclude this flow of resources from the calculations of basic economic indicators. If we display reluctance in using these resources in the calculations, the economic processes may become distorted.

CHAPTER 2

The Human Resource in a
Three-Dimensional Economic Space

At the first phase of this big theme we should consider what our predecessors in the economic theory have left to us. Here is, for example, one of the phrases stated by a great theorist: «the spare time of the population is the riches of a society». This maxim is about 200 years old, but it has not received further development till now. This statement has no ending. It is a familiar expression in which there are more questions than answers. He should have prompted the future generations in which direction they should move when considering this problem and what should be the first, the second and the third phases of research. But these things are absent in the theory. Yes, «the spare time of the population is the riches of a society», but after this statement the following subjects should be considered:

1. «The spare time of the population»—as a resource;

2. «The spare time of the population»—as an economic category;

3. Components of the spare time of the population;

4. Influence of economic relations on the structure of the resource of «the spare time of the population»;

5. «The spare time of the population»—as a component of GDP, NDP and NI;

6. Distribution of «the spare time of the population»;

7. The resource of «the spare time of the population» and relations of exchange;

8. The resource of «the spare time of the population» and relations of consumption, etc.;

9. Assimilation of the resource of «the spare time of the population» by the services of «Enlightenment», «Education» and «Entertainment»;

10. Increase of «the not-assimilated» part of the resource of the spare time of the population—one of the indicators of crisis in economy;

11. An economic estimation of the resources of «the spare time of the population» of different social groups, and layers of a society;

12. The spare time of the population of developed countries;

13. The spare time of poor and developing countries.

The Spare Time of the Population As an Economic Resource

We may have different attitudes to the economic problems of people's spare time.

The human resource in spare time may not be regarded as an economic one. In this case, all economic problems connected to it are absent. No resources, no problems.

However, as soon as we reject such a stand or a viewpoint and move over to the position of those who consider this resource as economic, we encounter a number of problems on all levels of investigation.

According to the existing theory the human resource of a country acts as an economic category only during working hours. In all other cases it is deprived of this privilege. Beyond the framework of working hours the human resource is not an economic resource. In the conditions of spare time it does not move in the economic space. In other words, the human resource during the spare time acts as the unidentified flying object (UFO).

It is necessary to object to the proponents of such a point of view.

Why is «the person in his spare time» not considered as an economic resource?

Why doesn't «the person in spare time» act as a bearer of economic relations?

These researchers should know that where there are no people, there are no economic relations, eg. on the peaks of the mountains—Elbrus and Everest; in the deserts—The Sahara and Kalahari; on snow spaces of the Arctic and Antarctica.

But as soon as people climb up these peaks or take part in the «Paris-Dakar» rally, economic relations appear immediately. Everything starts moving, rotating and whirling in economic space.

I suggest, therefore that we extend the formula: «time is money» to all parts of time budget of the population:

- working hours is money
- out of work hours is money
- spare time is money.

Should we economically estimate each of these vectors the total vector R will be written down as:

$$R = \left| \begin{array}{c} \text{Cost estimation of} \\ \text{working hours} \end{array} \right| + \left| \begin{array}{c} \text{Cost estimation of} \\ \text{non-working hours} \end{array} \right| + \left| \begin{array}{c} \text{Cost estimation} \\ \text{of spare time} \end{array} \right|$$

Here we have to deal with estimation problems which I suggest to examine in a three-dimensional space, by:

- placing vector R_1 on axis «X» = 8 hours—working time;
- placing vector R_2 on axis «Y» = 8 hours—non-working time;
- placing vector R_3 on axis «Z» = 8 hours—spare time.

Thus we shall receive a cube with equal sides 8, 8, 8 (this variant to be considered as a basis)

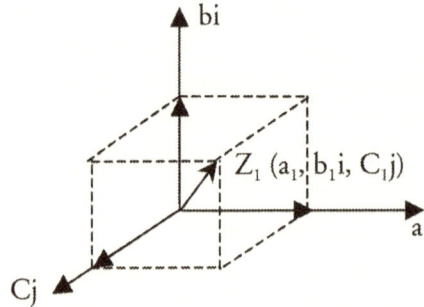

1. The time vector R_1 with the industrious part of the population» exceeds set up limits 8 hours. It may comprise e.g. 12 hours.

The non-working time vector (taking food, self-service etc.) may make up 8 hours. The spare time vector with the diligent people may come to 4 hours within twenty-four hours.

$$a_1 = 12, \; bi_2 = 8, \; Cj_3 = 4$$

A graphic interpretation of the above problem in a three-dimensional space allows to see that along with the increase of the working time vector the «cube» (8, 8, 8) is being transformed into a «parallelepiped» (12, 8, 4).

Non-working time:

1) The wasted time of sleeping
2) The wasted time of breakfast and dinner
3) The wasted time of transportation from home to work and vice versa
4) The wasted time of self-servicing

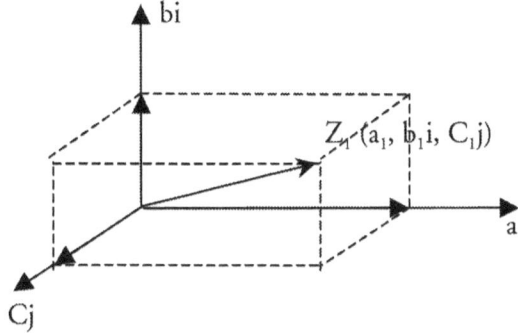

2. As to the non-industrious part of the population living in idleness most of the time, the «cube» is also transformed into a «parallelepiped» with sides 4, 8, 12 (vector $a_1 = 4$, $bi_2 = 8$, $Cj_3 = 12$).

In this variant the «parallelepiped» has other direction as compared with variant 2.

3. Hence we have two parallelepipeds with sides:

- 12, 8, 4;
- 4, 8, 12.

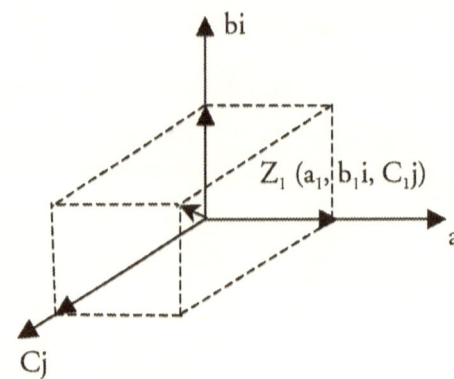

The question is which of these parallelepipeds is better: the first or the second one?

The answer lies in the plane of economic estimates.

Proceeding from the assumption that 1 working hour is estimated at 5 USD and 1 hour of non-working and spare time at 2 USD:

1. The cost value of the first «parallelepiped» is:

$R_1 = 12$	→	$ 5/per hour	=	$ 60
$R_2 = 8$	→	$ 2/per hour	=	$ 16
$R_3 = 4$	→	$ 2/per hour	=	$ 8
				$ 84

2. The cost value of the second «parallelepiped» is:

$R_1 = 4$	→	$ 5/per hour	=	$ 20
$R_2 = 8$	→	$ 2/per hour	=	$ 16
$R_3 = 12$	→	$ 2/per hour	=	$ 24
				$ 60

The estimates given above are to be specified proceeding from the presumption that the cost function of the spare time resource has the following shape:

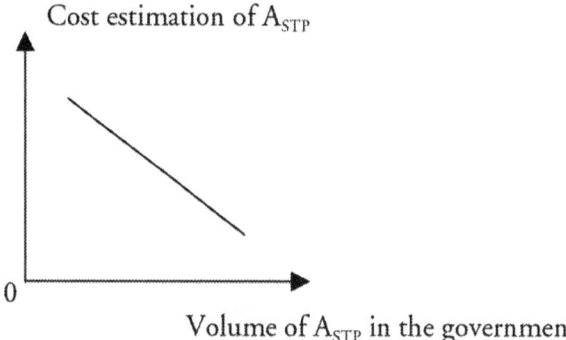

Cost estimation of A_{STP}

0

Volume of A_{STP} in the government

We can see on the graph that 1 hour of ASTP is changeable:

- the more ASTP the less expensive it is;
- the less ASTP the more expensive it is.

In developed countries with the lowest level of unemployment the cost of the A_{STP} resource will have a maximum value.

CHAPTER 3

The Problems of Construction of the Economic Theory of the Intellectual Sphere

In economic literature you can meet a pithy saying: «the intellectual element will take a worthy place in the theory of political economy». This idea was started 150 years ago but till now we have had a rather obscure conception of how this «economic element», as well as the system of «economic elements» of intellectual sphere look like.

This pithy saying has not got appropriate theoretical development till the present day. The author of this saying had to explain the essence of these «economic elements» pointing out their economic coordinates of «X», «Y», «Z». But all this is absent in theory.

Nobody doubts that «intellectual elements» will take a proper place in the economic theory of this sphere, provided that it has been created. Yes, these elements should be arranged in their places, roughly, of course, as it is in the table by Mendeleyev, but taking into account the economic component.

I suggest that we create: «A periodic table of the economic elements of the intellectual sphere» which should comprise.

- <u>Intellectual values</u>: books, newspapers, magazines and pictures placed in one part of the table;
- <u>Intellectual services</u>: enlightenment, education and entertainment shown in the other part;
- the criteria of intellectual provision taking their own part of the table;
- the criteria of the utilization of resources put into another relevant part, etc.

It is not easy to create a system of economic elements and here we should use the criteria of a «science of logics» and real, imaginary and complex numbers.

We should start the construction of the economic theory of the intellectual sphere by finding that certain initial «brick» on which the whole building will be erected.

While choosing that «brick», we meet a substantial number of problems of logic character. What economic category should be preferential as the basic one? It is difficult to answer this question since all the economic categories can be considered in a solitary key:

-   solitary factors of the production which take part in the creation of intellectual values in material and service form;
-   solitary productive force of the intellectual sphere;
-   solitary economic relations;
-   solitary intellectual values;
-   solitary intellectual services;
-   a solitary aggregate product of intellectual production.

Let us start from the very beginning, from the solitary resources entering the intellectual sphere.

A. Solitary Resources Entering the Intellectual Sphere

It is a long, monotonous process to enumerate all the resources entering the intellectual sphere. I suggest that we classify them using the following criteria:

Criterion 1—resources entering the intellectual sphere and directed to the creation of material, intellectual values: books, paintings, films etc.

Criterion 2—resources entering the intellectual sphere directed to the creation of intellectual services—non-material results of activity; services of the enlightenment, education and entertaining character.

A. The entering of the resources directed to the creation of intellectual values:

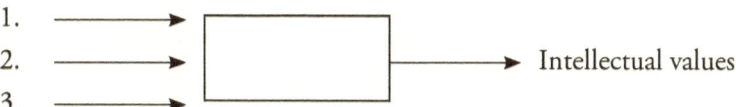

Here the resources entering are:

- means of labor;
- objects of labor;
- labor resources;
- power supply sources.

B. The resources entering directed to creating intellectual services:

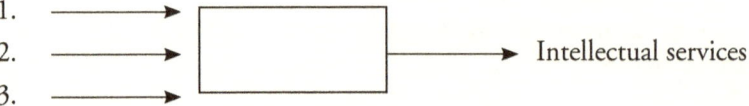

Here the resources entering are:

- means of labor;
- objects of labor;
- labor resources;
- power supply sources.
- plus a stream of visitors: pupils, students, cinema-goers, radio listeners, television viewers etc.

Considering the resources entering the intellectual sphere is the first step without which it is impossible to further realize the construction of the economic theory of the intellectual sphere.

Logic prompts us that we should use an aggregate (complex) intellectual product as a solitary basic economic category.

But a question arises: what is it? What does it look like?

I see the inner structure of a solitary intellectual product as:

THESIS	Solitary intellectual value in a material form a book, a picture, a film, a newspaper, a magazine.
ANTITHESIS	Solitary intellectual service
SYNTHESIS	Complex intellectual product consisting of a material and non-material (service) form.

1. If we carry out the construction of the economic theory using a solitary intellectual value, intellectual services will remain aside. Somehow they are beyond the line of consideration.

2. If we carry out the construction of the economic theory using a solitary intellectual service, (material) intellectual values are beyond the line of consideration.

B. Economic Relations in the Intellectual Sphere

The movement of intellectual values and intellectual services is not considered in the publications on problems of intellectual sphere.

Why are these values and services not considered in a process of movement?

If these values represent economic products they should move in economic space. And why not?

Some readers will object and that is why?

St. Peter's cathedral in Vatican can not move as well as any other cathedral.

Yes, I agree with this. But here there is a substitution of concepts. If these cathedrals are exploited, they are in a process of movement in the economic sense of this word.

The movement of intellectual values and intellectual services takes place in economic space and only in this case these values and services act as such.

If they are out of this space they do not act as economic products. We should not interpret economic space just as a flat surface.

Everything is much more complicated. There is economic space, it exists, yet it is not a materially tangible thing.

Economic space is economic relations that act in a non-material form. We can not bite them or stroke them tenderly with a hand. They are non-material.

This fact, through, must not be an obstacle on our way.

So, what is the structure of economic space?

What is the «linen» of economic space made of?

Economic space—if considered in a «horizontal» plane—represents four types of economic relations:

production, distribution, exchange, consumption.

Along with a horizontal structure, economic space has a vertical structure.

Thesis	Economic relations connected to intellectual values
Antithesis	Economic relations connected to intellectual services
Synthesis	Economic relations connected to aggregate (complex) intellectual products.

In the context of each economic relation the space under consideration has the following peculiarities.

Production

Thesis	Economic relations connected to the production of intellectual values
Antithesis	Economic relations connected to the production of intellectual services
Synthesis	Economic relations connected to the production of aggregate (complex) intellectual products.

Distribution

Thesis	Economic relations connected to the distribution of intellectual values
Antithesis	Economic relations connected to the distribution of intellectual services
Synthesis	Economic relations connected to the distribution of aggregate (complex) intellectual products.

Exchange

Thesis	Economic relations connected to the exchange of intellectual values
Antithesis	Economic relations connected to the exchange of intellectual services
Synthesis	Economic relations connected to the exchange of aggregate (complex) intellectual products.

<u>Consumption</u>

Thesis	Economic relations connected to the consumption of intellectual values
Antithesis	Economic relations connected to the consumption of intellectual services
Synthesis	Economic relations connected to the consumption of aggregate (complex) intellectual products.

The process of creating of intellectual values and intellectual services means the beginning of their movement. Everything starts from there.

You come into a museum—and it is only the beginning of creation of an intellectual service of an enlightenment character. A lecture starts at the university and you, as a listener, take part in the creation of an intellectual service of an educational character. Everything starts from moving—administrations, professors and students.

All these movements take place when the administrations, the students of the university enter economic relations.

Without economic relations everything stops.

The people's entry into economic relations makes it possible to create complex and necessary intellectual values and intellectual services. Without these relations, intellectual values and services will not act as an economic product for others.

The economic relations have their own specification and particular nature of origin. They are not material.

This circumstance raises a substantial number of questions:

What is happening at the phase of the «production» of intellectual values and intellectual services?

What is happening at the phase of the «distribution» of intellectual values and intellectual services?

What is happening at the phase of the «exchange» of intellectual values and intellectual services?

What is happening at the phase of the «consumption» of intellectual values and intellectual services?

These problems need better understanding. The movement of intellectual values and intellectual services, of a complex intellectual product within the economic space can be presented as:

Production	Distribution	Exchange	Consumption
Process of the movement of intellectual values in the framework of production	Process of the movement of intellectual values in the framework of distribution	Process of the movement of intellectual values in the framework of exchange	Process of the movement of intellectual values in the framework of consumption
Process of the movement of intellectual services in the framework of production	Process of the movement of intellectual services in the framework of distribution	Process of the movement of intellectual services in the framework of exchange	Process of the movement of intellectual services in the framework of consumption
Process of the movement of aggregate intellectual product in the framework of production	Process of the movement of aggregate intellectual product in the framework of distribution	Process of the movement of aggregate intellectual product in the framework of exchange	Process of the movement of aggregate intellectual product in the framework of consumption

In the frame I have outlined the processes which are clear:

- the process of the creation of intellectual values (books, magazines etc.);
- the process of the distribution of intellectual values;
- the process of the exchange of intellectual values;
- the process of the consumption of intellectual values.

But everything that has remained beyond the dashed line is not investigated.

CHAPTER 4

The Movement of Intellectual Values, Intellectual Services and of the Aggregate Intellectual Product

The reader may be required to know what necessitates the examination of the process of the movement of intellectual values, intellectual services and of the aggregate intellectual product?

The answer may be as follows. Any product of human activity, if it is not in a state of motion (i.e. from the economic point of view it is not exploited) is considered to be a dead product. This concept is also valid for intellectual values, intellectual services, and the aggregate intellectual product.

If intellectual values are not distributed that will mean they are neither sold nor consumed. They are stagnant, immovable. Within economic space they are lifeless products.

The consumption of intellectual services is possible only in the process of their creation e.g. in the museum, the theatre, the cinema, the church or during a football match.

The absence of any process of creating intellectual services would mean absence of their movement. Intellectual services are not produced. They are non-existent. Their beneficial effect is equal to nil. And intellectual values and intellectual services brought to «nought» cannot be examined. The object of motion is absent.

Today problems related to the movement of intellectual values and intellectual services and of the aggregate intellectual product in the economic space have not been given proper consideration.

The movement of economic values of the intellectual character has not been adequately researched. There is no formularized picture (sines and cosines of the vector of movement).

This provokes a number of questions, e.g.:

What are the trajectories of the movement of intellectual values?

What are the trajectories of the movement of intellectual services?

What mathematical formulas refer to the movement of intellectual values and services?

Are there sines and cosines in these formulas?

How are the separate parts of intellectual values and intellectual services moving?

Are there any economic estimates, criteria and indicators revealing the rate of movement of intellectual values and services?

Perhaps it is necessary to use trigonometric functions here?

Perhaps we have to apply complex numbers?

What is the specific feature of the movement of intellectual product?

What happens to the aggregate intellectual product while on move?

What types of graphs and curves, related to the movement of intellectual product are obtained?

I suggest that the movement of the aggregate intellectual product should be examined in time and space with the assumption that it consists of two parts: intellectual values and intellectual services.

The Movement of a Single (Complex) Intellectual Product

A single intellectual product represents a complex formation. It consists of:

- a single intellectual value;
- a single intellectual service.

Interpreted graphically a single intellectual product appears as follows:

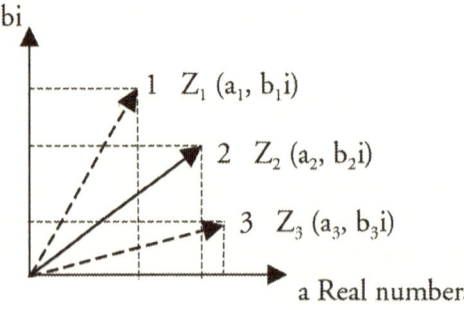

where

a—a single intellectual value (material form);

bi—a single intellectual services (service form);

Z = a + bi—an aggregate vector, revealing a complex intellectual product.

If vector Z occupies the first position, intellectual services are prevalent in the complex intellectual product.

If vector Z occupies the second position, the correlation of values and service is 50/50.

If vector Z occupies the third position, that would mean that intellectual values prevail in the complex intellectual product.

The movement of intellectual values and services takes place in economic environment.

- economic environment № 1
    - production of intellectual values;
    - production of intellectual services;
    - production of the aggregate intellectual product;

- economic environment № 2
    - distribution of intellectual values;
    - distribution of intellectual services;
    - distribution of the aggregate intellectual product;

- economic environment № 3
    - exchange of intellectual values;
    - exchange of intellectual services;
    - exchange of the aggregate intellectual services;

- economic environment № 4
    - consumption of intellectual values;
    - consumption of intellectual services;
    - consumption of the aggregate intellectual product.

Indeed, intellectual values and intellectual services exist and perform within economic space. In every economic environment intellectual values and intellectual services move in their particular way. In some cases they will have the configuration of «8», in other cases the motion will be spiral.

The movement of intellectual values and services occurs at different speeds depending on their economic property, particularly on the quality and the price. Since they are in permanent motion they should be investigated in the state of economic movement.

For intellectual values:
1. The movement of intellectual values within relations of production.
2. The movement of intellectual values within relations of distribution.
3. The movement of intellectual values within relations of exchange.
4. The movement of intellectual values within relations of consumption.

For intellectual services:
1. The movement of intellectual services within relations of production.
2. The movement of intellectual services within relations of distribution.
3. The movement of intellectual services within relations of exchange.
4. The movement of intellectual services within relations of consumption.

For aggregate intellectual product:
1. The movement of the aggregate intellectual product within relations of production.
2. The movement of the aggregate intellectual product within relations of distribution.
3. The movement of the aggregate intellectual product within relations of exchange.
4. The movement of the aggregate intellectual product within relations of consumption.

It is also apparent that the movement of intellectual values and services does not occur as a Brownian (random) motion. They move within the effect of «magnetic forces» introduced and performed by economic interests.

A. ECONOMIC INTERESTS OF THE MOVEMENT OF INTELLECTUAL VALUES

Economic properties of intellectual values: a_1—use value; b_1i—value; Z_1—exchange value: $Z_1 = a_1 + b_1i$	+	Economic interests, connected to the movement of intellectual values	$\rightarrow$	Economic results of movement

B. ECONOMIC INTERESTS OF THE MOVEMENT OF INTELLECTUAL SERVICES

Economic properties of intellectual services: a_2—use value; b_2i—value; Z_2—exchange value: $Z_2 = a_2 + b_2i$	+	Economic interests, connected to the movement of intellectual services	$\rightarrow$	Economic results of movement

C. ECONOMIC INTERESTS OF THE MOVEMENT OF THE AGGREGATE INTELLECTUAL PRODUCT

Economic properties of a complex intellectual product: a_3—use value; b_3i—value; Z_3—exchange value: $Z_3 = a_3 + b_3i$	+	Economic interests, connected to the movement of the aggregate intellectual product	$\rightarrow$	Economic results of movement

In different economic environments a «value» of interest is different, at creation it is one, at distribution it is another, etc.

1. In process of production

A. ECONOMIC INTERESTS OF THE MOVEMENT OF INTELLECTUAL VALUES

Economic properties of intellectual values: a—use value; bi—value; Z—exchange value: Z = a + bi	+	Economic interests, connected to the movement of intellectual values	→	Economic results of movement

B. ECONOMIC INTERESTS OF THE MOVEMENT OF INTELLECTUAL SERVICES

Economic properties of intellectual services: a—use value; bi—value; Z—exchange value: Z = a + bi	+	Economic interests, connected to the movement of intellectual services	→	Economic results of movement

C. ECONOMIC INTERESTS OF THE MOVEMENT OF THE AGGREGATE INTELLECTUAL PRODUCT

Economic properties of a complex intellectual product: a—use value; bi—value; Z—exchange value: Z = a + bi	+	Economic interests, connected to the movement of the aggregate intellectual product	→	Economic results of movement

2. In process of distribution

A. ECONOMIC INTERESTS OF THE MOVEMENT OF INTELLECTUAL VALUES

Economic properties of intellectual values: a—use value; bi—value; Z—exchange value: $Z = a + bi$	+	Economic interests, connected to the movement of intellectual values	→	Economic results of movement

B. ECONOMIC INTERESTS OF THE MOVEMENT OF INTELLECTUAL SERVICES

Economic properties of intellectual services: a—use value; bi—value; Z—exchange value: $Z = a + bi$	+	Economic interests, connected to the movement of intellectual services	→	Economic results of movement

C. ECONOMIC INTERESTS OF THE MOVEMENT OF THE AGGREGATE INTELLECTUAL PRODUCT

Economic properties of a complex intellectual product: a—use value; bi—value; Z—exchange value: $Z = a + bi$	+	Economic interests, connected to the movement of the aggregate intellectual product	→	Economic results of movement

3. In process of exchange

A. ECONOMIC INTERESTS OF THE MOVEMENT OF INTELLECTUAL VALUES

Economic properties of
intellectual values:
  a—use value;
  bi—value;
Z—exchange value:
  $Z = a + bi$

  +

Economic interests,
connected to the
movement of
intellectual values

  →

Economic results
of movement

B. ECONOMIC INTERESTS OF THE MOVEMENT OF INTELLECTUAL SERVICES

Economic properties of
intellectual services:
  a—use value;
  bi—value;
Z—exchange value:
  $Z = a + bi$

  +

Economic interests,
connected to the
movement of
intellectual services

  →

Economic results
of movement

C. ECONOMIC INTERESTS OF THE MOVEMENT OF THE AGGREGATE INTELLECTUAL PRODUCT

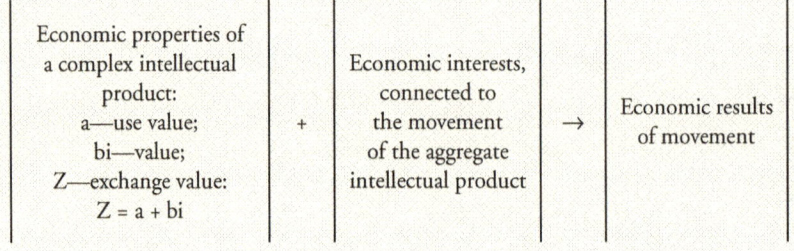

Economic properties of
a complex intellectual
product:
  a—use value;
  bi—value;
Z—exchange value:
  $Z = a + bi$

  +

Economic interests,
connected to
the movement
of the aggregate
intellectual product

  →

Economic results
of movement

4. In process of consumption

A. ECONOMIC INTERESTS OF THE MOVEMENT OF INTELLECTUAL VALUES

Economic properties of intellectual values: a—use value; bi—value; Z—exchange value: $Z = a + bi$	+	Economic interests, connected to the movement of intellectual values	$\rightarrow$	Economic results of movement

B. ECONOMIC INTERESTS OF THE MOVEMENT OF INTELLECTUAL SERVICES

Economic properties of intellectual services: a—use value; bi—value; Z—exchange value: $Z = a + bi$	+	Economic interests, connected to the movement of intellectual services	$\rightarrow$	Economic results of movement

C. ECONOMIC INTERESTS OF THE MOVEMENT OF THE AGGREGATE INTELLECTUAL PRODUCT

Economic properties of a complex intellectual product: a—use value; bi—value; Z—exchange value: $Z = a + bi$	+	Economic interests, connected to the movement of aggregate intellectual product	$\rightarrow$	Economic results of movement

CHAPTER 5

The Economic Estimations of the Services of the «Educational», «Enlightenment» and «Entertainment» Branches Including A$_{STP}$

The «Education», «Enlightenment» and «Entertainment» branches are directed to the assimilation of population's spare time.

The application of the spare time of population (A$_{STP}$) in three functionally different planes may be drawn up in the Cartesian coordinates as follows:

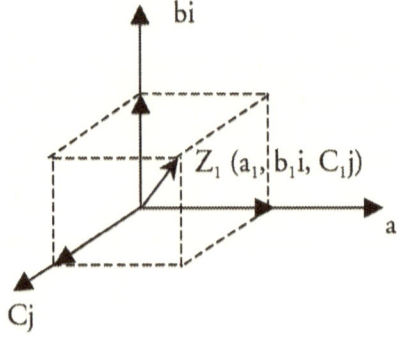

where

  a—the vector revealing the amount of time spent by the population while consuming Education services;

  bi—the vector revealing the amount of time spent by the population while consuming Enlightenment services;

Cj—the vector revealing the amount of time spent by the population while consuming Entertainment services.

The aggregate development vector of the three branches for this indicator will be recorded as:

$$R = a + bi + Cj$$

For every specified state vector a, bi, Cj have different values and lengths. The main task facing economists is to establish each of the development vectors that would subsequently enable us to calculate the total vector R.

Such a classification is founded on the people's choice of spending their free time.

The usage of the three-dimensional system of coordinates makes it possible to examine the correlation of the «Education», «Enlightenment» and «Entertainment» branches.

Proceeding from that we shall place:

- on axis «X»—the volume of intellectual services put at the disposal of people by the «Education» branches—vector «a»;
- on axis «Y»—the volume of intellectual services at people's disposal from the «Enlightenment» branches—vector «bi»;
- on axis «Z»—the volume of intellectual services given to people by the «Entertainment» branches—vector «C»;

As a result we shall receive a record of the activity of these three groups of branches in a vector form:

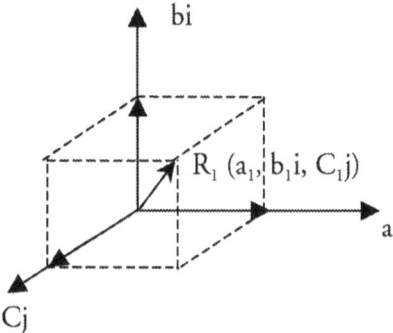

Aggregate efficiency vector of the «Education», «Enlightenment» and «Entertainment» branches will be written as follows:

$$R = a + bi + Cj$$

where

i, j—are indices denoting the different nature of the origin of intellectual services.

Education services—are services of the first kind

Enlightenment services—are services of the second kind

Entertainment services—are services of the third kind

The value of a, b, C vectors is changed every year, one of them becomes longer, the other shorter, etc.

Firstly, if within the three-dimensional system of coordinates the «Entertainment» vector in the longest, the aggregate vector R will naturally have a certain inclination (angle α, β, γ).

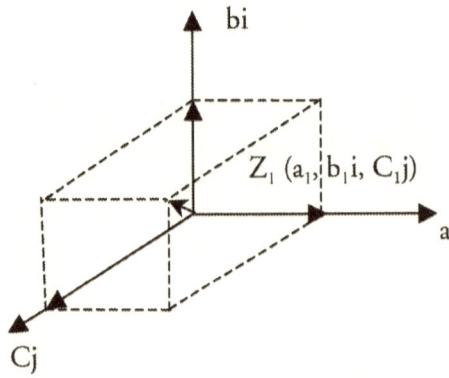

Second. If the greater part of the people's spare time is spent on «Education» and «Enlightenment», the vector R will have a different direction, other inclination (angle α_2, β_2, γ_2).

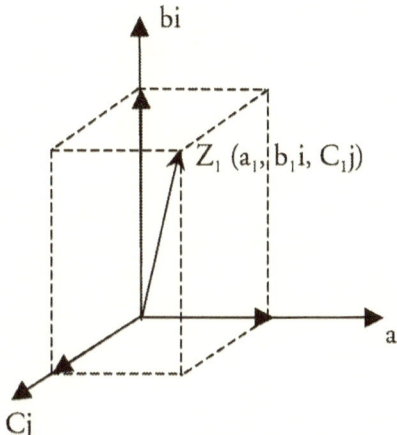

The application of the three-dimensional system of economic coordinates allows to examine the process of movement from several angles.

In applying Decarts coordinates, any of the services of «Education», «Enlightenment» and «Entertainment»can be reproduced in a three-dimensional space with a, b, C vectors.

Depending on the values of a, bi, Cj, the parallelepiped will change its values. It can be stretched on the axis «a», or «b», or «C» etc.

There is a number of various combinations here.

Calculation of the Services of the Educational, Enlightenment and Entertainment Character (Expenses + A_{STP})

For example, if about 227.4 million man-hours per year is assimilated by the system of museums, the total amount of museum services can be drawn up graphically as follows:

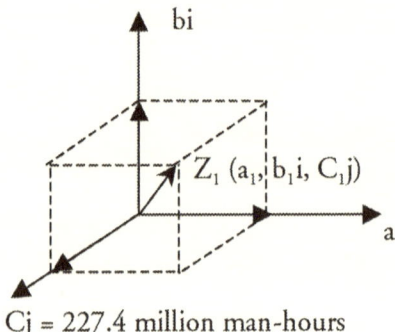

Cj = 227.4 million man-hours

where

a—past labor expenses;

bi—real labor expenses;

Cj—the assimilated A_{STP} resource.

For concert activity. For example, if 299 million man-hours of spare time are assimilated by the concert activity, the total amount of these services can be represented as:

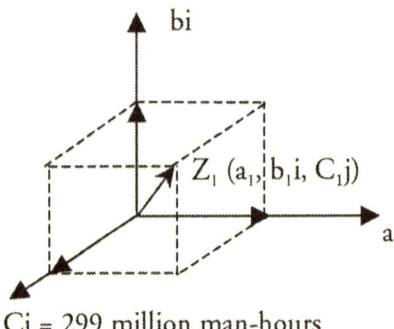

Cj = 299 million man-hours

where

$R_{CONCERT}$ = a + bi + 299 million man-hours

Or some other examples. If 320.6 million man-hours of spare time is assimilated by theatre activity, the total amount of these services can be shown as follows:

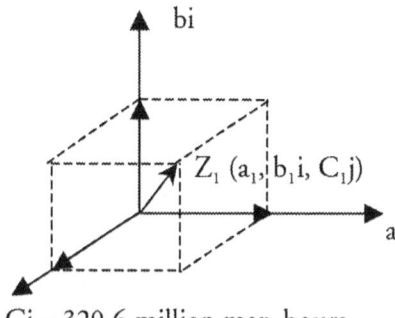

$$C_j = 320.6 \text{ million man-hours}$$

where

$$R_{THEATRE} = a + bi + 320.6 \text{ mln. man-hours.}$$

If 3,500 million man-hours of spare time is assimilated by the library activity, the total amount of these services can be represented:

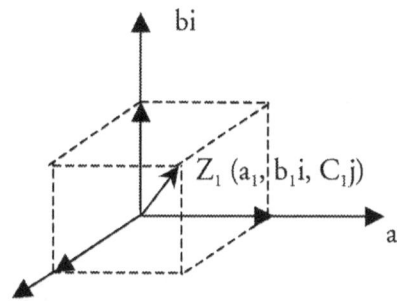

$$C_j = 3,500 \text{ million man-hours}$$

where

$$R_{ENLIGHTENMNET} = a + bi + 3,500 \text{ million man-hours}$$

For the film circulation activity. If 8,291 million man-hours of spare time is assimilated by the film circulation, the total amount of these services can be interpreted as follows:

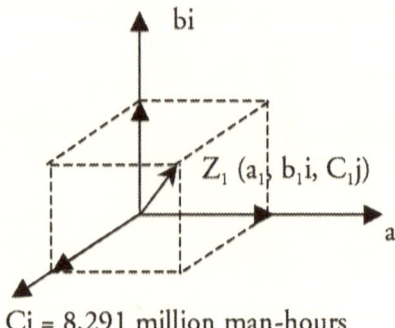

Cj = 8,291 million man-hours

where

R$_{FILM}$ = a + bi + 8,291 mln. man-hours.

For the radio. If 1,834 million man-hours of spare time is assimilated by the radio activity, the total amount of these services can be represented as follows:

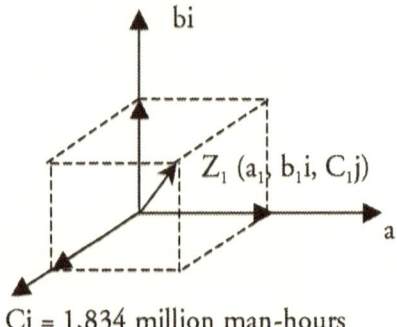

Cj = 1,834 million man-hours

where

R$_{RADIO}$ = a + bi + 1,834 million man-hours

For the television. If 55,400 million man-hours of spare time is assimilated by the TV, the total amount of these services can be shown:

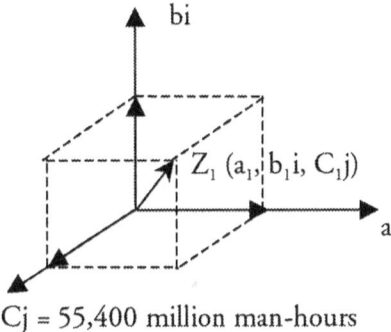

$C_j = 55,400$ million man-hours

where

$R_{TV} = a + bi + 55,400$ million man-hours

For example, according to the preliminary calculations for the USA:

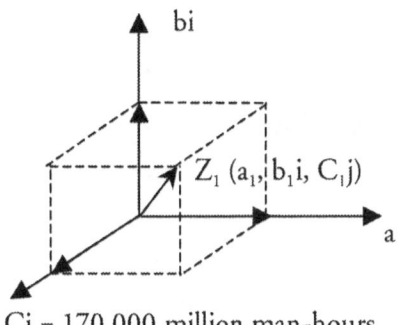

$C_j = 170,000$ million man-hours

where

$R_{TV} = a + bi + 170,000$ million man-hours

In the USA about 20,000 million man-hours are assimilated in the «Education» branch:

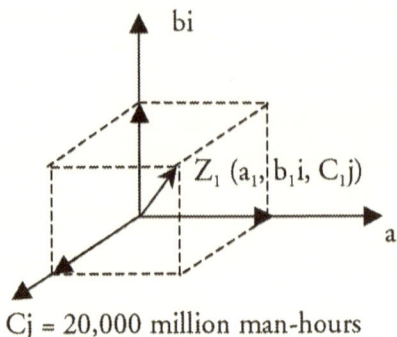

$C_j = 20{,}000$ million man-hours

where

$R_{TV} = a + bi + 20{,}000$ million man-hours

The «Education», «Enlightenment» and «Entertainment» branches are directed to the organization of the population's spare time.

They daily creation of a vast number of various intellectual services, such as:

- expenses connected with production school services + A_{STP};

- expenses connected with production college services + A_{STP};

- expenses connected with production university services + A_{STP};

- expenses connected with production library services + A_{STP};

- expenses connected with production exhibition services + A_{STP};

- expenses connected with production museum services + A_{STP};

- expenses connected with production concert services + A_{STP};

- expenses connected with production theatre services + A_{STP};

- expenses connected with production circus services + A_{STP};

- expenses connected with production Church services + A_{STP};

- expenses connected with production cinema services + A_{STP};

- expenses connected with the production services of the sports-entertainment character (attractions, aqua parks, DisneyLands) + A_{STP};

- expenses connected with the production services of entertainment character (summer sports) + A_{STP};

- expenses connected with the production services of the entertainment character (winter sports) + A_{STP};

- expenses connected with the production show services of football + A_{STP};

- expenses connected with the production show services of ice-hockey + A_{STP};

- expenses connected with the production show services of ball-hockey + A_{STP};

- expenses connected with the production show services of field hockey + A_{STP};

- expenses connected with the production show services of basketball + A_{STP};

- expenses connected with the production show services of volley-ball + A_{STP};

- expenses connected with the production show services of baseball + A_{STP};

- expenses connected with the production show services of rugby + A_{STP};

- expenses connected with the production show services of «Formula—1» + A_{STP};

- expenses connected with the production Radio services + A_{STP};

- expenses connected with the production TV services + A_{STP}.

CHAPTER 6

The Economic Estimates, Criteria and Indicators of the Movement of the Services of Education, Enlightenment and Entertainment in Economic Space

Each of the branches—«Education», «Enlightenment» and «Entertainment»— have a specific material and technical resource:

- labor resource structure;
- main funds structure (buildings, installations);
- economic relations structure;
- legal relations structure.

Labor resources of the «Education», «Enlightenment» and «Entertainment» branches differ from country to country. You have to count the age factor here. There is also a professional pattern (number of musicians, artists, cinema and theater people, radio and TV people, clergymen, etc.).

The above branches have other structures also liable for investigation. They may be of good, medium and bad quality which is possible to estimate.

However we should not examine them detachedly from economic relations. The interaction of the main assets, labor resources, and stream of visitors occur in the frames of economic relations (within an economic space) set up in the Intellectual sphere of society, namely:

- relations of production;
- relations of distribution;
- relations of consumption;
- relations of exchange.

When we take into account economic relations, everything becomes full of vigor and starts to function. Economic relations are like the elixir of life, representing a system of social relations among the people as regards the creation, distribution, consumption and exchange of «Education», «Enlightenment» and «Entertainment» services.

Outside economic relations the main assets of «Education», «Enlightenment» and «Entertainment», as well as the labor resources of the above branches, will not function. They will mean nothing but a pile of unnecessary, abandoned things.

If we ignore the exchange of intellectual services for other values and services, we shall find that the creation, distribution of «Education», «Enlightenment» and «Entertainment» services occur in a contracted version and that only a part of economic relations remains, the other part is absent.

Here we shall deliberate on that part of intellectual services which is consumed by the population free of charge, by-passing exchange relations, i.e. the stage of exchange. In other terms, we are in a situation when the chain of economic relations is missing a significant link. This is also shown below by a dotted line.

	Production		Distribution		Consumption		Exchange
A.	«Production» of Education services	→	«Distribution» of Education services	→	«Consumption» of Education services	→	«Exchange» of Education services
	↓		↓		↓		↓
B.	«Production» of Enlightenment services	→	«Distribution» of Enlightenment services	→	«Consumption» of Enlightenment services	→	«Exchange» of Enlightenment services
	↓		↓		↓		↓
C.	«Production» of Entertainment services	→	«Distribution» of Entertainment services	→	«Consumption» of Entertainment services	→	«Exchange» of Entertainment services

Below I give a system of economic relations without distributive functions (framed by dots).

	Production	Distribution	Consumption	Exchange
A.	«Production» of Education services $\rightarrow$	«Distribution» of Education services	$\rightarrow$ «Consumption» of Education services	$\rightarrow$ «Exchange» of Education services
	$\downarrow$	$\downarrow$	$\downarrow$	$\downarrow$
B.	«Production» of Enlightenment services $\rightarrow$	«Distribution» of Enlightenment services	$\rightarrow$ «Consumption» of Enlightenment services	$\rightarrow$ «Exchange» of Enlightenment services
	$\downarrow$	$\downarrow$	$\downarrow$	$\downarrow$
C.	«Production» of Entertainment services $\rightarrow$	«Distribution» of Entertainment services	$\rightarrow$ «Consumption» of Entertainment services	$\rightarrow$ «Exchange» of Entertainment services

However, on the way of the movement of services there is a significant number of problems of the economic character:

- in the process of the production (creation) of «Education», «Enlightenment» and «Entertainment» services, one of the resources joining them (i.e. the stream of visitors A_{STP}), is taken into account;
- in the process of the distribution of «Education», «Enlightenment» and «Entertainment» services, one of the resources joining them (i.e. the stream of visitors A_{STP}), is taken into account;
- in the process of the exchange of «Education», «Enlightenment» and «Entertainment» services one of the resources joining them (i.e. the stream of visitors A_{STP}), is taken into account;
- in the process of the consumption of «Education», «Enlightenment» and «Entertainment» services, one of the resources joining them (i.e. the stream of visitors A_{STP}), is taken into account.

At every stage of movement we shall have:

- economic estimates connected to the movement within each of these four relations;

If intellectual services estimates are as follows:

Intellectual services = $C + V + A_{STP} + m$, then the system of estimates of the movement of these services in economic space will be:

Table of Estimates Taking into Account the Economic Relations

Economic estimates of production	Economic estimates of distribution	Economic estimates of exchange	Economic estimates of consumption	Complex estimate
EEPM School services $+ A_{STP} + m$	EEDM School services $+ A_{STP} + m$	EECM School services $+ A_{STP} + m$	EEEMX School services $+ A_{STP} + m$	№ 1[1]
EEPM College services $+ A_{STP}$ $+ m$	EEDM College services $+ A_{STP}$ $+ m$	EECM College services $+ A_{STP}$ $+ m$	EEEMX College services $+ A_{STP}$ $+ m$	№ 2
EEPM University services $+ A_{STP}$ $+ m$	EEDM University services $+ A_{STP}$ $+ m$	EECM University services $+ A_{STP}$ $+ m$	EEEMX University services $+ A_{STP}$ $+ m$	№ 3
EEPM Library services $+ A_{STP}$ $+ m$	EEDM Library services $+ A_{STP}$ $+ m$	EECM Library services $+ A_{STP}$ $+ m$	EEEMX Library services $+ A_{STP}$ $+ m$	№ 4
EEPM Exhibition services $+ A_{STP}$ $+ m$	EEDM Exhibition services $+ A_{STP}$ $+ m$	EECM Exhibition services $+ A_{STP}$ $+ m$	EEEMX Exhibition services $+ A_{STP}$ $+ m$	№ 5
EEPM Museum services $+ A_{STP}$ $+ m$	EEDM Museum services $+ A_{STP}$ $+ m$	EECM Museum services $+ A_{STP}$ $+ m$	EEEMX Museum services $+ A_{STP}$ $+ m$	№ 6
EEPM Concert services $+ A_{STP}$ $+ m$	EEDM Concert services $+ A_{STP}$ $+ m$	EECM Concert services $+ A_{STP}$ $+ m$	EEEMX Concert services $+ A_{STP}$ $+ m$	№ 7

---

1   EEP—Economic estimates of production

EED—Economic estimates of distribution

EEC—Economic estimates of consumption

EEEX—Economic estimates of exchange

Economic estimates of production	Economic estimates of distribution	Economic estimates of exchange	Economic estimates of consumption	Complex estimate
EEPM Theatre services + A_{STP} + m	EEDM Theatre services + A_{STP} + m	EECM Theatre services + A_{STP} + m	EEEMX Theatre services + A_{STP} + m	№ 8
EEPM Circus services + A_{STP} + m	EEDM Circus services + A_{STP} + m	EECM Circus services + A_{STP} + m	EEEMX Circus services + A_{STP} + m	№ 9
EEPM Church services + A_{STP} + m	EEDM Church services + A_{STP} + m	EECM Church services + A_{STP} + m	EEEMX Church services + A_{STP} + m	№ 10
EEPM Cinema services + A_{STP} + m	EEDM Cinema services + A_{STP} + m	EECM Cinema services + A_{STP} + m	EEEMX Cinema services + A_{STP} + m	№ 11
EEPM Services of the sports-entertainment character (attractions, aqua parks, DisneyLands) + A_{STP} + m	EEDM Services of the sports-entertainment character (attractions, aqua parks, DisneyLands) + A_{STP} + m	EECM Services of the sports-entertainment character (attractions, aqua parks, DisneyLands) + A_{STP} + m	EEEMX Services of the sports-entertainment character (attractions, aqua parks, DisneyLands) + A_{STP} + m	№ 12
EEPM Services of the entertainment character (summer sports) + A_{STP} + m	EEDM Services of the entertainment character (summer sports) + A_{STP} + m	EECM Services of the entertainment character (summer sports) + A_{STP} + m	EEEMX Services of the entertainment character (summer sports) + A_{STP} + m	№ 13
EEPM Services of the entertainment character (winter sports) + A_{STP} + m	EEDM Services of the entertainment character (winter sports) + A_{STP} + m	EECM Services of the entertainment character (winter sports) + A_{STP} + m	EEEMX Services of the entertainment character (winter sports) + A_{STP} + m	№ 14

Economic estimates of production	Economic estimates of distribution	Economic estimates of exchange	Economic estimates of consumption	Complex estimate
EEPM Show services of football + A_{STP} + m	EEDM Show services of football + A_{STP} + m	EECM Show services of football + A_{STP} + m	EEEMX Show services of football + A_{STP} + m	№ 15
EEPM Show services of ice-hockey + A_{STP} + m	EEDM Show services of ice-hockey + A_{STP} + m	EECM Show services of ice-hockey + A_{STP} + m	EEEMX Show services of ice-hockey + A_{STP} + m	№ 16
EEPM Show services of ball-hockey + A_{STP} + m	EEDM Show services of ball-hockey + A_{STP} + m	EECM Show services of ball-hockey + A_{STP} + m	EEEMX Show services of ball-hockey + A_{STP} + m	№ 17
EEPM Show services of field hockey + A_{STP} + m	EEDM Show services of field hockey + A_{STP} + m	EECM Show services of field hockey + A_{STP} + m	EEEMX Show services of field hockey + A_{STP} + m	№ 18
EEPM Show services of basketball + A_{STP} + m	EEDM Show services of basketball + A_{STP} + m	EECM Show services of basketball + A_{STP} + m	EEEMX Show services of basketball + A_{STP} + m	№ 19
EEPM Show services of volley-ball + A_{STP} + m	EEDM Show services of volley-ball + A_{STP} + m	EECM Show services of volley-ball + A_{STP} + m	EEEMX Show services of volley-ball + A_{STP} + m	№ 20
EEPM Show services of baseball + A_{STP} + m	EEDM Show services of baseball + A_{STP} + m	EECM Show services of baseball + A_{STP} + m	EEEMX Show services of baseball + A_{STP} + m	№ 21
EEPM Show services of rugby + A_{STP} + m	EEDM Show services of rugby + A_{STP} + m	EECM Show services of rugby + A_{STP} + m	EEEMX Show services of rugby + A_{STP} + m	№ 22

Economic estimates of production	Economic estimates of distribution	Economic estimates of exchange	Economic estimates of consumption	Complex estimate
EEPM Show services of «Formula—1» + A_{STP} + m	EEDM Show services of «Formula—1» + A_{STP} + m	EECM Show services of «Formula—1» + A_{STP} + m	EEEMX Show services of «Formula—1» + A_{STP} + m	№ 23
EEPM Radio services + A_{STP} + m	EEDM Radio services + A_{STP} + m	EECM Radio services + A_{STP} + m	EEEMX Radio services + A_{STP} + m	№ 24
EEPM TV services + A_{STP} + m	EEDM TV services + A_{STP} + m	EECM TV services + A_{STP} + m	EEEMX TV services + A_{STP} + m	№ 25

The economic criteria connected to the movement within each of these relations.

The criteria characterizing the movement of the intellectual sphere resources can be of four types:

$$\text{Criterion № 1} = \frac{\text{Estimate of the result of the production including } A_{STP}}{\text{Expenses}}$$

$$\text{Criterion № 2} = \frac{\text{Estimate of the result of the distribution including } A_{STP}}{\text{Expenses}}$$

$$\text{Criterion № 3} = \frac{\text{Estimate of the result of the consumption including } A_{STP}}{\text{Expenses}}$$

$$\text{Criterion № 4} = \frac{\text{Estimate of the result of the exchange including } A_{STP}}{\text{Expenses}}$$

Table of Criteria Taking into Account the Economic Relations

Economic criteria of production	Economic criteria of distribution	Economic criteria of consumption	Economic criteria of exchange	Complex criteria
ECP School services + A_{STP}	ECD School services + A_{STP}	ECC School services + A_{STP}	ECEX School services + A_{STP}	№ 1[2]
ECP College services + A_{STP}	ECD College services + A_{STP}	ECC College services + A_{STP}	ECEX College services + A_{STP}	№ 2
ECP University services + A_{STP}	ECD University services + A_{STP}	ECC University services + A_{STP}	ECEX University services + A_{STP}	№ 3
ECP Library services + A_{STP}	ECD Library services + A_{STP}	ECC Library services + A_{STP}	ECEX Library services + A_{STP}	№ 4
ECP Exhibition services + A_{STP}	ECD Exhibition services + A_{STP}	ECC Exhibition services + A_{STP}	ECEX Exhibition services + A_{STP}	№ 5
ECP Museum services + A_{STP}	ECD Museum services + A_{STP}	ECC Museum services + A_{STP}	ECEX Museum services + A_{STP}	№ 6
ECP Concert services + A_{STP}	ECD Concert services + A_{STP}	ECC Concert services + A_{STP}	ECEX Concert services + A_{STP}	№ 7
ECP Theatre services + A_{STP}	ECD Theatre services + A_{STP}	ECC Theatre services + A_{STP}	ECEX Theatre services + A_{STP}	№ 8

---

2   ECP—Economic criteria of production
ECD—Economic criteria of distribution
ECC—Economic criteria of consumption
ECEX—Economic criteria of exchange

Economic criteria of production	Economic criteria of distribution	Economic criteria of consumption	Economic criteria of exchange	Complex criteria
ECP Circus services + A_{STP}	ECD Circus services + A_{STP}	ECC Circus services + A_{STP}	ECEX Circus services + A_{STP}	№ 9
ECP Church services + A_{STP}	ECD Church services + A_{STP}	ECC Church services + A_{STP}	ECEX Church services + A_{STP}	№ 10
ECP Cinema services + A_{STP}	ECD Cinema services + A_{STP}	ECC Cinema services + A_{STP}	ECEX Cinema services + A_{STP}	№ 11
ECP Services of the sports-entertainment character (attractions, aqua parks, DisneyLands) + A_{STP}	ECD Services of the sports-entertainment character (attractions, aqua parks, DisneyLands) + A_{STP}	ECC Services of the sports-entertainment character (attractions, aqua parks, DisneyLands) + A_{STP}	ECEX Services of the sports-entertainment character (attractions, aqua parks, DisneyLands) + A_{STP}	№ 12
ECP Services of the entertainment character (summer sports) + A_{STP}	ECD Services of the entertainment character (summer sports) + A_{STP}	ECC Services of the entertainment character (summer sports) + A_{STP}	ECEX Services of the entertainment character (summer sports) + A_{STP}	№ 13
ECP Services of the entertainment character (winter sports) + A_{STP}	ECD Services of the entertainment character (winter sports) + A_{STP}	ECC Services of the entertainment character (winter sports) + A_{STP}	ECEX Services of the entertainment character (winter sports) + A_{STP}	№ 14
ECP Show services of football + A_{STP}	ECD Show services of football + A_{STP}	ECC Show services of football + A_{STP}	ECEX Show services of football + A_{STP}	№ 15

Economic criteria of production	Economic criteria of distribution	Economic criteria of consumption	Economic criteria of exchange	Complex criteria
ECP Show services of ice-hockey + A_{STP}	ECD Show services of ice-hockey + A_{STP}	ECC Show services of ice-hockey + A_{STP}	ECEX Show services of ice-hockey + A_{STP}	№ 16
ECP Show services of ball-hockey + A_{STP}	ECD Show services of ball-hockey + A_{STP}	ECC Show services of ball-hockey + A_{STP}	ECEX Show services of ball-hockey + A_{STP}	№ 17
ECP Show services of field hockey + A_{STP}	ECD Show services of field hockey + A_{STP}	ECC Show services of field hockey + A_{STP}	ECEX Show services of field hockey + A_{STP}	№ 18
ECP Show services of basketball + A_{STP}	ECD Show services of basketball + A_{STP}	ECC Show services of basketball + A_{STP}	ECEX Show services of basketball + A_{STP}	№ 19
ECP Show services of volley-ball + A_{STP}	ECD Show services of volley-ball + A_{STP}	ECC Show services of volley-ball + A_{STP}	ECEX Show services of volley-ball + A_{STP}	№ 20
ECP Show services of baseball + A_{STP}	ECD Show services of baseball + A_{STP}	ECC Show services of baseball + A_{STP}	ECEX Show services of baseball + A_{STP}	№ 21
ECP Show services of rugby + A_{STP}	ECD Show services of rugby + A_{STP}	ECC Show services of rugby + A_{STP}	ECEX Show services of rugby + A_{STP}	№ 22
ECP Show services of «Formula— 1» + A_{STP}	ECD Show services of «Formula— 1» + A_{STP}	ECC Show services of «Formula— 1» + A_{STP}	ECEX Show services of «Formula— 1» + A_{STP}	№ 23

Economic criteria of production	Economic criteria of distribution	Economic criteria of consumption	Economic criteria of exchange	Complex criteria
ECP Radio services + A_{STP}	ECD Radio services + A_{STP}	ECC Radio services + A_{STP}	ECEX Radio services + A_{STP}	№ 24
ECP TV services + A_{STP}	ECD TV services + A_{STP}	ECC TV services + A_{STP}	ECEX TV services + A_{STP}	№ 25

- Economic indicators revealing the rate of movement within each of these relations.

3. Economic indicators of distribution

Indicators characterizing the «rate» of the movement of the intellectual sphere resources can be of four types:

$$\text{Indicator № 1} = \frac{\Delta \text{ Results of production}}{\Delta \text{ Investments}}$$

$$\text{Indicator № 2} = \frac{\Delta \text{ Results of distribution}}{\Delta \text{ Investments}}$$

$$\text{Indicator № 3} = \frac{\Delta \text{ Results of consumption}}{\Delta \text{ Investments}}$$

$$\text{Indicator № 4} = \frac{\Delta \text{ Results of exchange}}{\Delta \text{ Investments}}$$

Until recently Δ of the assimilated spare time of the population resource has not been considered as a specific result.

Table of Indicators Taking into Account the Economic Relations

Economic indicators of production	Economic indicators of distribution	Economic indicators of consumption	Economic indicators of exchange	Complex indicator
EIP School services + A_{STP}	EID School services + A_{STP}	EIC School services + A_{STP}	EIEX School services + A_{STP}	№ 1[3]
EIP College services + A_{STP}	EID College services + A_{STP}	EIC College services + A_{STP}	EIEX College services + A_{STP}	№ 2
EIP University services + A_{STP}	EID University services + A_{STP}	EIC University services + A_{STP}	EIEX University services + A_{STP}	№ 3
EIP Library services + A_{STP}	EID Library services + A_{STP}	EIC Library services + A_{STP}	EIEX Library services + A_{STP}	№ 4
EIP Exhibition services + A_{STP}	EID Exhibition services + A_{STP}	EIC Exhibition services + A_{STP}	EIEX Exhibition services + A_{STP}	№ 5
EIP Museum services + A_{STP}	EID Museum services + A_{STP}	EIC Museum services + A_{STP}	EIEX Museum services + A_{STP}	№ 6
EIP Concert services + A_{STP}	EID Concert services + A_{STP}	EIC Concert services + A_{STP}	EIEX Concert services + A_{STP}	№ 7
EIP Theatre services + A_{STP}	EID Theatre services + A_{STP}	EIC Theatre services + A_{STP}	EIEX Theatre services + A_{STP}	№ 8

3   EIP—Economic indicator of production
EID—Economic indicator of distribution
EIC—Economic indicator of consumption
EIEX—Economic indicator of exchange

Economic indicators of production	Economic indicators of distribution	Economic indicators of consumption	Economic indicators of exchange	Complex indicator
EIP Circus services + A_{STP}	EID Circus services + A_{STP}	EIC Circus services + A_{STP}	EIEX Circus services + A_{STP}	№ 9
EIP Church services + A_{STP}	EID Church services + A_{STP}	EIC Church services + A_{STP}	EIEX Church services + A_{STP}	№ 10
EIP Cinema services + A_{STP}	EID Cinema services + A_{STP}	EIC Cinema services + A_{STP}	EIEX Cinema services + A_{STP}	№ 11
EIP Services of the sports-entertainment character (attractions, aqua parks, DisneyLands) + A_{STP}	EID Services of the sports-entertainment character (attractions, aqua parks, DisneyLands) + A_{STP}	EIC Services of the sports-entertainment character (attractions, aqua parks, DisneyLands) + A_{STP}	EIEX Services of the sports-entertainment character (attractions, aqua parks, DisneyLands) + A_{STP}	№ 12
EIP Services of the entertainment character (summer sports) + A_{STP}	EID Services of the entertainment character (summer sports) + A_{STP}	EIC Services of the entertainment character (summer sports) + A_{STP}	EIEX Services of the entertainment character (summer sports) + A_{STP}	№ 13
EIP Services of the entertainment character (winter sports) + A_{STP}	EID Services of the entertainment character (winter sports) + A_{STP}	EIC Services of the entertainment character (winter sports) + A_{STP}	EIEX Services of the entertainment character (winter sports) + A_{STP}	№ 14
EIP Show services of football + A_{STP}	EID Show services of football + A_{STP}	EIC Show services of football + A_{STP}	EIEX Show services of football + A_{STP}	№ 15

Economic indicators of production	Economic indicators of distribution	Economic indicators of consumption	Economic indicators of exchange	Complex indicator
EIP Show services of ice-hockey + A_{STP}	EID Show services of ice-hockey + A_{STP}	EIC Show services of ice-hockey + A_{STP}	EIEX Show services of ice-hockey + A_{STP}	№ 16
EIP Show services of ball-hockey + A_{STP}	EID Show services of ball-hockey + A_{STP}	EIC Show services of ball-hockey + A_{STP}	EIEX Show services of ball-hockey + A_{STP}	№ 17
EIP Show services of field hockey + A_{STP}	EID Show services of field hockey + A_{STP}	EIC Show services of field hockey + A_{STP}	EIEX Show services of field hockey + A_{STP}	№ 18
EIP Show services of basketball + A_{STP}	EID Show services of basketball + A_{STP}	EIC Show services of basketball + A_{STP}	EIEX Show services of basketball + A_{STP}	№ 19
EIP Show services of volley-ball + A_{STP}	EID Show services of volley-ball + A_{STP}	EIC Show services of volley-ball + A_{STP}	EIEX Show services of volley-ball + A_{STP}	№ 20
EIP Show services of baseball + A_{STP}	EID Show services of baseball + A_{STP}	EIC Show services of baseball + A_{STP}	EIEX Show services of baseball + A_{STP}	№ 21
EIP Show services of rugby + A_{STP}	EID Show services of rugby + A_{STP}	EIC Show services of rugby + A_{STP}	EIEX Show services of rugby + A_{STP}	№ 22
EIP Show services of «Formula—1» + A_{STP}	EID Show services of «Formula—1» + A_{STP}	EIC Show services of «Formula—1» + A_{STP}	EIEX Show services of «Formula—1» + A_{STP}	№ 23

Economic indicators of production	Economic indicators of distribution	Economic indicators of consumption	Economic indicators of exchange	Complex indicator
EIP Radio services + A_{STP}	EID Radio services + A_{STP}	EIC Radio services + A_{STP}	EIEX Radio services + A_{STP}	№ 24
EIP TV services + A_{STP}	EID TV services + A_{STP}	EIC TV services + A_{STP}	EIEX TV services + A_{STP}	№ 25

CHAPTER 7

The Peculiarities of the Reproduction of the Intellectual Sphere

Until recently we have been investigating the movement of intellectual values, intellectual services and the aggregate intellectual product as an integral process:

Production	Distribution	Exchange	Consumption
Intellectual values	Intellectual values	Intellectual values	Intellectual values
↓	↓	↓	↓
Intellectual services	Intellectual services	Intellectual services	Intellectual services
↓	↓	↓	↓
Intellectual product	Intellectual product	Intellectual product	Intellectual product

The problems with reproduction of intellectual sphere can be considered as three autonomous processes:

Process № 1—The reproduction process of the educational sphere;

Process № 2—The reproduction process of the enlightenment sphere;

Process № 3—The reproduction process of the entertainment sphere.

If on axis «X» we should set the reproduction vector of the educational sphere

On axis «Y» we should set the reproduction vector of the enlightenment sphere

On axis «Z» we should set the reproduction vector of the entertainment sphere

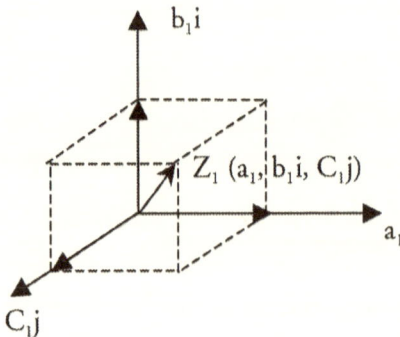

The aggregate vector of reproduction of the intellectual sphere:

$$R = a + bi + Cj$$

One of the problems arising while we are classifying the forms of activities in the educational sphere concerns the question of libraries, whether or not they should be included into this sphere.

As it is known, libraries perform both educational and enlightenment functions. I purpose the inclusion of libraries in the educational system will not be erroneous.[4]

The first thing we shall do in this connection is to establish the streams of resources flowing into and out of these spheres.

The Streams of Resources in the Educational Sphere

Inflowing		Outflowing
Resources A →	Production of books for the studying process →	Resource A
Inflowing		Outflowing
Resources B →	Pre-school/nursery establishments →	Resource B
Inflowing		Outflowing
Resources C →	Secondary/comprehensive schools →	Resource C

---

4   See. Macroeconomy of the Educational Sphere with Complex Numbers—Quaternions.

Inflowing Resources D	→	Colleges	→	Outflowing Resource D
Inflowing Resources E	→	Universities	→	Outflowing Resource E
Inflowing Resources F	→	Libraries	→	Outflowing Resource F

I suggest that a formalized record of educational values and services should be dine with the use of complex numbers.

Economic Estimates Connected to the Movement of Educational Values, Services and the Aggregate Educational Product

	Production	*Distribution*	*Exchange*	*Consumption*
A.	«Production» process of intellectual values educational character →	«Distribution» process of intellectual values educational character →	«Exchange» process of intellectual values educational character →	«Consumption» process of intellectual values educational character
	↓	↓	↓	↓
B.	«Production» process of intellectual services educational character →	«Distribution» process of Intellectual services educational character →	«Exchange» process of Intellectual services educational character →	«Consumption» process of intellectual services educational character
	↓	↓	↓	↓
C.	«Production» process of the aggregate intellectual product educational character →	«Distribution» process of the aggregate intellectual product educational character →	«Exchange» process of the aggregate intellectual product educational character →	«Consumption» process of the aggregate intellectual product educational character

The Expenses Connected to the Movement of Educational Values, Services and the Aggregate Educational Product

	Estimation of expenses of production	Estimation of expenses of distribution	Estimation of expenses of exchange	Estimation of expenses of consumption
A.	«Production» process of intellectual values educational character →	«Distribution» process of intellectual values educational character →	«Exchange» process of intellectual values educational character →	«Consumption» process of intellectual values educational character
	↓	↓	↓	↓
B.	«Production» process of intellectual services educational character →	«Distribution» process of Intellectual services educational character →	«Exchange» process of Intellectual services educational character →	«Consumption» process of intellectual services educational character
	↓	↓		↓
C.	«Production» process of the aggregate intellectual product educational character →	«Distribution» process of the aggregate intellectual product educational character →	«Exchange» process of the aggregate intellectual product educational character →	«Consumption» process of the aggregate intellectual product educational character

The Results Connected to the Movement of Educational Values, Services and the Aggregate Educational Product

	Estimation of results of production	Estimation of results of distribution	Estimation of results of exchange	Estimation of results of consumption
A.	«Production» process of intellectual values educational character →	«Distribution» process of intellectual values educational character →	«Exchange» process of intellectual values educational character →	«Consumption» process of intellectual values educational character
	↓	↓	↓	↓
B.	«Production» process of intellectual services educational character →	«Distribution» process of Intellectual services educational character →	«Exchange» process of Intellectual services educational character →	«Consumption» process of intellectual services educational character
	↓	↓	↓	↓

Estimation of results of production	Estimation of results of distribution	Estimation of results of exchange	Estimation of results of consumption
C. «Production» process of the aggregate intellectual product educational character →	«Distribution» process of the aggregate intellectual product educational character →	«Exchange» process of the aggregate intellectual product educational character →	«Consumption» process of the aggregate intellectual product educational character

The Criteria Connected to the Movement of Educational Values, Services and the Aggregate Educational Product

Economic criteria of production	Economic criteria of distribution	Economic criteria of exchange	Economic criteria of consumption
A. «Production» process of intellectual values educational character →	«Distribution» process of intellectual values educational character →	«Exchange» process of intellectual values educational character →	«Consumption» process of intellectual values educational character
↓	↓	↓	↓
B. «Production» process of intellectual services educational character →	«Distribution» process of Intellectual services educational character →	«Exchange» process of Intellectual services educational character →	«Consumption» process of intellectual services educational character
↓	↓	↓	↓
C. «Production» process of the aggregate intellectual product educational character →	«Distribution» process of the aggregate intellectual product educational character →	«Exchange» process of the aggregate intellectual product educational character →	«Consumption» process of the aggregate intellectual product educational character

The Indicators Connected to the Movement of Educational Values, Services and the Aggregate Educational Product

Economic indicators of production	*Economic indicators of distribution*	*Economic indicators of exchange*	*Economic indicators of consumption*
A. «Production» process of intellectual values educational character →	«Distribution» process of intellectual values educational character →	«Exchange» process of intellectual values educational character →	«Consumption» process of intellectual values educational character
↓	↓	↓	↓
B. «Production» process of intellectual services educational character →	«Distribution» process of Intellectual services educational character →	«Exchange» process of Intellectual services educational character →	«Consumption» process of intellectual services educational character
↓	↓	↓	↓
C. «Production» process of the aggregate intellectual product educational character →	«Distribution» process of the aggregate intellectual product educational character →	«Exchange» process of the aggregate intellectual product educational character →	«Consumption» process of the aggregate intellectual product educational character

B. The Streams of Resources in the Enlightenment Sphere

I consider enlightenment as an economic system which consists of eight subdivisions:

Inflowing		Outflowing
	Subdivision № 1	
Resources A →	Production of enlightenment values (material form)	→ Resource AA

Inflowing		Outflowing
	Subdivision № 2	
Resources B →	Production of exhibition services	→ Resource BB

| Inflowing | | Outflowing |
| Resources C → | Subdivision № 3
Production of museum services | → Resource CC |

| Inflowing | | Outflowing |
| Resources D → | Subdivision № 4
Production of concert services | → Resource DD |

| Inflowing | | Outflowing |
| Resources E → | Subdivision № 5
Production of theatre services | → Resource EE |

| Inflowing | | Outflowing |
| Resources F → | Subdivision № 6
Production of circus services | → Resource FF |

| Inflowing | | Outflowing |
| Resources G → | Subdivision № 7
Production of church services | → Resource GG |

| Inflowing | | Outflowing |
| Resources H → | Subdivision № 8
Production of cinema services | → Resource HH |

I suggest that a formalized record of enlightenment values and services should be done with the use of complex numbers.

1. A graphic interpretation of the <u>enlightenment values</u> in a three-dimensional space.

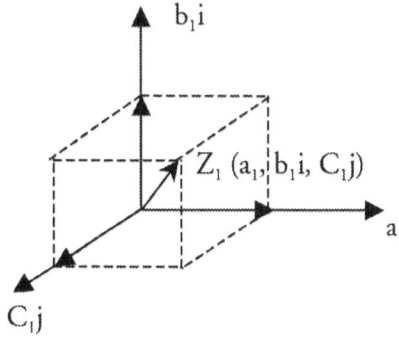

where

> a_1—the past labor expenses related to the production of enlightenment values (material form);
>
> b_1i—the direct labor expenses related to the production of enlightenment values;
>
> C_1j—income from subdivision I.
>
> Vector $Z_1 = a_1 + b_1i + C_1j$

2. Graphic interpretation of the second kind of <u>exhibition services</u> in the three-dimensional space will have the following shape:

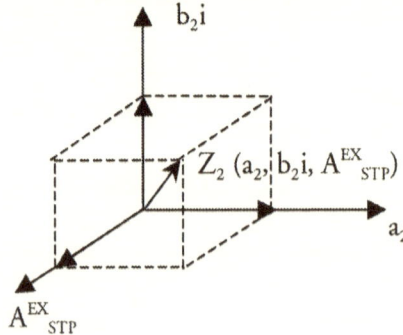

where

> a_2—the past labor expenses connected to the creation of the exhibition services of the second kind;
>
> b_2i—the direct labor expenses connected to the creation of exhibition services of the second kind;
>
> A^{EX}_{STP}—the spare time of the population resources assimilated by the exhibition services of the second kind.
>
> Vector $Z_2 = a_2 + b_2i + A^{EX}_{STP}$

We shall add one more vector—m_3j—income from exhibition services to the above recorded quaternions.

3. A graphic interpretation of the third kind of <u>museum services</u> in a three dimensional economic space will be shown as:

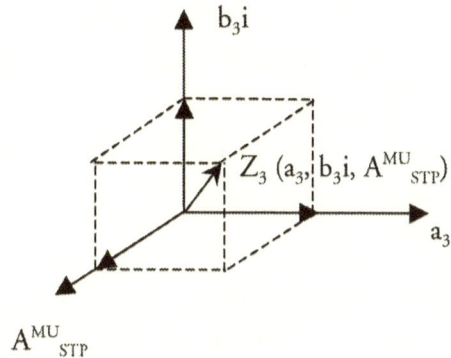

where

    a_3—the past labor expenses of the museum sphere subdivision 3;

    b_3i—the direct labor expenses of the museum sphere subdivision 3;

    A^{MU}_{STP}—the spare time of the population resource assimilated by the third kind of museum services.

    Vector $Z_3 = a_3 + b_3i + A^{MU}_{STP}$

We shall also add another vector—m_2j—income from the enlightenment services, or to the above recorded quaternion, in case private museum establishments are dealt with.

4. A graphic interpretation of the fourth kind of <u>concert services</u> in the three-dimensional economic space will be as follows:

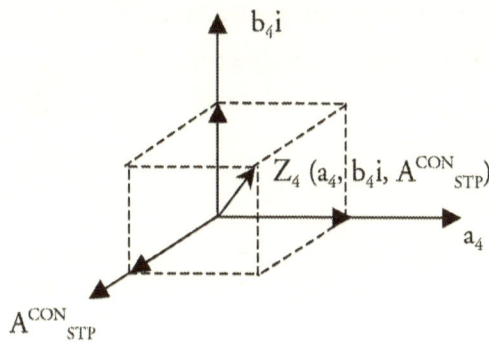

where

a$_4$—the past labor expenses of the concert sphere subdivision 4;

b$_4$i—the direct labor expenses of the concert sphere subdivision 4;

A^{CON}$_{STP}$—the spare time of the population resource assimilated by the fourth kind of concert services.

Vector $Z_4 = a_4 + b_4i + A^{CON}_{STP}$

We again adding another vector m$_4$j—income from the enlightenment services, income of subdivision 4, in case private concert establishments are under consideration.

5. A graphic interpretation of the fifth kind of <u>theatre services</u> in a three-dimensional economic space will be as follows:

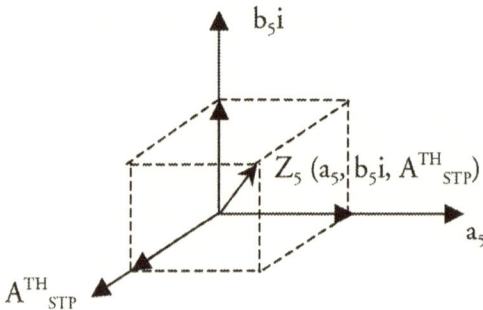

where

a$_5$—the past labor expenses of the theatre sphere subdivision 5;

b$_5$i—direct labor expenses of the theatre sphere subdivision 5;

ATH$_{STP}$—the spare time of the population resource assimilated by the fifth kind of theatre services.

Vector $Z_5 = a_5 + b_5i + A^{TH}_{STP}$

We again adding another vector m$_5$j—income from enlightenment services, income subdivision 5, in case private theatre establishment are under consideration.

6. A graphic interpretation of <u>circus services</u> in a three-dimensional space is seen as follows:

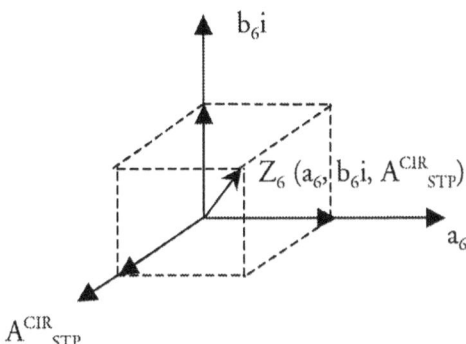

where

    a_6—the past labor expenses of the circus sphere subdivision 6;

    b_6i—the direct labor expenses of the circus sphere subdivision 6;

    A^{CIR}_{STP}—the spare time of the population resource assimilated by the circus services.

    Vector $Z_6 = a_6 + b_6i + A^{CIR}_{STP}$

7. A graphic interpretation of <u>church services</u> in a three-dimensional space (Z_7) is seen as follows:

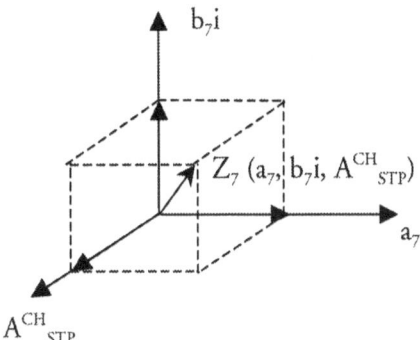

where

    a_7—the past labor expenses of church sphere subdivision 7;

    b_7i—the direct labor expenses of church sphere subdivision 7;

    A^{CH}_{STP}—the spare time of the population resource assimilated by the church services.

    Vector $Z_7 = a_7 + b_7i + A^{CH}_{STP}$

8. A graphic interpretation of <u>cinema services</u> in a three-dimensional space is seen as follows:

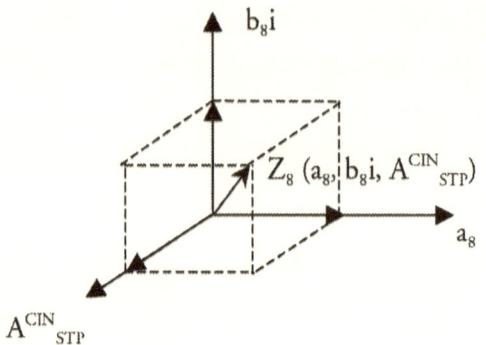

where

a_8—the past labor expenses of the cinema sphere subdivision 8;

b_8i—the direct labor expenses of the cinema sphere subdivision 8;

A^{CIN}_{STP}—the spare time of the population resource assimilated by the cinema services.

Vector $Z_8 = a_8 + b_8i + A^{CIN}_{STP}$

Provided that the cinema system is the one having its own income, we shall add the income of subdivision 8—m_3j to the above suggested quaternion.

The structure of the enlightenment sphere will be written down as follows:

$$
\begin{cases}
C_1 + V_1i + m_1j & = Z_1 & \text{- First subdivision—enlightenment values} \\
C_2 + V_2i + m_2j + A^{EX}_{STP}d_1 & = Z_2 & \text{- Second subdivision} \\
C_3 + V_3i + m_3j + A^{MU}_{STP}d_2 & = Z_3 & \text{- Third subdivision} \\
C_4 + V_4i + m_4j + A^{CON}_{STP}d_3 & = Z_4 & \text{- Fourth subdivision} \\
C_5 + V_5i + m_5j + A^{TH}_{STP}d_4 & = Z_5 & \text{- Fifth subdivision} \\
C_6 + V_6i + m_6j + A^{CIR}_{STP}d_5 & = Z_6 & \text{- Sixth subdivision} \\
C_7 + V_7i + m_7j + A^{CH}_{STP}d_6 & = Z_7 & \text{- Seventh subdivision} \\
C_8 + V_8i + m_8j + A^{CIN}_{STP}d_7 & = Z_8 & \text{- Eighth subdivision}
\end{cases}
$$

This system of enlightenment is written in the vector form.

For a better understanding of the vector form of writing the results of the enlightenment sphere? I suggest that their graphical interpretation should be performed in the three and four dimensional space.

General scheme of the reproduction of the enlightenment sphere can be represented as:

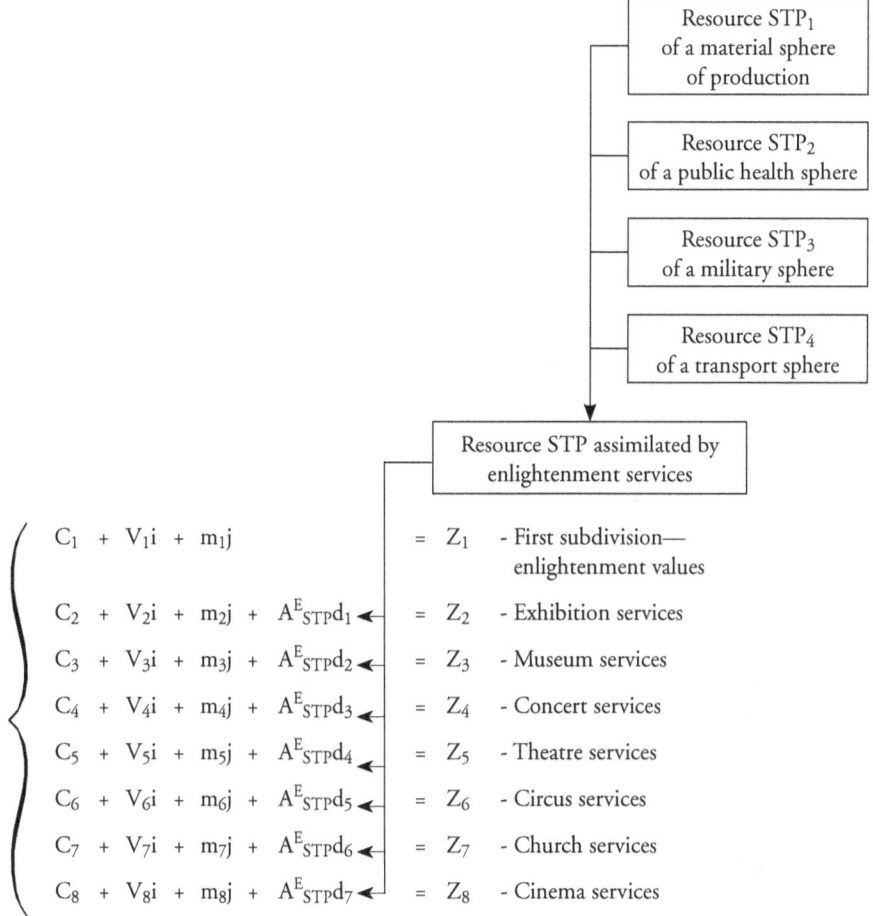

$A^E_{STPd_1}$—human stream of resources with the time factor A_{STP} assimilated by exhibitions;

$A^E_{STPd_2}$—human stream of resources with the time factor A_{STP} assimilated by museums;

$A^E_{STP}d_3$—human stream of resources with the time factor A_{STP} assimilated by concerts;

$A^E_{STP}d_4$—human stream of resources with the time factor A_{STP} assimilated by theatres;

$A^E_{STP}d_5$—human stream of resources with the time factor A_{STP} assimilated by circus;

$A^E_{STP}d_6$—human stream of resources with the time factor A_{STP} assimilated by churches;

$A^E_{STP}d_7$—human stream of resources with the time factor A_{STP} assimilated by cinema.

The human streams of resources of relatively autonomous spheres of the spare time of the population (A_{STP1}, A_{STP2}, A_{STP3}, A_{STP4}, A_{STP5}, A_{STP6}, A_{STP7}).

It is difficult to define what streams of resources should be channeled to the production needs of the enlightenment sphere.

It is also not easy to clarify what resources are being channeled to non-production aims of the enlightenment sphere.

What proportions should exist between these two main streams?

What proportions should be between past, direct and aggregate labor expenses in the process of the production, distribution, exchange and consumption of enlightenment values and services?

It is also essential to apply a logical criteria in the classification of reproductive schemes as well as of the «equality» and «inequality» between past labor expenses and direct labor expenses used for the creation of enlightenment values and services.

Below we shall investigate the patterns of the reproduction of the enlightenment sphere taking into account the human stream of resources assimilated by enlightenment services.

At this stage of research I shall examine the following options of the enlightenment sphere reproduction.

C. Classification of the Reproductive Processes in the Enlightenment Sphere

1) <u>Simple scale reproduction of the enlightenment sphere</u>.

In the reproductive scheme the used up part of Subdivisions I, II, III, IV, V, VI, VII, past labor is being restored. In other terms, all that has been carried over to renewed enlightenment values and services are restored.

Enlightenment sphere resources in the cost form can be represented as:

$$
\begin{cases}
C_1 + \boxed{V_1i + m_1j} = Z_1 & \text{- First subdivision—} \\
& \quad\text{enlightenment values} \\
\boxed{=} \\
C_2 + V_2i + m_2j + A^{EX}{}_{STP}d_1 = Z_2 \\
C_3 + V_3i + m_3j + A^{MU}{}_{STP}d_2 = Z_3 \\
C_4 + V_4i + m_4j + A^{CON}{}_{STP}d_3 = Z_4 \\
C_5 + V_5i + m_5j + A^{TH}{}_{STP}d_4 = Z_5 \\
C_6 + V_6i + m_6j + A^{CIR}{}_{STP}d_5 = Z_6 \\
C_7 + V_7i + m_7j + A^{CH}{}_{STP}d_6 = Z_7 \\
C_8 + V_8i + m_8j + A^{CIN}{}_{STP}d_7 = Z_8
\end{cases}
$$

where

$$(C1 + V1i + m1j) = C1 + C2 + C3 + C4 + C5 + C6 + C7 + C8$$

or

$$(V1i + m1j) = (C2 + C3 + C4 + C5 + C6 + C7 + C8).$$

Otherwise, we examine the case when the decreasing part of Subdivisions I, II, III material resources coincide with the restored amount of Subdivision I of enlightenment values

$$(V1i + m1j) = (C2 + C3 + C4 + C5 + C6 + C7 + C8)$$

or

$$(V1i + m1j) - (C2 + C3 + C4 + C5 + C6 + C7 + C8) = 0.$$

Enlarged scale reproduction of the enlightenment sphere

The reproduction of the enlightenment sphere on an enlarged scale is possible in case of additional investments, provided that more enlightenment values than what was required in the previous cycle have been created in Subdivision I.

In this option of the enlightenment sphere reproduction we have an excess of the volume of enlightenment values over the utilized part of the material base of subdivisions I, II, III, IV, V, VI, VII, VIII.

Enlightenment values are being created in such quantities that it would make it possible, not only to restore the utilized part of the material resources, but also to expand them.

$$
\begin{cases}
C_1 + \boxed{V_1i + m_1j} = Z_1 & \text{- First subdivision—enlightenment values} \\
\qquad\qquad \downarrow \\
\qquad\qquad \boxed{<} \\
\boxed{C_2} + V_2i + m_2j + A^E_{STP}d_1 = Z_2 \\
\boxed{C_3} + V_3i + m_3j + A^E_{STP}d_2 = Z_3 \\
\boxed{C_4} + V_4i + m_4j + A^E_{STP}d_3 = Z_4 \\
\boxed{C_5} + V_5i + m_5j + A^E_{TP}d_4 = Z_5 \\
\boxed{C_6} + V_6i + m_6j + A^E_{STP}d_5 = Z_6 \\
\boxed{C_7} + V_7i + m_7j + A^E_{STP}d_6 = Z_7 \\
\boxed{C_8} + V_8i + m_8j + A^E_{STP}d_7 = Z_8
\end{cases}
$$

where

$$(C1 + V1i + m1j) > (C1 + C2 + C3 + C4 + C5 + C6 + C7 + C8)$$

or

$$(V1i + m1j) > (C2 + C3 + C4 + C5 + C6 + C7 + C8)$$

or

$$(V1i + m1j)—(C2 + C3 + C4 + C5 + C6 + C7 + C8) > 0.$$

Reproduction of the enlightenment sphere

SCHEME C

This scheme reflects the option when the enlightenment sphere is functioning in conditions when the decreasing part of C_1, C_2, C_3, C_4, C_5, C_6, C_7, C_8 is partially restored. The amount of enlightenment values of subdivision I is insufficient for reproduction:

$$(C1 + C2 + C3 + C4 + C5 + C6 + C7 + C8) > Z1$$

or

$$(C2 + C3 + C4 + C5 + C6 + C7 + C8) > (V1i + m1j)$$

$$C_1 + V_1i + m_1j = Z_1 \quad \text{- First subdivision—enlightenment values}$$

$$> $$

$$C_2 + V_2i + m_2j + A^E_{STP}d_1 = Z_2$$
$$C_3 + V_3i + m_3j + A^E_{STP}d_2 = Z_3$$
$$C_4 + V_4i + m_4j + A^E_{STP}d_3 = Z_4$$
$$C_5 + V_5i + m_5j + A^E_{TP}d_4 = Z_5$$
$$C_6 + V_6i + m_6j + A^E_{STP}d_5 = Z_6$$
$$C_7 + V_7i + m_7j + A^E_{STP}d_6 = Z_7$$
$$C_8 + V_8i + m_8j + A^E_{STP}d_7 = Z_8$$

Here we face a problem of the distribution of the renewed enlightenment sphere Subdivision I product Z_1 among Subdivision I, II, III, IV, V, VI, VII, VIII.

Examining the reproduction schemes in such a key is the first stage to be passed while revealing the contours of the inner problems existing in this sphere of economy.

Having examined the vector form of interpreting enlightenment values and services we shall get over to the next stage of our research. The essence of it consists in the need to perform arithmetic operations with enlightenment values and services. However, we have to deal with the problem of the addition, subtraction, multiplication and division of vectors Z_1, Z_2, Z_3, Z_4, Z_5, Z_6, Z_7 and Z_8.

They are recorded with the aid of specific complex numbers—quaternions, which have their own arithmetic and algebraic rules. Thus we have to apply other version of arithmetic and algebra, different from that we have been accustomed to, since complex numbers shall be treated otherwise.

The Estimates Connected to the Movement of Enlightenment Values, Services and the Aggregate Enlightenment Product

	Production		Distribution		Exchange		Consumption
A.	«Production» process of intellectual values enlightenment character	→	«Distribution» process of intellectual values enlightenment character	→	«Exchange» process of intellectual values enlightenment character	→	«Consumption» process of intellectual values enlightenment character
	↓		↓		↓		↓
B.	«Production» process of intellectual services enlightenment character	→	«Distribution» process of Intellectual services enlightenment character	→	«Exchange» process of Intellectual services enlightenment character	→	«Consumption» process of intellectual services enlightenment character
	↓		↓		↓		↓
C.	«Production» process of the aggregate intellectual product enlightenment character	→	«Distribution» process of the aggregate intellectual product enlightenment character	→	«Exchange» process of the aggregate intellectual product enlightenment character	→	«Consumption» process of the aggregate intellectual product enlightenment character

The Expenses Connected to the Movement of Enlightenment Values, Services and the Aggregate Enlightenment Product

Economic estimates of production	Economic estimates of distribution	Economic estimates of consumption	Economic estimates of exchange	Indices
Enlightenment values	Enlightenment values	Enlightenment values	Enlightenment values	Index AA
Enlightenment services	Enlightenment services	Enlightenment services	Enlightenment services	Index BB
Aggregate enlightenment product	Aggregate enlightenment product	Aggregate enlightenment product	Aggregate enlightenment product	Index CC

The Criteria Connected to the Movement of Enlightenment Values, Services and the Aggregate Enlightenment Product

Economic criteria of production	Economic criteria of distribution	Economic criteria of consumption	Economic criteria of exchange	Criteria
Enlightenment values	Enlightenment values	Enlightenment values	Enlightenment values	Criterion AA
Enlightenment services	Enlightenment services	Enlightenment services	Enlightenment services	Criterion BB
Aggregate enlightenment product	Aggregate enlightenment product	Aggregate enlightenment product	Aggregate enlightenment product	Criterion CC

The Indicators Connected to the Movement of Enlightenment Values, Services and the Aggregate Enlightenment Product

Economic indicators of production	Economic indicators of distribution	Economic indicators of consumption	Economic indicators of exchange	Criteria
Enlightenment values	Enlightenment values	Enlightenment values	Enlightenment values	Criterion AA
Enlightenment services	Enlightenment services	Enlightenment services	Enlightenment services	Criterion BB
Aggregate enlightenment product	Aggregate enlightenment product	Aggregate enlightenment product	Aggregate enlightenment product	Criterion CC

CHAPTER 8

The Reproduction of the Entertainment Sphere

I consider the entertainment sphere as an economic system which consists of two large autonomous divisions:

$\left\{\begin{array}{ll} 1^{st} \text{ Division} & \text{Production of entertainment values} \\ 2^{nd} \text{ Division} & \text{Production of entertainment services} \end{array}\right.$

Entertainment values and services are organically connected.

A following dialectical scheme could be drawn based on the above:

DIALECTICAL SCHEME
OF A SOLITARY ENTERTAINMENT PRODUCT

Thesis: Solitary entertainment value (material form)

Antithesis: Solitary entertainment service (non-material form)

Synthesis: Solitary (aggregate) entertainment product (complex form)

The entertainment sphere of production as an economic system is not only a complex of the production processes of entertainment values and services, but also a distribution and consumption of these values and services and their exchange for other values and services, etc.

The peculiarities of the economic relations in the «entertainment sphere» are:

- *firstly,* **the process of creating (producing)** entertainment values, services and the aggregate entertainment product;

- *secondly,* **the process of distribution** of entertainment values, services and the aggregate entertainment product;

- *thirdly,* **the process of exchange** entertainment values, services and the aggregate entertainment product;

- *fourthly,* **the consumption process** is divided into two parts: production consumption and non-production consumption.

The complex of these specific economic relations makes up an economic structure of this entertainment sphere. This is the reality of what we reproduce every day.

The Estimates Connected to the Movement of Entertainment Values, Services and the Aggregate Entertainment Product

	Production	*Distribution*	*Exchange*	*Consumption*
A.	«Production» process of intellectual values entertainment character $\rightarrow$	«Distribution» process of intellectual values entertainment character $\rightarrow$	«Exchange» process of intellectual values entertainment character $\rightarrow$	«Consumption» process of intellectual values entertainment character
	$\downarrow$	$\downarrow$	$\downarrow$	$\downarrow$
B.	«Production» process of intellectual services entertainment character $\rightarrow$	«Distribution» process of Intellectual services entertainment character $\rightarrow$	«Exchange» process of Intellectual services entertainment character $\rightarrow$	«Consumption» process of intellectual services entertainment character
	$\downarrow$	$\downarrow$	$\downarrow$	$\downarrow$
C.	«Production» process of the aggregate intellectual product entertainment character $\rightarrow$	«Distribution» process of the aggregate intellectual product entertainment character $\rightarrow$	«Exchange» process of the aggregate intellectual product entertainment character $\rightarrow$	«Consumption» process of the aggregate intellectual product entertainment character

Today «entertainment branches» are a special part of the economy. They consists of huge enterprises and institutions:

Subdivision B «Sports-entertainment branches»:

- «Entertainment» services (attractions, aqua parks, DisneyLands);
- «Entertainment» services (summer sports);
- «Entertainment» services (winter sports);
- «Football» services;
- «Ice-hockey» services;
- «Ball-hockey» services;
- «Field hockey» services;
- «Basketball» services;
- «Volley-ball» services;
- «Baseball» services;
- «Rugby» services;
- «Formula—1» services;

Subdivision C entertainment branches:

- «Radio» services;
- «TV» services.

Scheme A

We consider a variant of an excess of direct labor expenses in the entertainment sphere Division I that go for the production of the entertainment values which are to enter EN Divisions II & III replacing a quitting portion (IIc and IIIc). The entertainment values are produced at such an amount that it allows us to restore and add a new portion to the quitting material and technical basis of IP Divisions II & III.

$$
\begin{cases}
C_1 + \boxed{V_1 i + m_1 j} & = D_1 \\
\qquad\quad \boxed{<} \\
\boxed{C_2} + V_2 i + m_2 j + A^E_{STP}d & = D_2 \\
C_3 + V_3 i + m_3 j + A^S_{STP}d & = D_3
\end{cases}
$$

$$I (C1 + Vli + m1j) > (C1 + C2 + C3)$$

or

$$I (Vli + m1j) > (C2 + C3)$$

or

$$I (Vli + m1j) - (C2 + C3) > 0.$$

As per Scheme A, the product of the labor of the EN Division I exceeds the past labor expenses $C_1 + C_2 + C_3$, which are transferred onto the newly created entertainment values (D_1) and entertainment services (D_2) and (D_3).

The scheme considers a problem of direct labor expenses in EN Division I ($V_1 + m_1$) with an amount of investments (of past labor) that go for the creation of the technical basis of entertainment Divisions II & III (IIc + IIIc).

Scheme B

Direct labor expenses in EN Division I are equal to a quitting portion of the past labor in EN Divisions II & III in the reproduction scheme proposed here. In other words, all and everything that has been transferred into the newly created «entertainment» services is restored.

$$\begin{cases} C_1 + \boxed{V_1i + m_1j} & = D_1 \\ \quad\ \ \boxed{=} & \\ \boxed{\begin{aligned} C_2 \\ C_3 \end{aligned}} + V_2i + m_2j + A^E_{STP}d & = D_2 \\ \ \ \ + V_3i + m_3j + A^S_{STP}d & = D_3 \end{cases}$$

Scheme B holds the following equalities

$$(C1 + Vli + m1j) = (C1 + C2 + C3)$$

or

$$(Vli + m1j) = (C2 + C3).$$

And this means that all past labor expenses spent for the production of the entertainment values and services are compensated within the sphere.

In other words, we are considering the variant of a coincidence of the quitting portion of the technical basis of Divisions II & III with a newly created volume of the entertainment values of IP Division I.

$$I(V1i + m1j) = (C2 + C3)$$

or

$$I(V1i + m1j) - (C2 + C3) = 0.$$

Scheme C

Scheme C reflects a variant of the entertainment sphere functioning when past labor expenses are partially restored in it, i.e. an insufficient amount of the entertainment values required for a reproduction is produced within Division I.

$$(C_1 + C_2 + C_3) > D_1$$

or

$$(C_2 + C_3) > I(V_1 + m_1)$$

$$
\left\{
\begin{array}{l}
C_1 \;+\; \boxed{V_1i \;+\; m_1j} \qquad\qquad = \; D_1 \\[2ex]
\qquad\; \boxed{>} \\[2ex]
\boxed{\begin{array}{l} C_2 \end{array}} \;+\; V_2i \;+\; m_2j \;+\; A^E_{STP}d \;=\; D_2 \\[1ex]
\boxed{\begin{array}{l} C_3 \end{array}} \;+\; V_3i \;+\; m_3j \;+\; A^S_{STP}d \;=\; D_3
\end{array}
\right.
$$

Apart from the above, some problems arise concerning the distribution of the newly created product of EN Division I—D_1 between Divisions I, II & III. And three variants appear here.

Firstly, the entertainment values are to be more directed into EN Division II than into the «Entertainment» branch $II_c > III_c$;

Secondly, the quantity of the entertainment values directed into Divisions II & III is equal, i.e. $II_c = III_c$;

Thirdly, the quantity of the entertainment values directed into Division III exceeds the same directed into Division II, i.e. $II_c < III_c$.

The Expenses Connected to the Movement of Entertainment Values, Services and the Aggregate Entertainment Product

Estimation of expenses of production	*Estimation of expenses of distribution*	*Estimation of expenses of exchange*	*Estimation of expenses of consumption*
A. «Production» process of intellectual values entertainment character →	«Distribution» process of intellectual values entertainment character →	«Exchange» process of intellectual values entertainment character →	«Consumption» process of intellectual values entertainment character
↓	↓	↓	↓
B. «Production» process of intellectual services entertainment character →	«Distribution» process of Intellectual services entertainment character →	«Exchange» process of Intellectual services entertainment character →	«Consumption» process of intellectual services entertainment character
↓	↓	↓	↓
C. «Production» process of the aggregate intellectual product entertainment character →	«Distribution» process of the aggregate intellectual product entertainment character →	«Exchange» process of the aggregate intellectual product entertainment character →	«Consumption» process of the aggregate intellectual product entertainment character

The Results Connected to the Movement of Entertainment Values, Services and the Aggregate Entertainment Product

Estimation of results of production	*Estimation of results of distribution*	*Estimation of results of exchange*	*Estimation of results of consumption*
A. «Production» process of intellectual values entertainment character →	«Distribution» process of intellectual values entertainment character →	«Exchange» process of intellectual values entertainment character →	«Consumption» process of intellectual values entertainment character
↓	↓	↓	↓

Estimation of results of production	Estimation of results of distribution	Estimation of results of exchange	Estimation of results of consumption
B. «Production» process of intellectual services entertainment character	«Distribution» process of Intellectual services entertainment character	«Exchange» process of Intellectual services entertainment character	«Consumption» process of intellectual services entertainment character
↓	↓	↓	↓
C. «Production» process of the aggregate intellectual product entertainment character	«Distribution» process of the aggregate intellectual product entertainment character	«Exchange» process of the aggregate intellectual product entertainment character	«Consumption» process of the aggregate intellectual product entertainment character

The Criteria Connected to the Movement of Entertainment Values, Services and the Aggregate Entertainment Product

Economic criteria of production	Economic criteria of distribution	Economic criteria of exchange	Economic criteria of consumption
A. «Production» process of intellectual values entertainment character	«Distribution» process of intellectual values entertainment character	«Exchange» process of intellectual values entertainment character	«Consumption» process of intellectual values entertainment character
↓	↓	↓	↓
B. «Production» process of intellectual services entertainment character	«Distribution» process of Intellectual services entertainment character	«Exchange» process of Intellectual services entertainment character	«Consumption» process of intellectual services entertainment character
↓	↓	↓	↓
C. «Production» process of the aggregate intellectual product entertainment character	«Distribution» process of the aggregate intellectual product entertainment character	«Exchange» process of the aggregate intellectual product entertainment character	«Consumption» process of the aggregate intellectual product entertainment character

The Indicators Connected to the Movement of Entertainment Values, Services and the Aggregate Entertainment Product

Economic indicators of production	Economic indicators of distribution	Economic indicators of exchange	Economic indicators of consumption
A. «Production» process of intellectual values entertainment character →	«Distribution» process of intellectual values entertainment character →	«Exchange» process of intellectual values entertainment character →	«Consumption» process of intellectual values entertainment character
↓	↓	↓	↓
B. «Production» process of intellectual services entertainment character →	«Distribution» process of Intellectual services entertainment character →	«Exchange» process of Intellectual services entertainment character →	«Consumption» process of intellectual services entertainment character
↓	↓	↓	↓
C. «Production» process of the aggregate intellectual product entertainment character →	«Distribution» process of the aggregate intellectual product entertainment character →	«Exchange» process of the aggregate intellectual product entertainment character →	«Consumption» process of the aggregate intellectual product entertainment character

CHAPTER 9

The Proportions as a System of Economic Estimations of Distribution

A. Inherent Aspect of Distribution in the Intellectual Sphere

I proceed from the assumption that if there are estimates, criteria and indicators related to the creation of intellectual values and intellectual services, there will be no exceptions for the other forms of economic relations:

- within «distributive» relations there should be estimates, criteria and indicators;

- within «consumption» relations there should be estimates, criteria and indicators;[5]

- within «exchange» relations there should be estimates, criteria and indicators.

In this fragment of my work I suggest that the question of estimates, criteria and indicators be investigated for the relations of «distribution» in the intellectual sphere.

It should also be noted that the proportions of development of the intellectual sphere appear as a system of economic estimates. The proportions of the intellectual sphere streams of resources change every day, week and month. Each of the ratio options represents a system of economic estimates.

The distribution estimates are closely connected to the resources:

---

5   The reader will agree with me that the economic theory should not contain any dark corners. Every thing should be clear and intelligible.

It is essential to know what is going on in the framework of economic relations.

- if there are 10 streams of resources in the intellectual sphere, there should be 10 economic estimates of distribution;
- if there are 25 streams of resources in the intellectual sphere, there should be 25 economic estimates of distribution;
- if there are 30 streams of resources in the intellectual sphere, there should be 30 economic estimates, respectively, etc.

In other terms the quantity of the resource streams explains the number of estimates which will be at our disposal while examining the relations of distribution in the intellectual sphere.

Proportions should be referred to a special class of estimates, applicable in the spectrum of economic relations of «distribution». We shall not simplify the problem of establishing the proportionate «distribution» estimates.

It can be noted that:

a)   proportions which are logically well-grounded will have a system of corresponding estimates;

b)   proportions can be randomly and logically ungrounded (which is also a system of evaluation).

A number of examples can be given when interrelated branches of proportions in the intellectual sphere have been formed irrespective of economic logic. These refer to the cases when non-economic principles are used by:

- residual principle of financing;
- principle of the intellectual sphere financing in percentage to GDP;
- non-inclusion of the assimilated spare time of the population into the value of intellectual services.

In these cases the estimation of the movement of resources will have gross logical errors.

A. Inherent Aspects of Distribution in the Intellectual Sphere

Estimates of distribution can be of three forms:

First—economic estimates of incoming resources;

Second—proportions inside the intellectual sphere (correlation of resources);

Third—economic estimations of outgoing resources.

The problem of establishing proportions in the intellectual sphere should be neither simplified nor complicated.

Proportions outline the quantitative and qualitative aspects of distributive relations in the intellectual sphere.

In case priority is given to the growth of intellectual services of the entertainment character, whereas services of education and enlightenment are assigned an auxiliary part, we would observe an imbalanced development of the intellectual sphere branches.

Now we shall investigate the variant of the resource distribution in the intellectual sphere without the A_{STP} resource. I have enclosed that part of resources which is not taken into consideration in the intellectual sphere reproduction schemes.

$$
\begin{cases}
C_1 + V_1i + m_1j & = R_1^6 \quad \text{Educational values} \\
C_2 + V_2i + m_2j & = R_2 \quad \text{Enlightenment values} \\
C_3 + V_3i + m_3j & = R_3 \quad \text{Entertainment values} \\
\\
C_4 + V_4i + m_4j + \boxed{A^{EN}_{STP}} & = R_4 \quad \text{- «Education» branches} \\
C_5 + V_5i + m_5j + \boxed{A^{EN}_{STP}} & = R_5 \quad \text{- «Enlightenment» branches} \\
C_6 + V_6i + m_6j + \boxed{A^{EN}_{STP}} & = R_6 \quad \text{- «Entertainment» branches}
\end{cases}
$$

In the above variant it is apparent that the absence of A^{ED}_{STP}, A^{EN}_{STP} and A^{SH}_{STP} resources results in the distortion of proportions in the intellectual sphere.

With the application of the above resources the proportions become real and flawless.

We shall examine these proportions in detail in the context of 3 + 25 intellectual sphere services branches.

$$
\begin{array}{llll}
C_1 + V_1 + m_1 + & = R_1 & \text{- Educational values} \\
C_2 + V_2 + m_2 + & = R_2 & \text{- Enlightenment values} \\
C_3 + V_3 + m_3 + & = R_3 & \text{- Entertainment values}
\end{array}
$$

---

6   R_1—estimation results of production of intellectual values № 1

R_2—estimation results of production of intellectual values № 2

R_3—estimation results of production of intellectual values № 3

$$C_4 + V_4 + m_4 + A_{STP4} = R_4$$
$$C_5 + V_5 + m_5 + A_{STP5} = R_5$$
$$C_6 + V_6 + m_6 + A_{STP6} = R_6$$
$$C_7 + V_7 + m_7 + A_{STP7} = R_7 \quad \text{Education services}$$
$$C_8 + V_8 + m_8 + A_{STP8} = R_8$$
$$C_9 + V_9 + m_9 + A_{STP9} = R_9$$
$$C_{10} + V_{10} + m_{10} + A_{STP10} = R_{10}$$
$$C_{11} + V_{11} + m_{11} + A_{STP11} = R_{11}$$
$$C_{12} + V_{12} + m_{12} + A_{STP12} = R_{12}$$
$$C_{13} + V_{13} + m_{13} + A_{STP13} = R_{13}$$
$$C_{14} + V_{14} + m_{14} + A_{STP14} = R_{14} \quad \text{Enlightenment services}$$
$$C_{15} + V_{15} + m_{15} + A_{STP15} = R_{15}$$
$$C_{16} + V_{16} + m_{16} + A_{STP16} = R_{16}$$
$$C_{17} + V_{17} + m_{17} + A_{STP17} = R_{17}$$
$$C_{18} + V_{18} + m_{18} + A_{STP18} = R_{18}$$
$$C_{19} + V_{19} + m_{19} + A_{STP19} = R_{19}$$
$$C_{20} + V_{20} + m_{20} + A_{STP20} = R_{20}$$
$$C_{21} + V_{21} + m_{21} + A_{STP21} = R_{21}$$
$$C_{22} + V_{22} + m_{22} + A_{STP22} = R_{22}$$
$$C_{23} + V_{23} + m_{23} + A_{STP23} = R_{23} \quad \text{Entertainment services}$$
$$C_{24} + V_{24} + m_{24} + A_{STP24} = R_{24}$$
$$C_{25} + V_{25} + m_{25} + A_{STP25} = R_{25}$$
$$C_{26} + V_{26} + m_{26} + A_{STP26} = R_{26}$$
$$C_{27} + V_{27} + m_{27} + A_{STP27} = R_{27}$$
$$C_{28} + V_{28} + m_{28} + A_{STP28} = R_{28}$$

If in scheme 3 + 25 we arrange coefficients before C, V, m and A_{STP}, we shall receive real proportions which have taken shape in the intellectual sphere.

The proportions existing in the intellectual branches will be different from country to country.

One of the key questions of the Intellectual sphere is what proportions are sustained in the process of its functioning? Here we may deal with several options:[7]

---

7   While drawing up an economic balance of the intellectual sphere it is necessary to take in account both the onward and rotatory movements of the resources. The development of the intellectual sphere is dependent on these two types of movement.

- if the proportion among the segments of Intellectual values, and services, the aggregate Intellectual product correlates with the logic of reproduction in this sphere, the results will be of one kind. They will rest within the spectrum of positive trends;

- if the proportion among the segments of Intellectual values, services and the aggregate Intellectual product are not sustained? the results of the Intellectual sphere movement in the economic space will be negative.

B. Balance Correlation of the Intellectual Sphere with Complex Numbers

Until recently we have been investigating the movement of intellectual values and services and the aggregate intellectual product as an integral process:

Production	Distribution	Exchange	Consumption
Intellectual values $\rightarrow$	Intellectual values $\rightarrow$	Intellectual values $\rightarrow$	Intellectual values
$\downarrow$	$\downarrow$	$\downarrow$	$\downarrow$
Intellectual services $\rightarrow$	Intellectual services $\rightarrow$	Intellectual services $\rightarrow$	Intellectual services
$\downarrow$	$\downarrow$	$\downarrow$	$\downarrow$
Intellectual product $\rightarrow$	Intellectual product $\rightarrow$	Intellectual product $\rightarrow$	Intellectual product

Such an insight into the structure of the economic products does not reveal their inner substance, all parts of which are in permanent movement. They pass the stages of production, distribution, exchange and consumption.

At every stage of the movement of the component parts of intellectual values and intellectual services? there are certain problems connected to the economic estimate of the stream of resources moving within the intellectual sphere.

What ratios should exist among the streams of resources in the intellectual sphere?

How to cognize the particulars of the balance method in the intellectual sphere?

Which balance ratios should be adhered to in the intellectual sphere?

These questions need to be answered right from the beginning of this chapter.

The essence of the balance method can be conceived by comparising a ring or? rather, a hula-hoop used in the fitness clubs.

To keep it whirling one has to perform:

-   onward movements;

-   rotatory movements;

-   onward-rotatory movements of the body.

The maintenance of balance between the two types of motion enables lengthy revolving of the hoop round one's torso.

The above paradigm visually demonstrates the interconnection between onward and rotary movements.

But how does the movement of the intellectual resources occur?

What economic impetus should be given to start the development of the intellectual sphere?

We shall keep to the principle of adequacy in reflecting economic estimates, criteria and indicators. All the streams of resources in the intellectual sphere should carry economic evaluations.

Now economic estimates are leveled up with the expenses connected to the production of these services.

Economic estimates of the intellectual services are understated by the cost amount of the assimilated spare time of the population resource which is not included in the resulting outcome of the intellectual sphere labor.

We shall examine the logic of the proportions bringing the intellectual sphere to:

a) simple reproduction;

b) extended reproduction;

c) imbalanced economic development.

The peculiarities of the first group of estimates—proportions of distribution in the intellectual sphere are as follows.

A) In the first variant the stream of resources is arranged in such a way that the intellectual sphere is expanding and all its economic parameters improve.

The movement of the component parts of the intellectual values, intellectual services and the aggregate intellectual product is happening according to the following scheme:

Scheme № 1

$$
\begin{cases}
C_1 + V_1 i + m_1 j & = R_1 \quad \text{Educational values} \\
C_2 + V_2 i + m_2 j & = R_2 \quad \text{Enlightenment values} \\
C_3 + V_3 i + m_3 j & = R_3 \quad \text{Entertainment values} \\
\\
< \\
\\
C_4 + V_4 i + m_4 j + A^{EN}_{STP} & = R_4{}^8 \quad \text{- «Education» branches} \\
C_5 + V_5 i + m_5 j + A^{EN}_{STP} & = R_5 \quad \text{- «Enlightenment» branches} \\
C_6 + V_6 i + m_6 j + A^{EN}_{STP} & = R_6 \quad \text{- «Entertainment» branches}
\end{cases}
$$

This is an option of extended reproduction.

$$[(V_1 i + m_1 j) + (V_2 i + m_2 j) + (V_3 i + m_3 j)] > (C_4 + C_5 + C_6)$$

If in scheme 3 + 25 we arrange coefficients before C, V, m and A_{STP}, we shall receive real proportions which have taken shape in the intellectual sphere. On their basis it is possible to write down the matrix of coefficients:

$$
\begin{vmatrix}
\alpha_1 & \beta_1 & \gamma_1 & \\
\alpha_2 & \beta_2 & \gamma_2 & \\
\alpha_3 & \beta_3 & \gamma_3 & \\
\alpha_4 & \beta_4 & \gamma_4 & S_4 \\
\alpha_5 & \beta_5 & \gamma_5 & S_5 \\
\alpha_6 & \beta_6 & \gamma_6 & S_6
\end{vmatrix}
$$

---

8   R_1—estimated results of the production of the intellectual services of education branches

R_2—estimated results of the production of the intellectual services of enlightenment branches

R_3—estimated results of the production of the intellectual services of entertainment branches

α_7	β_7	γ_7	S_7
α_8	β_8	γ_8	S_8
α_9	β_9	γ_9	S_9
α_{10}	β_{10}	γ_{10}	S_{10}
α_{11}	β_{11}	γ_{11}	S_{11}
α_{12}	β_{12}	γ_{12}	S_{12}
α_{13}	β_{13}	γ_{13}	S_{13}
α_{14}	β_{14}	γ_{14}	S_{14}
α_{15}	β_{15}	γ_{15}	S_{15}
α_{16}	β_{16}	γ_{16}	S_{16}
α_{17}	β_{17}	γ_{17}	S_{17}
α_{18}	β_{18}	γ_{18}	S_{18}
α_{19}	β_{19}	γ_{19}	S_{19}
α_{20}	β_{20}	γ_{20}	S_{20}
α_{21}	β_{21}	γ_{21}	S_{21}
α_{22}	β_{22}	γ_{22}	S_{22}
α_{23}	β_{23}	γ_{23}	S_{23}
α_{24}	β_{24}	γ_{24}	S_{24}
α_{25}	β_{25}	γ_{25}	S_{25}
α_{26}	β_{26}	γ_{26}	S_{26}
α_{27}	β_{27}	γ_{27}	S_{27}
α_{28}	β_{28}	γ_{28}	S_{28}

The above given matrix of coefficients, or rather, a matrix of the distribution of resources in the intellectual sphere has several peculiarities.[9]

I suggest that the distribution estimates be adjusted for complex numbers. In this case, the schemes of reproduction would be modified taking into account this new circumstance and the system of estimation will be as follows:

---

9   The proportions existing in intellectual branches will be different from country to country.

$$\alpha_1 C_1 + \beta_1 V_1 i + \gamma_1 m_1 j = R_1$$

$$\alpha_2 C_2 + \beta_2 V_2 i + \gamma_2 m_2 j = R_2$$

$$\alpha_3 C_3 + \beta_3 V_3 i + \gamma_3 m_3 j = R_3$$

$$<$$

$$\alpha_4 C_4 + \beta_4 V_4 i + \gamma_4 m_4 j + A_{STP} d = R_4$$

$$\alpha_5 C_5 + \beta_5 V_5 i + \gamma_5 m_5 j + A_{STP} d = R_5$$

$$\alpha_6 C_6 + \beta_6 V_6 i + \gamma_6 m_6 j + A_{STP} d = R_6$$

$$\alpha_7 C_7 + \beta_7 V_7 i + \gamma_7 m_7 j + A_{STP} d = R_7$$

$$\alpha_8 C_8 + \beta_8 V_8 i + \gamma_8 m_8 j + A_{STP} d = R_8$$

$$\alpha_9 C_9 + \beta_9 V_9 i + \gamma_9 m_9 j + A_{STP} d = R_9$$

$$\alpha_{10} C_{10} + \beta_{10} V_{10} i + \gamma_{10} m_{10} j + A_{STP} d = R_{10}$$

$$\alpha_{11} C_{11} + \beta_{11} V_{11} i + \gamma_{11} m_{11} j + A_{STP} d = R_{11}$$

$$\alpha_{12} C_{12} + \beta_{12} V_{12} i + \gamma_{12} m_{12} j + A_{STP} d = R_{12}$$

$$\alpha_{13} C_{13} + \beta_{13} V_{13} i + \gamma_{13} m_{13} j + A_{STP} d = R_{13}$$

$$\alpha_{14} C_{14} + \beta_{14} V_{14} i + \gamma_{14} m_{14} j + A_{STP} d = R_{14}$$

$$\alpha_{15} C_{15} + \beta_{15} V_{15} i + \gamma_{15} m_{15} j + A_{STP} d = R_{15}$$

$$\alpha_{16} C_{16} + \beta_{16} V_{16} i + \gamma_{16} m_{16} j + A_{STP} d = R_{16}$$

$$\alpha_{17} C_{17} + \beta_{17} V_{17} i + \gamma_{17} m_{17} j + A_{STP} d = R_{17}$$

$$\alpha_{18} C_{18} + \beta_{18} V_{18} i + \gamma_{18} m_{18} j + A_{STP} d = R_{18}$$

$$\alpha_{19} C_{19} + \beta_{19} V_{19} i + \gamma_{19} m_{19} j + A_{STP} d = R_{19}$$

$$\alpha_{20} C_{20} + \beta_{20} V_{20} i + \gamma_{20} m_{20} j + A_{STP} d = R_{20}$$

$$\alpha_{21} C_{21} + \beta_{21} V_{21} i + \gamma_{21} m_{21} j + A_{STP} d = R_{21}$$

$$\alpha_{22} C_{22} + \beta_{22} V_{22} i + \gamma_{22} m_{22} j + A_{STP} d = R_{22}$$

$$\alpha_{23} C_{23} + \beta_{23} V_{23} i + \gamma_{23} m_{23} j + A_{STP} d = R_{23}$$

$$\alpha_{24} C_{24} + \beta_{24} V_{24} i + \gamma_{24} m_{24} j + A_{STP} d = R_{24}$$

$$\alpha_{25} C_{25} + \beta_{25} V_{25} i + \gamma_{25} m_{25} j + A_{STP} d = R_{25}$$

$$\alpha_{26} C_{26} + \beta_{26} V_{26} i + \gamma_{26} m_{26} j + A_{STP} d = R_{26}$$

$$\alpha_{27} C_{27} + \beta_{27} V_{27} i + \gamma_{27} m_{27} j + A_{STP} d = R_{27}$$

$$\alpha_{28} C_{28} + \beta_{28} V_{28} i + \gamma_{28} m_{28} j + A_{STP} d = R_{28}$$

B) <u>The second variant</u>. The peculiarities of the second group of estimates—proportions of the distribution in the intellectual sphere.

This is the option of simple reproduction in the intellectual sphere when all its parameters remain changeless from year to year. They are neither expanding nor reducing.

Scheme № 2

$$
\begin{aligned}
C_1 + \boxed{V_1 i + m_1 j} &= R_1 \quad \text{Educational values} \\
C_2 + V_2 i + m_2 j &= R_2 \quad \text{Enlightenment values} \\
C_3 + V_3 i + m_3 j &= R_3 \quad \text{Entertainment values} \\
\\
\boxed{C_4} + V_4 i + m_4 j + A^{EN}_{STP} &= R_4{}^{10} \quad \text{- «Education» branches} \\
C_5 + V_5 i + m_5 j + A^{EN}_{STP} &= R_5 \quad \text{- «Enlightenment» branches} \\
C_6 + V_6 i + m_6 j + A^{EN}_{STP} &= R_6 \quad \text{- «Entertainment» branches}
\end{aligned}
$$

$$[(V_1 i + m_1 j) + (V_2 i + m_2 j) + (V_3 i + m_3 j)] = (C_4 + C_5 + C_6)$$

Scheme № 2 can be examined in detail in the context of 3 + 25 intellectual sphere services branches.

If in scheme 3 + 25 we arrange coefficients before C, V, m and A_{STP}, we shall receive real proportions which have taken shape in the intellectual sphere.

The proportions existing in the intellectual branches will be different from country to country.

I suggest that the distribution estimates be adjusted for the complex numbers. In this case, the schemes of reproduction would be modified taking into account this new circumstance and the system of estimation will be as follows:

---

10   R_4—estimation of the production of the intellectual services of educational branches
R_5—estimation of the production of the intellectual services of enlightenment branches
R_6—estimation of the production of the intellectual services of entertainment branches

$$\alpha_1 C_1 + \beta_1 V_1 i + \gamma_1 m_1 j = R_1$$

$$\alpha_2 C_2 + \beta_2 V_2 i + \gamma_2 m_2 j = R_2$$

$$\alpha_3 C_3 + \beta_3 V_3 i + \gamma_3 m_3 j = R_3$$

$$=$$

$$\alpha_4 C_4 + \beta_4 V_4 i + \gamma_4 m_4 j + A_{STP} d = R_4$$

$$\alpha_5 C_5 + \beta_5 V_5 i + \gamma_5 m_5 j + A_{STP} d = R_5$$

$$\alpha_6 C_6 + \beta_6 V_6 i + \gamma_6 m_6 j + A_{STP} d = R_6$$

$$\alpha_7 C_7 + \beta_7 V_7 i + \gamma_7 m_7 j + A_{STP} d = R_7$$

$$\alpha_8 C_8 + \beta_8 V_8 i + \gamma_8 m_8 j + A_{STP} d = R_8$$

$$\alpha_9 C_9 + \beta_9 V_9 i + \gamma_9 m_9 j + A_{STP} d = R_9$$

$$\alpha_{10} C_{10} + \beta_{10} V_{10} i + \gamma_{10} m_{10} j + A_{STP} d = R_{10}$$

$$\alpha_{11} C_{11} + \beta_{11} V_{11} i + \gamma_{11} m_{11} j + A_{STP} d = R_{11}$$

$$\alpha_{12} C_{12} + \beta_{12} V_{12} i + \gamma_{12} m_{12} j + A_{STP} d = R_{12}$$

$$\alpha_{13} C_{13} + \beta_{13} V_{13} i + \gamma_{13} m_{13} j + A_{STP} d = R_{13}$$

$$\alpha_{14} C_{14} + \beta_{14} V_{14} i + \gamma_{14} m_{14} j + A_{STP} d = R_{14}$$

$$\alpha_{15} C_{15} + \beta_{15} V_{15} i + \gamma_{15} m_{15} j + A_{STP} d = R_{15}$$

$$\alpha_{16} C_{16} + \beta_{16} V_{16} i + \gamma_{16} m_{16} j + A_{STP} d = R_{16}$$

$$\alpha_{17} C_{17} + \beta_{17} V_{17} i + \gamma_{17} m_{17} j + A_{STP} d = R_{17}$$

$$\alpha_{18} C_{18} + \beta_{18} V_{18} i + \gamma_{18} m_{18} j + A_{STP} d = R_{18}$$

$$\alpha_{19} C_{19} + \beta_{19} V_{19} i + \gamma_{19} m_{19} j + A_{STP} d = R_{19}$$

$$\alpha_{20} C_{20} + \beta_{20} V_{20} i + \gamma_{20} m_{20} j + A_{STP} d = R_{20}$$

$$\alpha_{21} C_{21} + \beta_{21} V_{21} i + \gamma_{21} m_{21} j + A_{STP} d = R_{21}$$

$$\alpha_{22} C_{22} + \beta_{22} V_{22} i + \gamma_{22} m_{22} j + A_{STP} d = R_{22}$$

$$\alpha_{23} C_{23} + \beta_{23} V_{23} i + \gamma_{23} m_{23} j + A_{STP} d = R_{23}$$

$$\alpha_{24} C_{24} + \beta_{24} V_{24} i + \gamma_{24} m_{24} j + A_{STP} d = R_{24}$$

$$\alpha_{25} C_{25} + \beta_{25} V_{25} i + \gamma_{25} m_{25} j + A_{STP} d = R_{25}$$

$$\alpha_{26} C_{26} + \beta_{26} V_{26} i + \gamma_{26} m_{26} j + A_{STP} d = R_{26}$$

$$\alpha_{27} C_{27} + \beta_{27} V_{27} i + \gamma_{27} m_{27} j + A_{STP} d = R_{27}$$

$$\alpha_{28} C_{28} + \beta_{28} V_{28} i + \gamma_{28} m_{28} j + A_{STP} d = R_{28}$$

C) <u>The third variant</u>. Peculiarities of the third group of estimates—proportions of distribution in the intellectual sphere.

This is the option of an imbalanced development of the intellectual sphere:

Scheme № 3

$$
\begin{cases}
C_1 + \boxed{V_1 i + m_1 j} & = R_1 \quad \text{Educational values} \\
C_2 + V_2 i + m_2 j & = R_2 \quad \text{Enlightenment values} \\
C_3 + V_3 i + m_3 j & = R_3 \quad \text{Entertainment values} \\
\qquad\boxed{>} \\
\boxed{C_4} + V_4 i + m_4 j + A^{EN}_{STP} = R_4 \quad \text{- «Education» branches} \\
C_5 + V_5 i + m_5 j + A^{EN}_{STP} = R_5 \quad \text{- «Enlightenment» branches} \\
C_6 + V_6 i + m_6 j + A^{EN}_{STP} = R_6 \quad \text{- «Entertainment» branches}
\end{cases}
$$

$$[(V_1 i + m_1 j) + (V_2 i + m_2 j) + (V_3 i + m_3 j)] < (C_4 + C_5 + C_6)$$

Scheme № 3 can be examined in detail in the context of 3 + 25 intellectual sphere services branches, or with complex numbers.

I suggest that distribution estimates be adjusted for the complex numbers. In this case schemes of reproduction would be modified taking into account this new circumstance and the system of estimation will be as follows:

$$\alpha_1 C_1 \quad + \quad \beta_1 V_1 i \quad + \quad \gamma_1 m_1 j \qquad\qquad = \quad R_1$$

$$\alpha_2 C_2 \quad + \quad \beta_2 V_2 i \quad + \quad \gamma_2 m_2 j \qquad\qquad = \quad R_2$$

$$\alpha_3 C_3 \quad + \quad \beta_3 V_3 i \quad + \quad \gamma_3 m_3 j \qquad\qquad = \quad R_3$$

$>$

$$\alpha_4 C_4 \quad + \quad \beta_4 V_4 i \quad + \quad \gamma_4 m_4 j \quad + \quad A_{STP} d \quad = \quad R_4$$

$$\alpha_5 C_5 \quad + \quad \beta_5 V_5 i \quad + \quad \gamma_5 m_5 j \quad + \quad A_{STP} d \quad = \quad R_5$$

$$\alpha_6 C_6 \quad + \quad \beta_6 V_6 i \quad + \quad \gamma_6 m_6 j \quad + \quad A_{STP} d \quad = \quad R_6$$

$$\alpha_7 C_7 \quad + \quad \beta_7 V_7 i \quad + \quad \gamma_7 m_7 j \quad + \quad A_{STP} d \quad = \quad R_7$$

$$\alpha_8 C_8 \quad + \quad \beta_8 V_8 i \quad + \quad \gamma_8 m_8 j \quad + \quad A_{STP} d \quad = \quad R_8$$

$$\alpha_9 C_9 \quad + \quad \beta_9 V_9 i \quad + \quad \gamma_9 m_9 j \quad + \quad A_{STP} d \quad = \quad R_9$$

$$\alpha_{10} C_{10} \quad + \quad \beta_{10} V_{10} i \quad + \quad \gamma_{10} m_{10} j \quad + \quad A_{STP} d \quad = \quad R_{10}$$

$$\alpha_{11} C_{11} \quad + \quad \beta_{11} V_{11} i \quad + \quad \gamma_{11} m_{11} j \quad + \quad A_{STP} d \quad = \quad R_{11}$$

$$\alpha_{12} C_{12} \quad + \quad \beta_{12} V_{12} i \quad + \quad \gamma_{12} m_{12} j \quad + \quad A_{STP} d \quad = \quad R_{12}$$

$$\alpha_{13} C_{13} \quad + \quad \beta_{13} V_{13} i \quad + \quad \gamma_{13} m_{13} j \quad + \quad A_{STP} d \quad = \quad R_{13}$$

$$\alpha_{14} C_{14} \quad + \quad \beta_{14} V_{14} i \quad + \quad \gamma_{14} m_{14} j \quad + \quad A_{STP} d \quad = \quad R_{14}$$

$$\alpha_{15} C_{15} \quad + \quad \beta_{15} V_{15} i \quad + \quad \gamma_{15} m_{15} j \quad + \quad A_{STP} d \quad = \quad R_{15}$$

$$\alpha_{16} C_{16} \quad + \quad \beta_{16} V_{16} i \quad + \quad \gamma_{16} m_{16} j \quad + \quad A_{STP} d \quad = \quad R_{16}$$

$$\alpha_{17} C_{17} \quad + \quad \beta_{17} V_{17} i \quad + \quad \gamma_{17} m_{17} j \quad + \quad A_{STP} d \quad = \quad R_{17}$$

$$\alpha_{18} C_{18} \quad + \quad \beta_{18} V_{18} i \quad + \quad \gamma_{18} m_{18} j \quad + \quad A_{STP} d \quad = \quad R_{18}$$

$$\alpha_{19} C_{19} \quad + \quad \beta_{19} V_{19} i \quad + \quad \gamma_{19} m_{19} j \quad + \quad A_{STP} d \quad = \quad R_{19}$$

$$\alpha_{20} C_{20} \quad + \quad \beta_{20} V_{20} i \quad + \quad \gamma_{20} m_{20} j \quad + \quad A_{STP} d \quad = \quad R_{20}$$

$$\alpha_{21} C_{21} \quad + \quad \beta_{21} V_{21} i \quad + \quad \gamma_{21} m_{21} j \quad + \quad A_{STP} d \quad = \quad R_{21}$$

$$\alpha_{22} C_{22} \quad + \quad \beta_{22} V_{22} i \quad + \quad \gamma_{22} m_{22} j \quad + \quad A_{STP} d \quad = \quad R_{22}$$

$$\alpha_{23} C_{23} \quad + \quad \beta_{23} V_{23} i \quad + \quad \gamma_{23} m_{23} j \quad + \quad A_{STP} d \quad = \quad R_{23}$$

$$\alpha_{24} C_{24} \quad + \quad \beta_{24} V_{24} i \quad + \quad \gamma_{24} m_{24} j \quad + \quad A_{STP} d \quad = \quad R_{24}$$

$$\alpha_{25} C_{25} \quad + \quad \beta_{25} V_{25} i \quad + \quad \gamma_{25} m_{25} j \quad + \quad A_{STP} d \quad = \quad R_{25}$$

$$\alpha_{26} C_{26} \quad + \quad \beta_{26} V_{26} i \quad + \quad \gamma_{26} m_{26} j \quad + \quad A_{STP} d \quad = \quad R_{26}$$

$$\alpha_{27} C_{27} \quad + \quad \beta_{27} V_{27} i \quad + \quad \gamma_{27} m_{27} j \quad + \quad A_{STP} d \quad = \quad R_{27}$$

$$\alpha_{28} C_{28} \quad + \quad \beta_{28} V_{28} i \quad + \quad \gamma_{28} m_{28} j \quad + \quad A_{STP} d \quad = \quad R_{28}$$

CHAPTER 10

The System of the Criteria of Intellectual Provision (With Complex Numbers — Quaternions)

A. Classification of the Criteria of Intellectual Provision

According to constitutional provisions we have the right to receive open information. Our rights in this part are protected, but there are certain difficulties here.

If you have a desire to find out what the level of the intellectual welfare of the population is at present, or what it was three years ago, or what level is expected the next year, statisticians will enumerate you the number of museums, theatres, schools the radios and TV sets in the country.

Other information on he intellectual welfare of the population is not collected and is not provided.

There is some kind of misinterpretation of intellectual welfare; we can not get full information and therefore all the time we only use some fragments. This situation arises not because somebody conceals something. No. Everything is very simple. Statisticians will not answer the questions because till now the economic theory of the intellectual sphere has not been developed including the section concerning the intellectual welfare of society.

We are in a situation when the conception of the «intellectual welfare of the population» exists in everyday life though there is no information about our intellectual development.

This contradiction has been existing for decades. The problem of intellectual provision is not solved in the economic theory. It has not been worked up yet.

In the everyday arsenal of journalists, there are no criteria with the help of which they could ascertain the level of the intellectual provision of the population of a region, a city or a country. The reason may be that there are no sections or books on this problem in the theory. In such a non-standard situation journalists have to use emotional estimations and slang.

Journalists explain the necessity of the application of «means of effect» by emphasizing the meaning of the problems under consideration. They say that it is some kind of sauce «Chili» for intellectual food. It is possible to agree with such position: really, the intellectual food should not be «dietary».

Their position can be criticized.

But it is necessary to put yourself in their place. How can they answer the question about the level of Intellectual provision of the population in the conditions of absence of theory? This is the first.

The second: they are forced to write 1-2 newspaper articles on the topic of welfare. If you were them, after the fourth article you would also start using non-standard words.

There is a way out of the situation. It is necessary to work up a section in the theory: «The intellectual provision of the population». Then journalists will be able to widely use the values of these indicators. They will gradually give up using emotional expressions. They will estimate an intellectual component of our everyday life in a new way.

We use our spare time in different functional planes regarding services: Education, Enlightenment and Entertainment. Exactly in such a way we should consider the intellectual welfare of the population.

Proceeding from the above I offer:

- on axis «X»—to set values of time spent by the population connected with consumption of the services of the Educational character;
- on axis «Y»—to set values of time spent by the population connected with consumption of the services of the Enlightenment character;
- on axis «Z»—to set values of time spent by the population connected with consumption of the services of the Entertainment character.

Time spent by the population on the consumption of the services of Education, Enlightenment and Entertainment can be written down graphically:

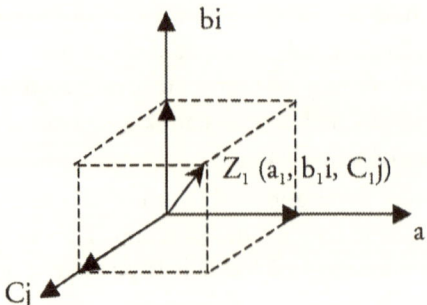

$$Z_1 = a_1 + b_1i + C_1j$$

Depending on what values the vectors a, bi, Cj obtain the total vector R changes its position in economic space.

If society spends more time connected with the consumption of the services of Education the graph will be as follows:

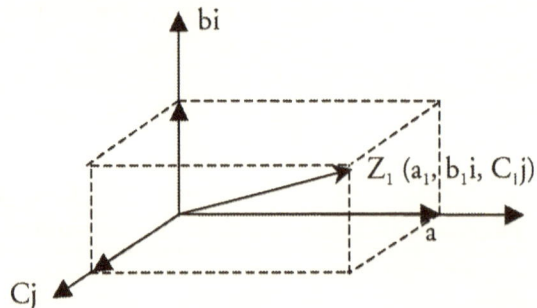

2) If the society spends more time connected with consumption of the services of the Entertainment the graph will be as follows:

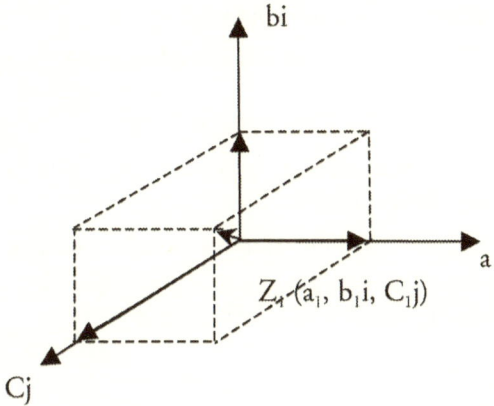

The aggregate vector R will be calculated in the following way:

$$R_{ASTP} = a_l + b_1i + C_lj.$$

Vector R_{ASTP} reveals the absolute expenses of the time spent by the population connected with consumption services of Education, Enlightenment and Entertainment. Estimations can be carried out in hours or in cost units.

At the second phase of the construction of the criteria of the intellectual welfare of the population it is necessary to work up estimations determining a volume of the services of Education, Enlightenment and Entertainment. For this purpose we should add up expenses of past labor ($R_C = R_C^{ED} + R_C^{EN}i + R_C^{SH}j$) and direct labor ($R_V = R_V^{ED} + R_V^{EN}i + RV_C^{SH}j$) connected to the creation of services—Education, Enlightenment and Entertainment—to the «assimilated resource of the spare time of the population»—(a_1, b_1i, C_1j).

$$R_{ASTP} = R_{ASTP}^{ED} + R_{ASTP}^{EN}i + R_{ASTP}^{SH}j$$

On axis «X»—the cost estimation of the services of the Educational character—a_2

$$a_2 = C_{ED} + V_{ED}i + A^{ED}_{STP}j$$

on axis «Y»—cost estimation of the services of Enlightenment—b_2

$$B_2i = C_{EN} + V_{EN}i + A^{EN}_{STP}j$$

on axis «Z»—cost estimation of the services of Entertaining character—C_2

$$C_2j = C_{SH} + V_{SH}i + A^{SH}_{STP}j$$

The aggregate vector will be calculated in the following way:

$$R_2 = a_2 + b_2i + C_2j = (C_{ED} + V_{ED}i + A^{ED}_{STP}j) + (C_{EN} + V_{EN}i + A^{EN}_{STP}j)i + (C_{SH} + V_{SH}i + A^{SH}_{STP}j)j$$

It reveals the total volume of intellectual services created by the branches of Education, Enlightenment and Entertainment.

<u>At the third step of construction</u> of criteria it is necessary to introduce relative estimations (vertical indicators) revealing the provision of the population with the services of Education, Enlightenment and Entertainment.

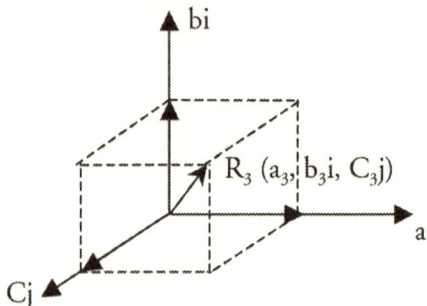

Where, on axis «X»—the provision of the population with the services of the Educational character

on axis «Y»—the provision of the population with the services of the Enlightenment character

on axis «Z»—the provision of the population with the services of the Entertaining character.

The aggregate vector R_3 revealing the general level of the provision of the population with intellectual services will be written down in the following way:

$$R_3 = \frac{a_2}{\text{Number of population}} + \frac{b_2i}{\text{Number of population}} + \frac{C_2j}{\text{Number of population}}$$

There are some other modifications of the criteria of the intellectual provision of the population.

$$R_3 = \frac{(C_{ED} + V_{ED}i + A^{ED}_{STP}j)}{\text{Number of population}}$$

$$+ \frac{(C_{EN} + V_{EN}i + A^{ENL}_{STP}j)}{\text{Number of population}}$$

$$+ \frac{(C_{SH} + V_{SH}i + A^{SH}_{STP}j)}{\text{Number of population}}$$

$$R_4 = \frac{(C_{ED} + V_{ED}i + A^{ED}_{STP}j + m_k)}{\text{Number of population}}$$

$$+ \frac{(C_{EN} + V_{EN}i + A^{ENL}_{STP}j + m_k)}{\text{Number of population}}$$

$$+ \frac{(C_{SH} + V_{SH}i + A^{SH}_{STP}j + m_k)}{\text{Number of population}}$$

$$R_5 = \frac{(V_{ED}i + A^{ED}_{STP}j + m_k)}{\text{Number of population}}$$

$$+ \frac{(V_{EN}i + A^{ENL}_{STP}j + m_k)}{\text{Number of population}}$$

$$+ \frac{(V_{SH}i + A^{SH}_{STP}j + m_k)}{\text{Number of population}}$$

$$R_6 = \frac{(A^{ED}_{STP}j + m_k)}{\text{Number of population}}$$

$$+ \frac{(A^{ENL}_{STP}j + m_k)}{\text{Number of population}}$$

$$+ \frac{(A^{SH}_{STP}j + m_k)}{\text{Number of population}}$$

At this stage of construction the system of the criteria of provision with intellectual values and services, it is necessary to look into those streams of resources that exist in the intellectual sphere.

The stream of resources coming out of the intellectual sphere has different functional purposes. A book can be purchased for a public library—this is a productive utilization. But the book can be purchased and utilized for personal purpose at your home in your private library—this is personal consumption.

More examples can be given.

But the main idea is that the entire volume of intellectual values and intellectual services created during a year should be divided into two components:

- intellectual values and intellectual services of the production character (including all those which are directed to production and are consumed within it);

- intellectual values and intellectual services of the non-production character (which are consumed by the population for personal, non-production purposes).

1. I suggest that we consider the productive consumption of intellectual values and intellectual services in a three-dimensional space.

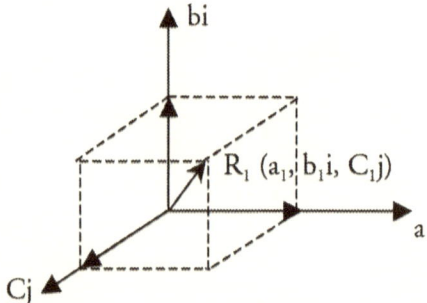

where

a_1—the volume of intellectual values consumed by production—economic estimation № 1

b_1i—the volume of intellectual services (without A_{STP} resource) consumed by production—economic estimation № 2

C_1j—the volume of the human resource A_{STP} involved in the process of the creation of intellectual services—economic estimation № 3

An aggregate economic estimation of <u>production consumption</u> will be as follows:

$$R_1 = a_1 + b_1i + C_1j$$

Vector R changes it values subject to the first, the second and the third components—Cj.

2. <u>Non-production</u> character consumption of intellectual values and intellectual services.

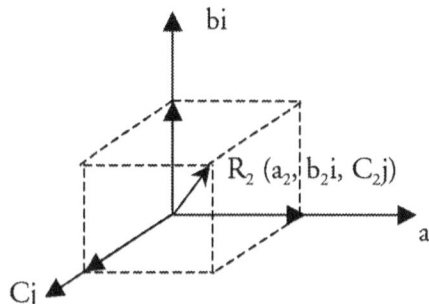

where

a₂—the volume of intellectual values for the non-productive character of consumption—economic estimation № 5

b₂i—the entire volume of intellectual services (without A_{STP} resource) for the non-productive character of consumption—economic estimation № 6

C₂j—the cost estimation of the human A_{STP} resource acting as an «object of labor» involved in the process of the creation of intellectual services—economic estimation № 7.

An aggregate economic estimation of non-production consumption will be as follows:

$$R_2 = a_2 + b_2 i + C_2 j$$

Vector R changes its values subject to the values of the 1st, 2nd and 3rd components.

The more A_{STP} resource is assimilated the more value R has. And, vice versa, the less the A_{STP} resource is assimilated the less the vector R is.

3. <u>Complex consumption</u> of intellectual values and intellectual services. I suggest that we consider this problem in a three-dimensional space.

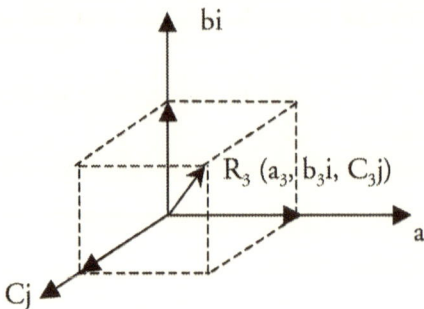

$$R_3 (a_3, b_3i, C_3j)$$

where

a$_3$—the entire volume of intellectual values consumed for productive and non-productive consumption—economic estimation № 9

b$_3$i—the volume of intellectual services (without A$_{STP}$) consumed for productive and non-productive consumption—economic estimation № 10.

C$_3$j—cost estimation of the human resource A$_{STP}$ involved in the process of the creation of intellectual services—economic estimation № 11.

An aggregate economic estimation of non-productive consumption will be as follows:

$$R_3 = a_3 + b_3i + C_3j$$

A functional division of the whole stream of intellectual values and intellectual services into two streams—productive and non-productive consumption—allows us to substantially increase the logic component of our discussion.

A) Productive Provision with Intellectual Values and Services.

1. Provision of production with intellectual values

2. Provision of production with intellectual services

3. Complex provision of production with intellectual values and services.

B) Non-Production Provision with Intellectual Values and Services.

1 Provision of the population with intellectual values

2 Provision of the population with intellectual services

3 Complex provision of the population with intellectual values and services.

1. Intellectual values

Branches	Complex product (production use)				Complex product (non-production use)				Aggregate complex product						
	№ 1	№ 2	№ 3	№ 4	№ 5	№ 6	№ 7	№ 8	№ 9	№ 10	№ 11	№ 12	Estimations	Criteria	Indicators
I branch	■												Estimations	Criteria	Indicators
		■											Estimations	Criteria	Indicators
			■										Estimations	Criteria	Indicators
				■									Estimations	Criteria	Indicators
(Production needs of intellectual values (estimations))					■								Estimations	Criteria	Indicators
II branch						■							Estimations	Criteria	Indicators
							■						Estimations	Criteria	Indicators
								■					Estimations	Criteria	Indicators
(Non-production needs of intellectual values (estimations))									■				Estimations	Criteria	Indicators
III branch										■			Estimations	Criteria	Indicators
											■		Estimations	Criteria	Indicators
(Complex needs of intellectual values (estimations))												■	Estimations	Criteria	Indicators
													Estimations	Criteria	Indicators

2. Intellectual services

Branches	Complex product (production use)				Complex product (non-production use)				Aggregate complex product				Estimations	Criteria	Indicators
	№ 1	№ 2	№ 3	№ 4	№ 5	№ 6	№ 7	№ 8	№ 9	№ 10	№ 11	№ 12	Estimations	Criteria	Indicators
I branch	Production needs of intellectual services (estimations)												Estimations	Criteria	Indicators
II branch					Non-production needs of intellectual services (estimations)								Estimations	Criteria	Indicators
III branch									Complex needs of intellectual services (estimations)				Estimations	Criteria	Indicators

3) Classification of the Criteria of Provision for the Educational Sphere

Educational needs are being met along two interopposed planes:
- part of the educational needs have a production character;
- part of the educational needs are of non-production character.

In general, the structure of production needs of educational values and services is as follows:
a) production needs of educational values;
b) production needs of educational services;
c) production needs of the aggregate educational product.

The non-production character of meeting educational needs has the following structure:
a) non-production needs of educational values;
b) non-production needs of educational services;
c) non-production needs of the aggregate educational product.

The above mentioned can be interpreted by the following logical table:

Productive consumption	Non-productive consumption	Aggregate consumption
Educational values	Educational values	Educational values
Educational services	Educational services	Educational services
Aggregate educational product	Aggregate educational product	Aggregate educational product

I) Indicators of the Long-Term Provision of Educational Values and Services

A. Structure of The Long-Term Needs of Educational Values

Thesis	An increment (Δ) of the volume of the production needs of educational values
Antithesis	An increment (Δ) of the volume of the non-production needs of educational values
Synthesis	An increment (Δ) of the volume of aggregate needs (both a production and non-production character) of educational values

1. Educational values

Branches	Volume of educational values (EDV) (production use)				Volume of educational values (EDV) (non-production use)				Aggregate volume of educational values (EDV)						
	№ 1	№ 2	№ 3	№ 4	№ 5	№ 6	№ 7	№ 8	№ 9	№ 10	№ 11	№ 12	Estimations	Criteria	Indicators
I branch — Production needs of education values (estimation)													Estimations	Criteria	Indicators
													Estimations	Criteria	Indicators
													Estimations	Criteria	Indicators
													Estimations	Criteria	Indicators
II branch — Non-production needs of education values (estimation)													Estimations	Criteria	Indicators
													Estimations	Criteria	Indicators
													Estimations	Criteria	Indicators
													Estimations	Criteria	Indicators
III branch — Complex needs of education values (estimation)													Estimations	Criteria	Indicators
													Estimations	Criteria	Indicators
													Estimations	Criteria	Indicators
													Estimations	Criteria	Indicators

AA. Indicator of the Long-Term «Provision of Educational Values» (of a Production Purpose)

Thesis	Increment (Δ) of the volume of educational values production purpose (ΔVED-VAL-P)
Antithesis	Increment (Δ) production needs of educational values

Synthesis
$$\frac{(\Delta\text{VED-VAL-P})}{\text{Increment } (\Delta) \text{ production needs of educational values}} \text{ - indicator}$$

AAA. Indicator of the Long-Term «Provision of Educational Values» (of a Non-Production Purpose)

Thesis	Increment (Δ) of the volume of educational values non-production purpose (ΔVED-VAL-NP)
Antithesis	Increment (Δ) non-production needs of educational values

Synthesis
$$\frac{(\Delta\text{VED-VAL-NP})}{\text{Increment } (\Delta) \text{ non-production needs of educational values}} \text{ - indicator}$$

B. Dialectical Structure of Long-Term Needs of Educational Services

Thesis	Long-term increment (Δ) of the volume of the educational services of a production character
Antithesis	Long-term increment (Δ) of the volume of educational services of a non-production character
Synthesis	Long-term increment (Δ) of the volume of the educational services of the aggregate needs (production and non-production character)

2. Educational services

Branches	Volume of educational services (EDS) (production use)				Volume of educational services (EDS) (non-production use)				Aggregate volume of educational services (EDS)						
	№ 1	№ 2	№ 3	№ 4	№ 5	№ 6	№ 7	№ 8	№ 9	№ 10	№ 11	№ 12			
I branch	Production needs of education services (estimation)												Estimations	Criteria	Indicators
II branch					Non-production needs of education services (estimation)								Estimations	Criteria	Indicators
III branch									Complex needs of education services (estimation)				Estimations	Criteria	Indicators

BB. Dialectical Structure of an Indicator of the Long-Term Provision of Educational Services

Thesis An increment (Δ) of the volume of educational services production purpose

Antithesis Long-term increment (Δ) of the social needs of educational services production purpose

Synthesis

$$\frac{\text{An increment (Δ) of the volume of educational services production purpose}}{\text{Long-term increment (Δ) of the social needs of educational services production purpose}}$$

BBB. Dialectical Structure of An Indicator of Long-Term Provision of Educational Services

Thesis An increment (Δ) of the volume of educational services non-production purpose

Antithesis Long-term increment (Δ) of the social needs for educational services non-production purpose

Synthesis

$$\frac{\text{An increment (Δ) of the volume of educational services non-production purpose}}{\text{Long-term increment (Δ) of the social needs of educational services non-production purpose}}$$

SYSTEM OF INDICATORS OF THE «LONG-TERM PROVISION» OF EDUCATIONAL SERVICES (FUNCTIONAL INDICATION)

Thesis Dialectical structure of a division of the aggregate of educational services as per functional indication.

   Thesis An increment (Δ) of the volume of the educational services of a production purpose.

   Antithesis An increment (Δ) of the volume of the educational services of a non-production purpose.

   Synthesis An increment (Δ) of the volume of aggregate educational services.

Antithesis Dialectical structure of the needs for educational services

   Thesis An increment (Δ) of the production needs in educational services.

   Antithesis An increment (Δ) of the non-production needs in educational services.

   Synthesis An increment (Δ) of the aggregate needs of a society in educational services.

Synthesis Dialectical system of the criteria of «provision» with educational services.

Thesis

$$\frac{\text{An increment } (\Delta) \text{ of the volume of the educational services of a production purpose}}{\text{An increment } (\Delta) \text{ of the production needs}} = \text{an indicator of the «long-term provision» of a production purpose}$$

Antithesis

$$\frac{\text{An increment } (\Delta) \text{ of the volume of the educational services of a non-production purpose}}{\text{An increment } (\Delta) \text{ of non-production needs}} = \text{an indicator of the «long-term provision» of a non-production purpose.}$$

Synthesis

$$\frac{\text{An increment } (\Delta) \text{ of an aggregate volume of educational services*}}{\text{An increment } (\Delta) \text{ of aggregate needs}} = \text{a complex indicator of the «long-term educational provision»}$$

A SYSTEM OF THE INDICATORS OF EDUCATIONAL PROVISION
AS PER A FUNCTIONAL INDICATION

Thesis

Aggregate criterion of a long-term production provision

$$\frac{\text{An increment } (\Delta) \text{ of the volume of educational values and educational services of a production character}}{\text{An increment } (\Delta) \text{ of the production needs in educational values and services}}$$

«thesis» indicator

Antithesis

Aggregate criterion of a long-term non-production provision

$$\frac{\text{An increment } (\Delta) \text{ of the volume of educational values and educational services of a non-production character}}{\text{An increment } (\Delta) \text{ of the non-production needs in educational values and services}}$$

«antithesis» indicator

Synthesis

Criterion of an aggregate long-term provision

$$\frac{\text{An increment } (\Delta) \text{ of the volume of educational values and services}}{\text{An increment } (\Delta) \text{ of the aggregate needs in educational values and services (of a production and non-production character)}}$$

«synthesis» indicator

B. Classification of the Criteria of the Provision of the Enlightenment Sphere

Enlightenment needs are being met along two interopposed planes:

- part of the enlightenment needs have a production character;
- part of the enlightenment needs are of non-production character.

In general, the structure of the production needs of enlightenment values and services is as follows:

a) production character needs of enlightenment values;
b) production character needs of enlightenment services;
c) production character needs of the aggregate enlightenment product.

The non-production character of meeting enlightenment needs has the following structure:

a) non-production character needs of enlightenment values;
b) non-production character needs of enlightenment services;

c) non-production character needs of the aggregate enlightenment product.

Production and non-production character enlightenment consumption are closely interrelated.

The above mentioned can be interpreted by the following logical table:

Process of production consumption	Process of non-production consumption	Process of aggregate consumption
Process of the production consumption of enlightenment values	Process of non-the production consumption of enlightenment values	Process of the aggregate (production and non-production) consumption of enlightenment values
Process of the production consumption of enlightenment services	Process of the non-production consumption of enlightenment services	Process of the aggregate (production and non-production) consumption of enlightenment services
Process of the production consumption of the aggregate enlightenment product	Process of the non-production consumption of the aggregate enlightenment product	Process of the aggregate (production and non-production) consumption of the enlightenment product

II) Indicators of the Long-Term Provision of Enlightenment Values and Services

A. Structure of the Long-Term Needs of Enlightenment Values

Thesis An increment (Δ) of the volume of the production needs of enlightenment values

Antithesis An increment (Δ) of the volume of the non-production needs of enlightenment values

Synthesis An increment (Δ) of the volume of the aggregate needs (both of a production and non-production character) of enlightenment values

1. Enlightenment values

Branches	Volume of enlightenment values (ENVL) (production use)				Volume of enlightenment values (ENVL) (non-production use)				Volume of enlightenment values (ENVL)						
	№ 1	№ 2	№ 3	№ 4	№ 5	№ 6	№ 7	№ 8	№ 9	№ 10	№ 11	№ 12	Estimations	Criteria	Indicators
I branch	Production needs of enlightenment values (estimations)														
II branch	Non-production needs of enlightenment values (estimations)														
III branch	Complex needs of enlightenment values (estimations)														

AA. Indicator of the Long-Term «Provision of Enlightenment Values» (of a Production Purpose)

Thesis — Increment (Δ) of the volume of enlightenment values production purpose (ΔENL-VAL-P)

Antithesis — Increment (Δ) the production needs of enlightenment values

Synthesis —
$$\frac{(\Delta\text{ENL-VAL-P})}{\text{Increment }(\Delta)\text{ production needs of enlightenment values}} \text{ - indicator}$$

AAA. Indicator of the Long-Term «Provision of Enlightenment Values» (of a Non-Production Purpose)

Thesis — Increment (Δ) of the volume of enlightenment values non-production purpose (ΔENL-VAL-NP)

Antithesis — Increment (Δ) non-production needs of enlightenment values

Synthesis —
$$\frac{(\Delta\text{ENL-VAL-NP})}{\text{Increment }(\Delta)\text{ non-production needs of enlightenment values}} \text{ - indicator}$$

B. Dialectical Structure of the Long-Term Needs of Enlightenment Services

Thesis — Long-term increment (Δ) of the volume of the enlightenment services of a production character

Antithesis — Long-term increment (Δ) of the volume of the enlightenment services of a non-production character

Synthesis — Long-term increment (Δ) of the volume of the enlightenment services of the aggregate needs (of a production and non-production character)

2. Enlightenment services

Branches	Volume of enlightenment services (ENLS) (production use)				Volume of enlightenment services (ENLS) (non-production use)				Volume of enlightenment services (ENLS)					Estimations	Criteria	Indicators
	№ 1	№ 2	№ 3	№ 4	№ 5	№ 6	№ 7	№ 8	№ 9	№ 10	№ 11	№ 12			
I branch	▓	▓	▓	▓	Production needs of enlightenment services (estimations)								Estimations	Criteria	Indicators
II branch					▓	▓	▓	▓	Non-production needs of enlightenment services (estimations)				Estimations	Criteria	Indicators
III branch									▓	▓	▓	▓	Complex needs of enlightenment services (estimations)	Estimations	Criteria	Indicators

BB. Dialectical Structure of an Indicator of the Long-Term Provision of Enlightenment Services

Thesis An increment (Δ) of the volume of enlightenment services production purpose

Antithesis Long-term increment (Δ) of the social needs for enlightenment services production purpose

Synthesis $$\frac{\text{An increment } (\Delta) \text{ of the volume of enlightenment services production purpose}}{\text{Long-term increment } (\Delta) \text{ of the social needs for enlightenment services production purpose}} \text{ - indicator}$$

BBB. Dialectical Structure of an Indicator of the Long-Term Provision of Enlightenment Services

Thesis An increment (Δ) of the volume of enlightenment services non-production purpose

Antithesis Long-term increment (Δ) of the social needs for enlightenment services non-production purpose

Synthesis $$\frac{\text{An increment } (\Delta) \text{ of the volume of enlightenment services non-production purpose}}{\text{Long-term increment } (\Delta) \text{ of the social needs for enlightenment services non-production purpose}} \text{ - indicator}$$

SYSTEM OF INDICATORS OF THE «LONG-TERM PROVISION» OF ENLIGHTENMENT SERVICES (FUNCTIONAL INDICATION)

Thesis — Dialectical structure of a division of the aggregate of enlightenment services as per functional indication.

  Thesis — An increment (Δ) of the volume of the enlightenment services of a production purpose.

  Antithesis — An increment (Δ) of the volume of the enlightenment services of a non-production purpose.

  Synthesis — An increment (Δ) of the volume of the aggregate enlightenment services.

Antithesis — Dialectical structure of the needs for enlightenment services

  Thesis — An increment (Δ) of the production needs in enlightenment services.

  Antithesis — An increment (Δ) of non-production needs in enlightenment services.

  Synthesis — An increment (Δ) of the aggregate needs of a society in enlightenment services.

Synthesis — Dialectical system of the criteria of «provision» with enlightenment services.

Thesis

$$\frac{\text{An increment }(\Delta)\text{ of the volume of enlightenment services of a production purpose}}{\text{An increment }(\Delta)\text{ of the production needs}} = \begin{array}{l}\text{an indicator of the «long-term provision» of a production purpose}\end{array}$$

Antithesis

$$\frac{\text{An increment }(\Delta)\text{ of the volume of the enlightenment services of a non-production purpose}}{\text{An increment }(\Delta)\text{ of non-production needs}} = \begin{array}{l}\text{an indicator of the «long-term provision» of a non-production purpose.}\end{array}$$

Synthesis

$$\frac{\text{An increment }(\Delta)\text{ of an aggregate volume of enlightenment services*}}{\text{An increment }(\Delta)\text{ of aggregate needs}} = \begin{array}{l}\text{a complex indicator of the «long-term enlightenment provision»}\end{array}$$

**A SYSTEM OF THE INDICATORS OF ENLIGHTENMENT PROVISION AS PER A
FUNCTIONAL INDICATION**

Thesis	**Aggregate criterion of a long-term production provision**	
	$$\frac{\text{An increment } (\Delta) \text{ of the volume of enlightenment values and services of a production character}}{\text{An increment } (\Delta) \text{ of the production needs in enlightenment values and services}}$$	«**thesis**» **indicator**
Antithesis	**Aggregate criterion of a long-term non-production provision**	
	$$\frac{\text{An increment } (\Delta) \text{ of the volume of enlightenment values and services of a non-production character}}{\text{An increment } (\Delta) \text{ of the non-production needs in enlightenment values and services}}$$	«**antithesis**» **indicator**
Synthesis	**Criterion of an aggregate long-term provision**	
	$$\frac{\text{An increment } (\Delta) \text{ of the volume of enlightenment values and services}}{\text{An increment } (\Delta) \text{ of the aggregate needs in enlightenment values and services (of a production and non-production character)}}$$	«**synthesis**» **indicator**

C. Classification of the Indicators of the Provision of the Entertainment Sphere

In general the structure of the production consumption of entertainment values and services is as follows:

a) production character consumption of entertainment values;

b) production character consumption of entertainment services;

c) production character consumption of the aggregate entertainment product.

The non-production character of meeting entertainment consumption has the following structure:

a) non-production character consumption of entertainment values;

b) non-production character consumption of entertainment services;

c) non-production character consumption of the aggregate entertainment product.

The above mentioned can be interpreted by the following logical table:

Process of production consumption	Process of non-production consumption	Process of aggregate consumption
Process of the production consumption of entertainment values	Process of the non-production consumption of entertainment values	Process of the aggregate (production and non-production) consumption of entertainment values
Process of the production consumption of entertainment services	Process of the non-production consumption of entertainment services	Process of the aggregate (production and non-production) consumption of entertainment services
Process of the production consumption of the aggregate entertainment product	Process of the non-production consumption of the aggregate entertainment product	Process of the aggregate (production and non-production) consumption of the entertainment product

III) Indicators of the Long-Term Provision of Entertainment Values and Services

A. Structure of the Long-Term Needs of Entertainment Values

Thesis An increment (Δ) of the volume of the production needs of entertainment values

Antithesis An increment (Δ) of the volume of the non-production needs of entertainment values

Synthesis An increment (Δ) of the volume of the aggregate needs (both of a production and non-production character) of entertainment values

1. Entertainment values

Branches	Volume of entertainment values (ENTV) (production use)				Volume of entertainment values (ENTV) (non-production use)				Aggregate volume of entertainment values (ENTV)						
	№ 1	№ 2	№ 3	№ 4	№ 5	№ 6	№ 7	№ 8	№ 9	№ 10	№ 11	№ 12	Estimations	Criteria	Indicators
I branch	Production needs of entertainment values (estimations)												Estimations	Criteria	Indicators
II branch					Non-production needs of entertainment values (estimations)								Estimations	Criteria	Indicators
III branch									Complex needs of entertainment values (estimations)				Estimations	Criteria	Indicators

AA. Indicator of the Long-Term «Provision of Entertainment Values» (of a Production Purpose)

Thesis	Increment (Δ) of the volume of entertainment values production purpose (ΔVEN-VAL-P)
Antithesis	Increment (Δ) the production needs of entertainment values

Synthesis

$$\frac{(\Delta\text{VEN-VAL-P})}{\text{Increment } (\Delta) \text{ production needs of entertainment values}} \text{ - indicators}$$

AAA. Indicator of the Long-Term «Provision of Entertainment Values» (of a Non-Production Purpose)

Thesis	Increment (Δ) of the volume of entertainment values non-production purpose (ΔVEN-VAL-NP)
Antithesis	Increment (Δ) non-production needs of entertainment values

Synthesis

$$\frac{(\Delta\text{VEN-VAL-NP})}{\text{Increment } (\Delta) \text{ non-production needs of entertainment values}} \text{ - indicators}$$

B. Dialectical Structure of the Long-Term Needs of Entertainment Services

Thesis	Long-term increment (Δ) of the volume of the entertainment services of a production character
Antithesis	Long-term increment (Δ) of the volume of the entertainment services of non-production character
Synthesis	Long-term increment (Δ) of the volume of the entertainment services of the aggregate needs (of a production and non-production character)

2. Entertainment services

Branches	Volume of entertainment services (ENTS) (production use)				Volume of entertainment services (ENTS) (non-production use)				Aggregate volume of entertainment services (ENTS)						
	№ 1	№ 2	№ 3	№ 4	№ 5	№ 6	№ 7	№ 8	№ 9	№ 10	№ 11	№ 12	Estimations	Criteria	Indicators
	▓												Estimations	Criteria	Indicators
		▓											Estimations	Criteria	Indicators
			▓										Estimations	Criteria	Indicators
I branch				▓									Estimations	Criteria	Indicators
Production needs of entertainment services (estimations)					▓								Estimations	Criteria	Indicators
						▓							Estimations	Criteria	Indicators
							▓						Estimations	Criteria	Indicators
II branch								▓					Estimations	Criteria	Indicators
Non-production needs of entertainment services (estimations)									▓				Estimations	Criteria	Indicators
										▓			Estimations	Criteria	Indicators
											▓		Estimations	Criteria	Indicators
III branch												▓	Estimations	Criteria	Indicators
Complex needs of entertainment services (estimations)													Estimations	Criteria	Indicators
													Estimations	Criteria	Indicators

BB. Dialectical Structure of an Indicator of Long-Term Provision of Entertainment Services

Thesis   An increment (Δ) of the volume of entertainment services production purpose

Antithesis   Long-term increment (Δ) of the social needs for entertainment services production purpose

Synthesis $$\frac{\text{An increment } (\Delta) \text{ of the volume of entertainment services production purpose}}{\text{Long-term increment } (\Delta) \text{ of the social needs for entertainment services production purpose}} \text{ - indicators}$$

BBB. Dialectical Structure of an Indicator of Long-Term Provision of Entertainment Services

Thesis   An increment (Δ) of the volume of the entertainment services non-production purpose

Antithesis   Long-term increment (Δ) of the social needs for entertainment services non-production purpose

Synthesis $$\frac{\text{An increment } (\Delta) \text{ of the volume of entertainment services non-production purpose}}{\text{Long-term increment } (\Delta) \text{ of the social needs for entertainment services non-production purpose}} \text{ - indicators}$$

SYSTEM OF CRITERIA OF THE «LONG-TERM PROVISION» OF ENTERTAINMENT SERVICES (FUNCTIONAL INDICATION)

Thesis Dialectical structure of a division of the aggregate of entertainment services as per functional indication.

  Thesis An increment (Δ) of the volume of the entertainment services of a production purpose.

  Antithesis An increment (Δ) of the volume of the entertainment services of a non-production purpose.

  Synthesis An increment (Δ) of the volume of the aggregate entertainment services.

Antithesis Dialectical structure of needs for entertainment services

  Thesis An increment (Δ) of the production needs in entertainment services.

  Antithesis An increment (Δ) of the non-production needs in entertainment services.

  Synthesis An increment (Δ) of the aggregate needs of a society in entertainment services.

Synthesis Dialectical system of the criteria of «provision» with entertainment services.

Thesis
$$\frac{\text{An increment (Δ) of the volume of the entertainment services of a production purpose}}{\text{An increment (Δ) of production needs}} = \text{an indicator of «long-term provision» of production purpose}$$

Antithesis
$$\frac{\text{An increment (Δ) of volume of the entertainment services of a non-production purpose}}{\text{An increment (Δ) of non-production needs}} = \text{an indicator of «long-term provision» of a non-production purpose}$$

Synthesis
$$\frac{\text{An increment (Δ) of an aggregate volume of entertainment services*}}{\text{An increment (Δ) of aggregate needs}} = \text{a complex indicator of the «long-term entertainment provision»}$$

A SYSTEM OF THE INDICATORS OF ENTERTAINMENT PROVISION AS PER A FUNCTIONAL INDICATION

Thesis   **Aggregate criterion of a long-term production provision**

$$\frac{\text{An increment } (\Delta) \text{ of the volume of entertainment values and entertainment services of a production character}}{\text{An increment } (\Delta) \text{ of the production needs in entertainment values and services}} \quad \begin{array}{l} \text{«thesis»} \\ \text{indicator} \end{array}$$

Antithesis   **Aggregate criterion of a long-term non-production provision**

$$\frac{\text{An increment } (\Delta) \text{ of the volume of entertainment values and entertainment services of a non-production character}}{\text{An increment } (\Delta) \text{ of the non-production needs in entertainment values and services}} \quad \begin{array}{l} \text{«antithesis»} \\ \text{indicator} \end{array}$$

Synthesis   **Criterion of an aggregate long-term provision**

$$\frac{\text{An increment } (\Delta) \text{ of the volume of entertainment values and services}}{\text{An increment } (\Delta) \text{ of the aggregate needs in entertainment values and services (of a production and non-production character)}} \quad \begin{array}{l} \text{«synthesis»} \\ \text{indicator} \end{array}$$

CHAPTER 11

The Economic Arithmetic's in Intellectual Sphere Taking into Account of Services of the Three Branches of Power

The reader will create no illusions that the movement of intellectual values and services in the economic space may happen without the services of legislative, executive and judicial power.

These three branches of power will affect processes such as production, distribution, exchange and consumption. The services of the branches of power should be separately evaluated.

The aggregate vector of services will be recorded as follows:

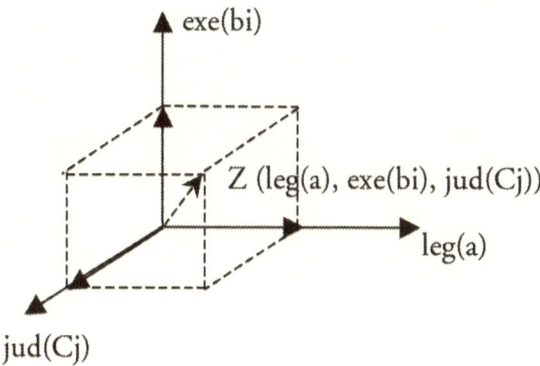

$$R = \pm\, leg(a) \pm exe(bi) \pm jud(Cj)$$

where

- - on axis X—the economic estimate of services of legislative power (± leg);
- - on axis Y—the economic estimate of services of executive power (± exe);
- - on axis Z—the economic estimate of services of judicial power (± jud);

Signs of «+» and «-» applied before vectors leg, exe, jud, reveal the positive or negative inclination of each of the power branches.[11]

Nothing here is contradictory to elementary logic:

- - once there is influence there should also be estimates;
- - no influence would mean absence of estimates.

If the provisions of law do not meet the requirements of the present day development, the services of the executive and judicial powers will be confined to old conceptions impeding the accomplishment of the intellectual sphere.

In other terms, failure in adopting necessary laws by the legislature will have negative effect on the performance of the executive and judicial powers.

It should also be born in mind that the executive and judicial powers may exceed the limits established by the law.

In case these services have specific judicial rating as, for example, e.g. criminal (trespassing), they will accordingly receive a negative economic estimation.

Double accountancy in the intellectual sphere.

---

11   I introduce the following symbols to indicate the three branches of power:
   - leg(a)—legislative power services;
   - exe(a)—executive power services;
   - jud(a)—judicial power services.

1) Economic estimation of production of intellectual values	+	± leg—economic estimate of influence of legislative power services on the process of production of intellectual values ± exe—economic estimate of influence of legislative power services on the process of production of intellectual values ± jud—economic estimate of influence of legislative power services on the process of production of intellectual values
2) Economic estimation of production of intellectual services	+	± leg—economic estimate of influence of legislative power services on the process of production of intellectual services ± exe—economic estimate of influence of legislative power services on the process of production of intellectual services ± jud—economic estimate of influence of legislative power services on the process of production of intellectual services
1) Economic estimation of distribution of intellectual values		± leg—economic estimate of influence of legislative power services on the process of distribution of intellectual values ± exe—economic estimate of influence of legislative power services on the process of distribution of intellectual values ± jud—economic estimate of influence of legislative power services on the process of distribution of intellectual values
2) Economic estimation of distribution of intellectual services		± leg—economic estimate of influence of legislative power services on the process of distribution of intellectual services ± exe—economic estimate of influence of legislative power services on the process of distribution of intellectual services ± jud—economic estimate of influence of legislative power services on the process of distribution of intellectual services

1)

Economic
estimation of
exchange of
intellectual values

± leg—economic estimate of influence of legislative power services on the process of exchange of intellectual values

± exe—economic estimate of influence of legislative power services on the process of exchange of intellectual values

± jud—economic estimate of influence of legislative power services on the process of exchange of intellectual values

2)

Economic
estimation of
exchange of
intellectual services

± leg—economic estimate of influence of legislative power services on the process of exchange of intellectual services

± exe—economic estimate of influence of legislative power services on the process of exchange of intellectual services

± jud—economic estimate of influence of legislative power services on the process of exchange of intellectual services

1)

Economic
estimation of
consumption of
intellectual values

± leg—economic estimate of influence of legislative power services on the process of consumption of intellectual values

± exe—economic estimate of influence of legislative power services on the process of consumption of intellectual values

± jud—economic estimate of influence of legislative power services on the process of consumption of intellectual values

2)

Economic
estimation of
consumption of
intellectual services

± leg—economic estimate of influence of legislative power services on the process of consumption of intellectual services

± exe—economic estimate of influence of legislative power services on the process of consumption of intellectual services

± jud—economic estimate of influence of legislative power services on the process of consumption of intellectual services

Today we try to make the first steps in the creation of the three dimensional estimates of power services. I suggest we imagine these services in vector form, for a better understanding of the three power branches problem:[12]

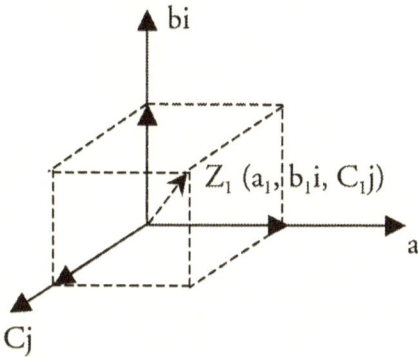

where

- the vector of the services of legislative power
- the vector of the services of executive power
- the vector of the services of judicial power

The aggregate vector of the three branches of power can be presented as follows:

$$Z = a + bi + Cj \text{—complex services of power}$$

By examining state power in a holographic variant we begin to realize that power creates specific services, which support the system of legal and economic relations existing in society.

---

12 The civilized calculation of resources of government state of power should exist in economic theory.

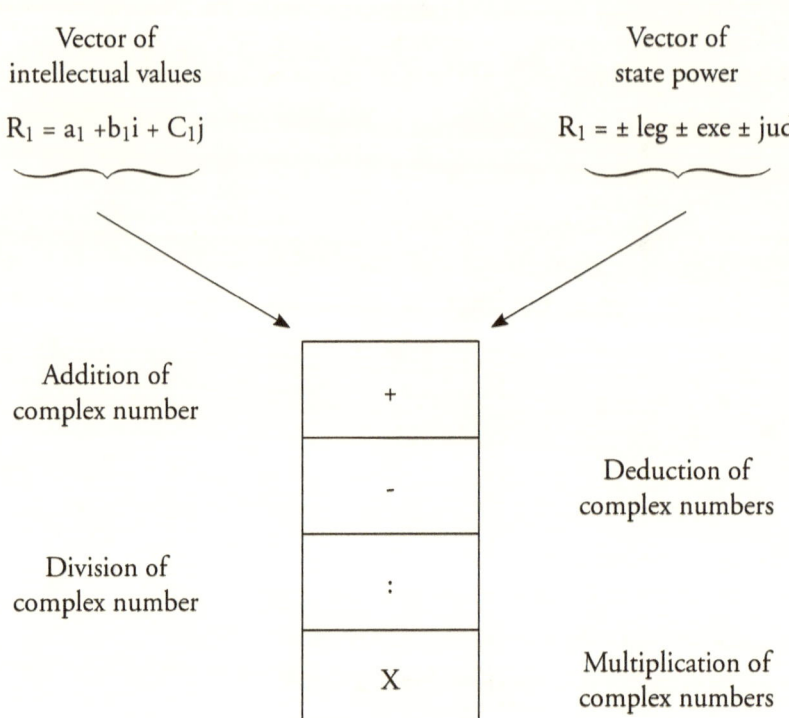

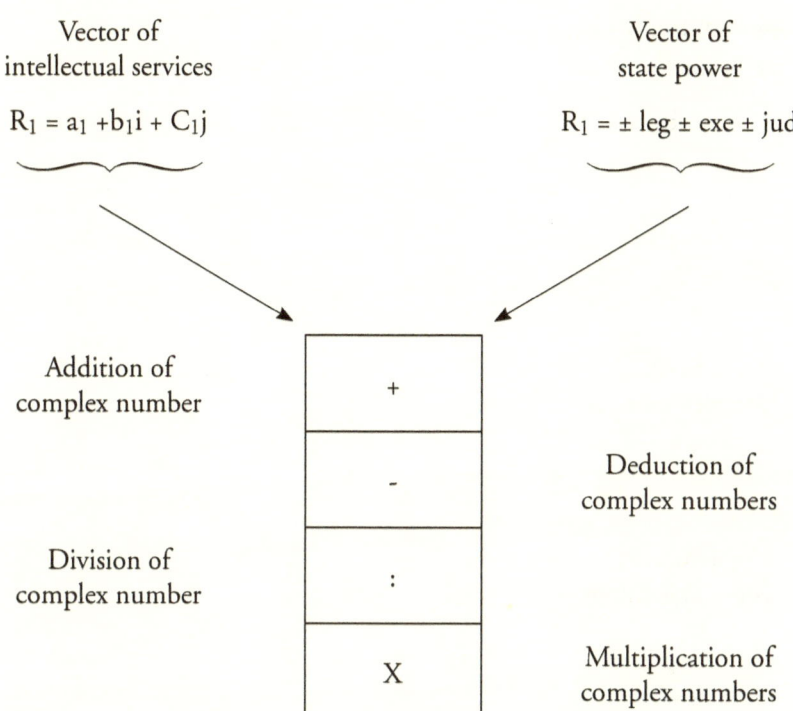

Vector of
intellectual services

$R_1 = a_1 + b_1i + C_1j$

Vector of
state power

$R_1 = \pm \text{leg} \pm \text{exe} \pm \text{jud}$

Addition of
complex number

+

Deduction of
complex numbers

−

Division of
complex number

:

Multiplication of
complex numbers

X

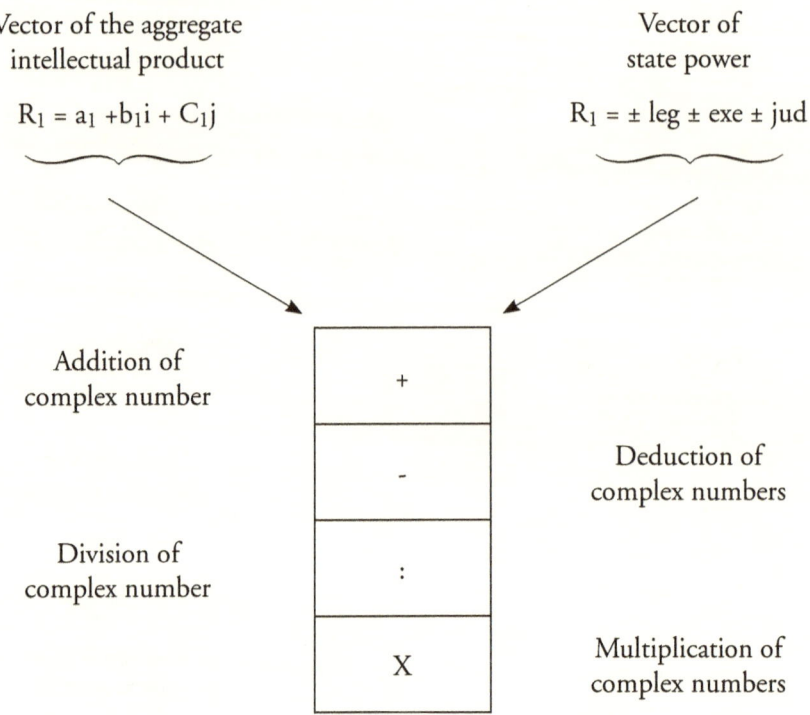

Double accountancy in the educational sphere.

1)

Economic estimation of production of education values	+	± leg—economic estimate of influence of legislative power services on the process of production of education value ± exe—economic estimate of influence of legislative power services on the process of production of education values ± jud—economic estimate of influence of legislative power services on the process of production of education values

2)

Economic estimation of production of education services	+	± leg—economic estimate of influence of legislative power services on the process of production of education services ± exe—economic estimate of influence of legislative power services on the process of production of education services ± jud—economic estimate of influence of legislative power services on the process of production of education services

1)

Economic estimation of distribution of education values	+	± leg—economic estimate of influence of legislative power services on the process of distribution of education values ± exe—economic estimate of influence of legislative power services on the process of distribution of education values ± jud—economic estimate of influence of legislative power services on the process of distribution of education values

2)

Economic estimation of distribution of education services	+	± leg—economic estimate of influence of legislative power services on the process of distribution of education services ± exe—economic estimate of influence of legislative power services on the process of distribution of education services ± jud—economic estimate of influence of legislative power services on the process of distribution of education services

1)

Economic estimation of exchange of education values

+

± leg—economic estimate of influence of legislative power services on the process of exchange of education values

± exe—economic estimate of influence of legislative power services on the process of exchange of education values

± jud—economic estimate of influence of legislative power services on the process of exchange of education values

2)

Economic estimation of exchange of education services

+

± leg—economic estimate of influence of legislative power services on the process of exchange of education services

± exe—economic estimate of influence of legislative power services on the process of exchange of education services

± jud—economic estimate of influence of legislative power services on the process of exchange of education services

1)

Economic estimation of consumption of education values

+

± leg—economic estimate of influence of legislative power services on the process of consumption of education values

± exe—economic estimate of influence of legislative power services on the process of consumption of education values

± jud—economic estimate of influence of legislative power services on the process of consumption of education values

2)

Economic estimation of consumption of education services

+

± leg—economic estimate of influence of legislative power services on the process of consumption of education services

± exe—economic estimate of influence of legislative power services on the process of consumption of education services

± jud—economic estimate of influence of legislative power services on the process of consumption of education services

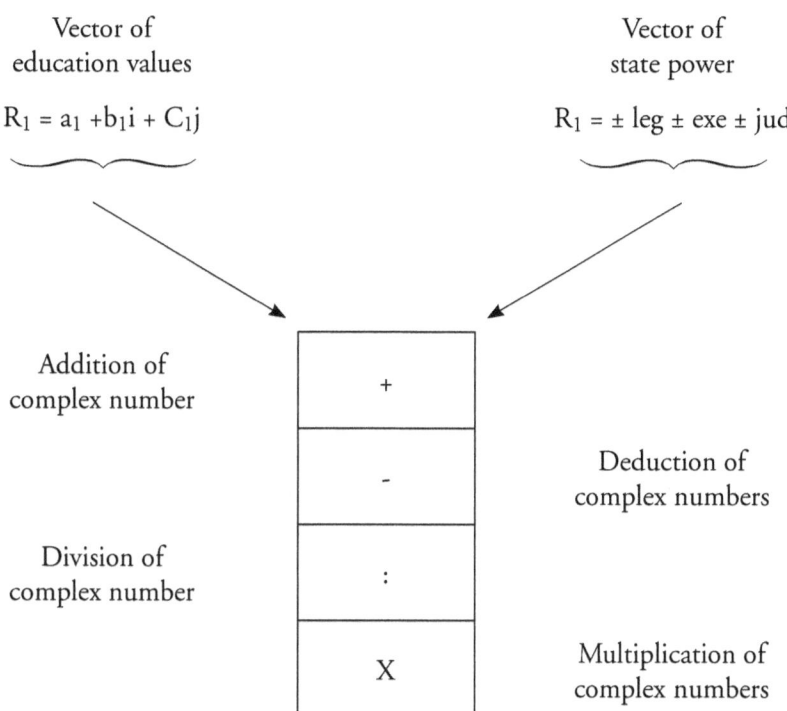

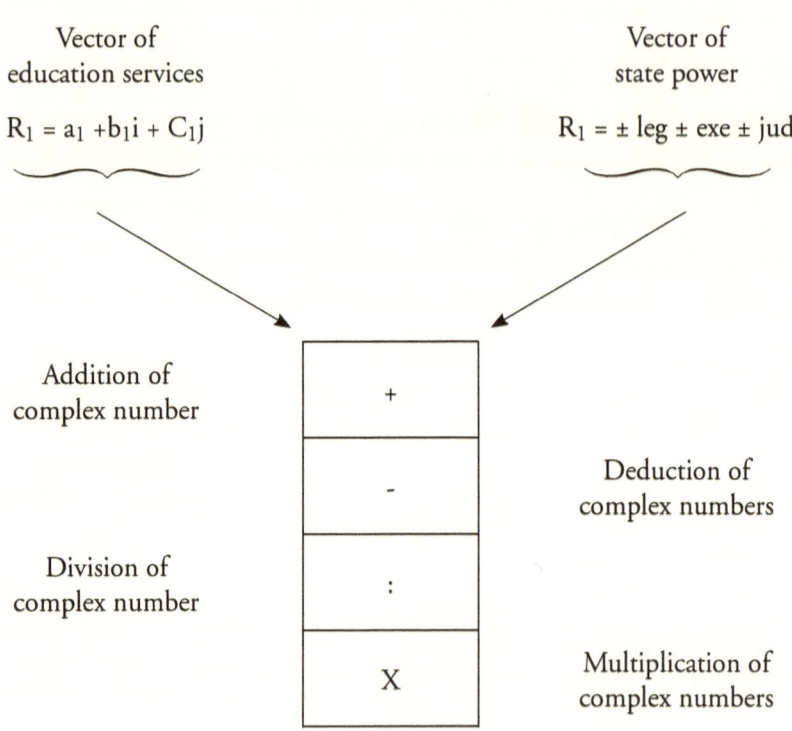

Vector of
education services

$R_1 = a_1 + b_1i + C_1j$

Vector of
state power

$R_1 = \pm \text{leg} \pm \text{exe} \pm \text{jud}$

Addition of
complex number

$+$

Deduction of
complex numbers

$-$

Division of
complex number

$:$

Multiplication of
complex numbers

X

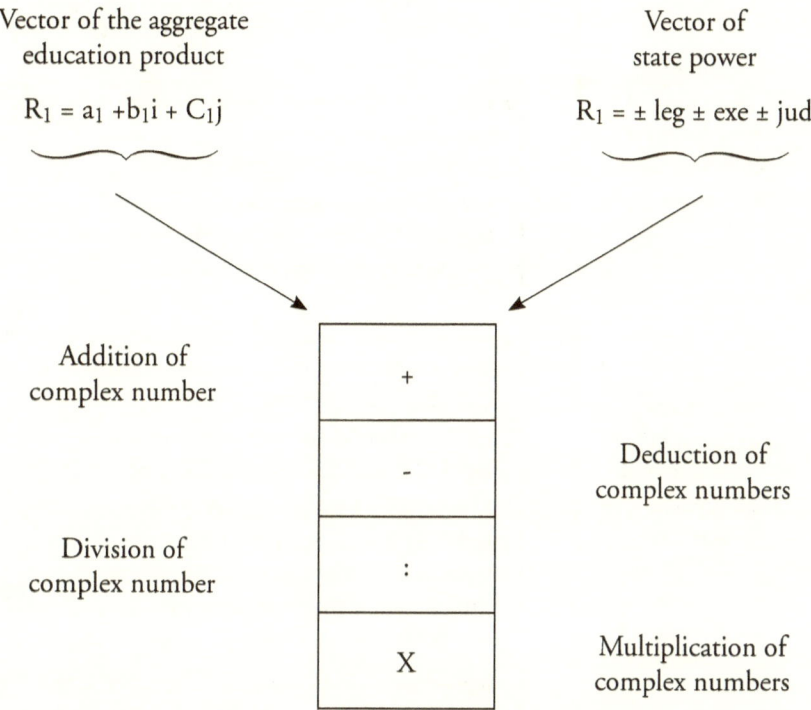

Vector of the aggregate
education product

$R_1 = a_1 + b_1i + C_1j$

Vector of
state power

$R_1 = \pm \, leg \pm exe \pm jud$

Addition of
complex number

$+$

Deduction of
complex numbers

$-$

Division of
complex number

$:$

Multiplication of
complex numbers

X

Double accountancy in the economic relation in the enlightenment sphere.

1)

Economic estimation of production of enlightenment values	+	± leg—economic estimate of influence of legislative power services on the process of production of enlightenment values
		± exe—economic estimate of influence of legislative power services on the process of production of enlightenment values
		± jud—economic estimate of influence of legislative power services on the process of production of enlightenment values

2)

Economic estimation of production of enlightenment services	+	± leg—economic estimate of influence of legislative power services on the process of production of enlightenment services
		± exe—economic estimate of influence of legislative power services on the process of production of enlightenment services
		± jud—economic estimate of influence of legislative power services on the process of production of enlightenment services

1)

Economic estimation of distribution of enlightenment values	+	± leg—economic estimate of influence of legislative power services on the process of distribution of enlightenment values
		± exe—economic estimate of influence of legislative power services on the process of distribution of enlightenment values
		± jud—economic estimate of influence of legislative power services on the process of distribution of enlightenment values

2)

Economic estimation of distribution of enlightenment services	+	± leg—economic estimate of influence of legislative power services on the process of distribution of enlightenment services
		± exe—economic estimate of influence of legislative power services on the process of distribution of enlightenment services
		± jud—economic estimate of influence of legislative power services on the process of distribution of enlightenment services

1)

Economic estimation of exchange of enlightenment values	+	± leg—economic estimate of influence of legislative power services on the process of exchange of enlightenment values
		± exe—economic estimate of influence of legislative power services on the process of exchange of enlightenment values
		± jud—economic estimate of influence of legislative power services on the process of exchange of enlightenment values

2)

Economic estimation of exchange of enlightenment services	+	± leg—economic estimate of influence of legislative power services on the process of exchange of enlightenment services
		± exe—economic estimate of influence of legislative power services on the process of exchange of enlightenment services
		± jud—economic estimate of influence of legislative power services on the process of exchange of enlightenment services

1)

Economic estimation of consumption of enlightenment values	+	± leg—economic estimate of influence of legislative power services on the process of consumption of enlightenment values
		± exe—economic estimate of influence of legislative power services on the process of consumption of enlightenment values
		± jud—economic estimate of influence of legislative power services on the process of consumption of enlightenment values

2)

Economic estimation of consumption of enlightenment services	+	± leg—economic estimate of influence of legislative power services on the process of consumption of enlightenment services
		± exe—economic estimate of influence of legislative power services on the process of consumption of enlightenment services
		± jud—economic estimate of influence of legislative power services on the process of consumption of enlightenment services

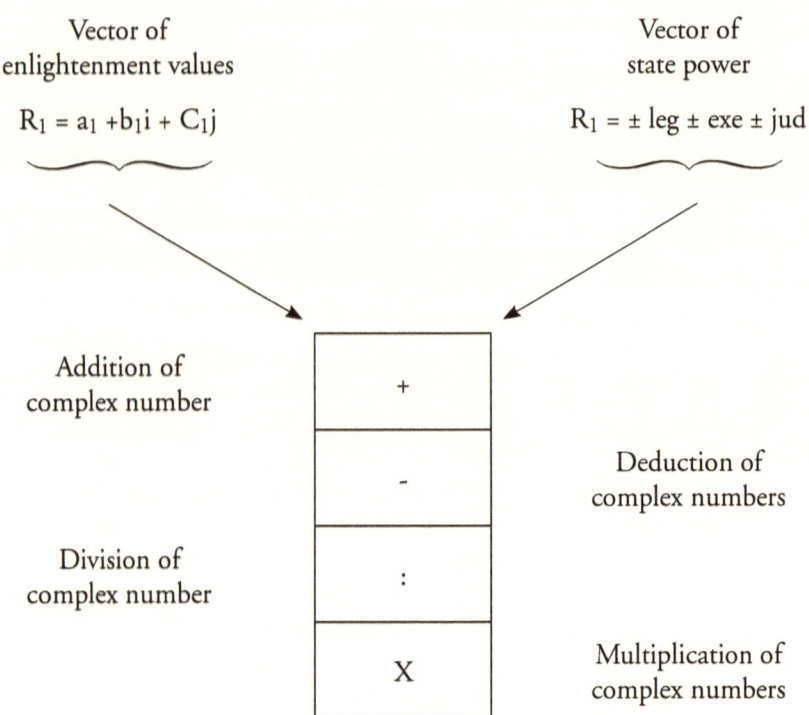

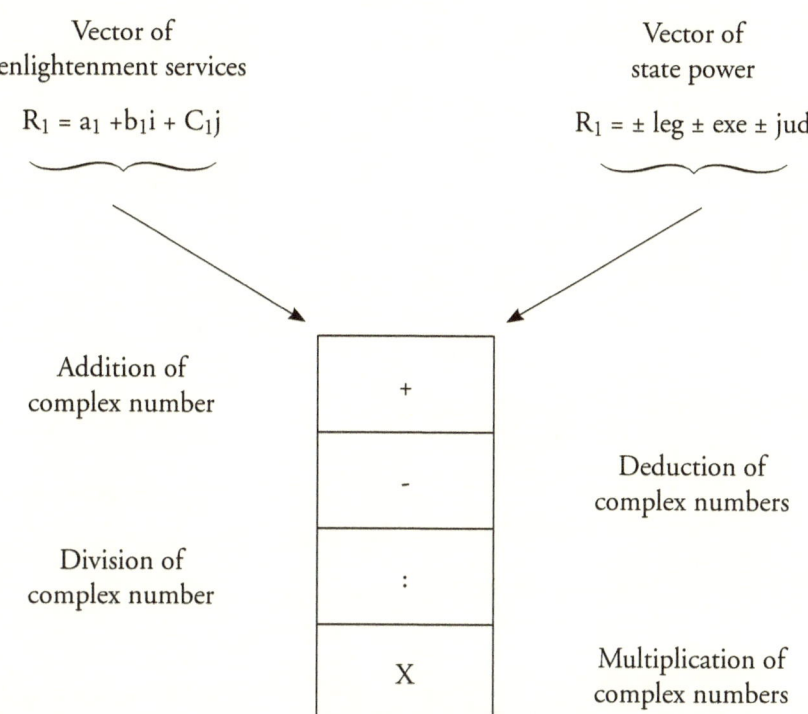

Vector of
enlightenment services

$$R_1 = a_1 + b_1 i + C_1 j$$

Vector of
state power

$$R_1 = \pm \, leg \pm exe \pm jud$$

Addition of
complex number

+

Deduction of
complex numbers

−

Division of
complex number

:

X

Multiplication of
complex numbers

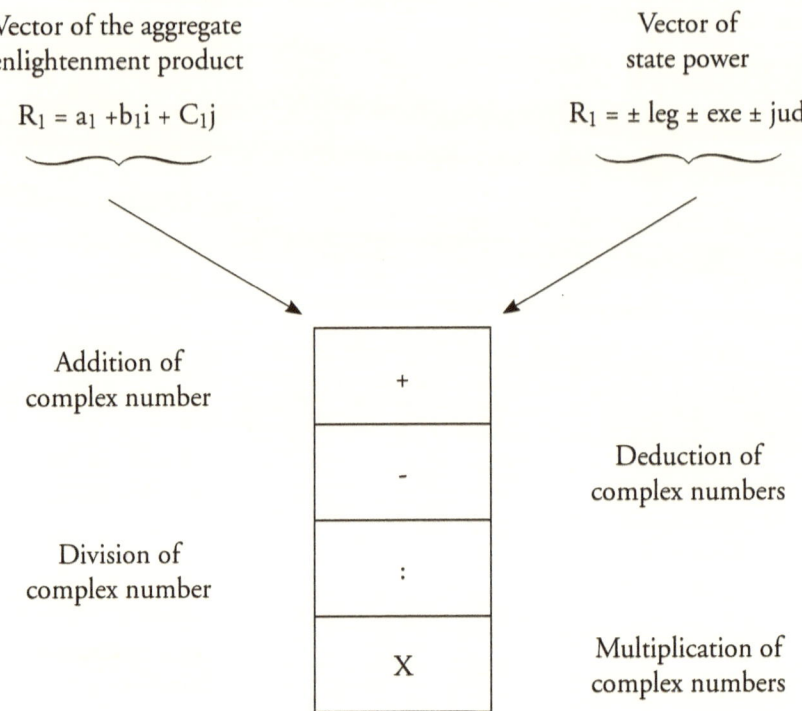

Vector of the aggregate enlightenment product

$$R_1 = a_1 + b_1i + C_1j$$

Vector of state power

$$R_1 = \pm \text{leg} \pm \text{exe} \pm \text{jud}$$

Addition of complex number

\+

Deduction of complex numbers

\-

Division of complex number

:

Multiplication of complex numbers

X

Double accountancy in the economic relation in the entertainment sphere.

1)

Economic
estimation of
production of
entertainment
values

+

± leg—economic estimate of influence of legislative
power services on the process of production of
entertainment values

± exe—economic estimate of influence of
legislative power services on the process of
production of entertainment values

± jud—economic estimate of influence of
legislative power services on the process of
production of entertainment values

2)

Economic
estimation of
production of
entertainment
services

+

± leg—economic estimate of influence of legislative
power services on the process of production of
entertainment services

± exe—economic estimate of influence of
legislative power services on the process of
production of entertainment services

± jud—economic estimate of influence of
legislative power services on the process of
production of entertainment services

1)

Economic
estimation of
distribution of
entertainment
values

+

± leg—economic estimate of influence of legislative
power services on the process of distribution of
entertainment values

± exe—economic estimate of influence of legislative
power services on the process of distribution of
entertainment values

± jud—economic estimate of influence of legislative
power services on the process of distribution of
entertainment values

2)

Economic
estimation of
distribution of
entertainment
services

+

± leg—economic estimate of influence of legislative
power services on the process of distribution of
entertainment services

± exe—economic estimate of influence of legislative
power services on the process of distribution of
entertainment services

± jud—economic estimate of influence of legislative
power services on the process of distribution of
entertainment services

1)

Economic estimation of exchange of entertainment values	+	± leg—economic estimate of influence of legislative power services on the process of exchange of entertainment values
		± exe—economic estimate of influence of legislative power services on the process of exchange of entertainment values
		± jud—economic estimate of influence of legislative power services on the process of exchange of entertainment values

2)

Economic estimation of exchange of entertainment services	+	± leg—economic estimate of influence of legislative power services on the process of exchange of entertainment services
		± exe—economic estimate of influence of legislative power services on the process of exchange of entertainment services
		± jud—economic estimate of influence of legislative power services on the process of exchange of entertainment services

1)

Economic estimation of consumption of entertainment values	+	± leg—economic estimate of influence of legislative power services on the process of consumption of entertainment values
		± exe—economic estimate of influence of legislative power services on the process of consumption of entertainment values
		± jud—economic estimate of influence of legislative power services on the process of consumption of entertainment values

2)

Economic estimation of consumption of entertainment services	+	± leg—economic estimate of influence of legislative power services on the process of consumption of entertainment services
		± exe—economic estimate of influence of legislative power services on the process of consumption of entertainment services
		± jud—economic estimate of influence of legislative power services on the process of consumption of entertainment services

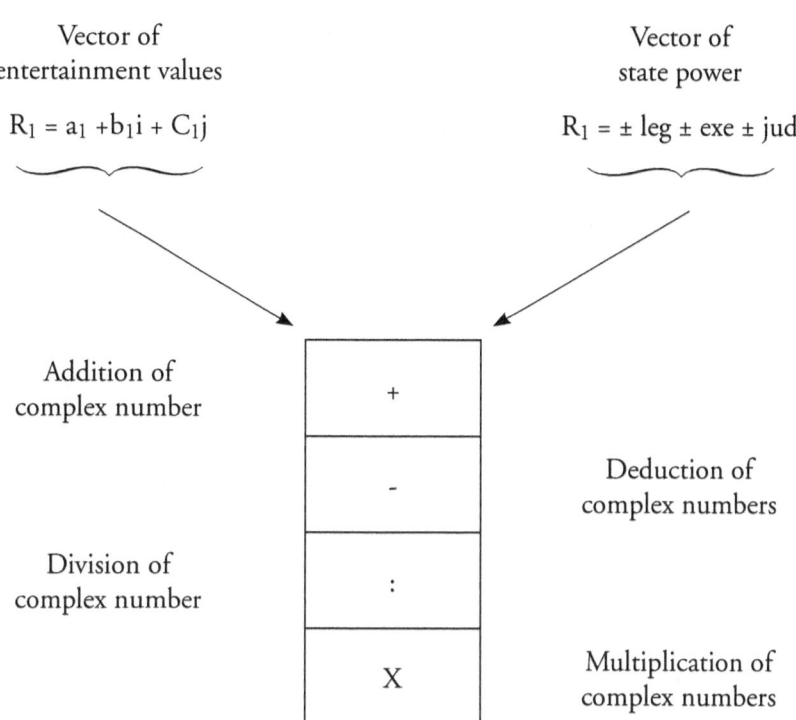

Vector of
entertainment values

$R_1 = a_1 + b_1 i + C_1 j$

Vector of
state power

$R_1 = \pm \text{leg} \pm \text{exe} \pm \text{jud}$

Addition of
complex number

$+$

Deduction of
complex numbers

$-$

Division of
complex number

$:$

Multiplication of
complex numbers

X

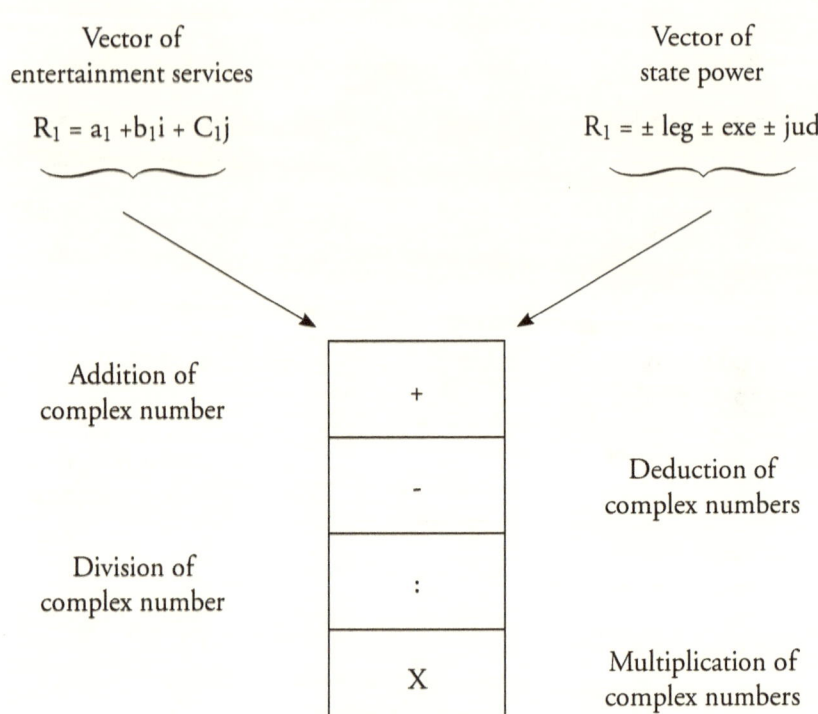

Vector of
entertainment services

$$R_1 = a_1 + b_1 i + C_1 j$$

Vector of
state power

$$R_1 = \pm \, \text{leg} \pm \text{exe} \pm \text{jud}$$

Addition of
complex number

$+$

Deduction of
complex numbers

$-$

Division of
complex number

$:$

Multiplication of
complex numbers

X

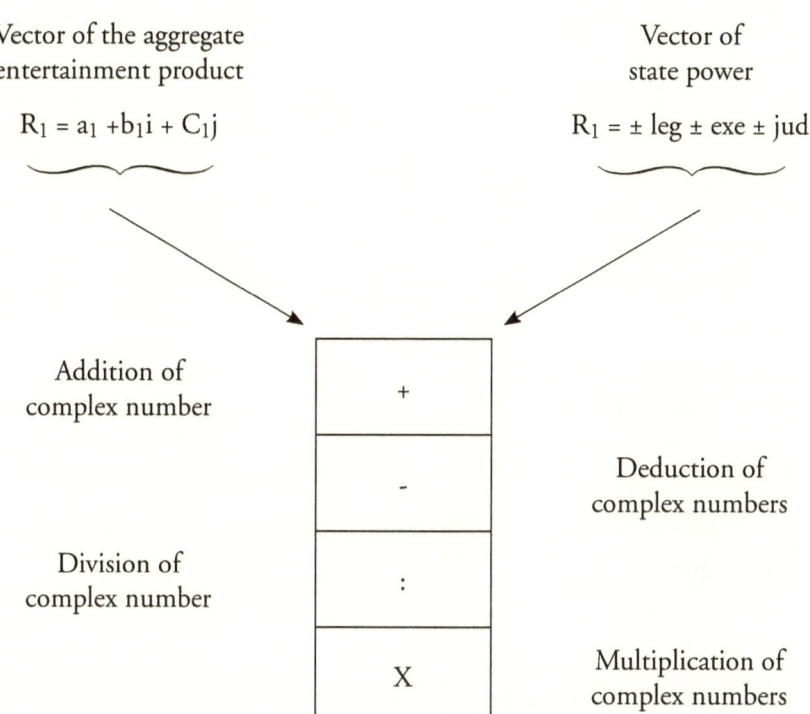

Vector of the aggregate
entertainment product

$$R_1 = a_1 + b_1 i + C_1 j$$

Vector of
state power

$$R_1 = \pm leg \pm exe \pm jud$$

Addition of
complex number

+

Deduction of
complex numbers

−

Division of
complex number

:

Multiplication of
complex numbers

X

IP Division I

$\pm$ leg(a) $\pm$ exe(bi) $\pm$ jud(Cj) + C_1 + V_1i + m_1j = GDP created in the Intellectual sphere (Subdivision I)

$\pm$ leg(a) $\pm$ exe(bi) $\pm$ jud(Cj) + V_1i + m_1j = NDP created in the Intellectual sphere (Subdivision I)

$\pm$ leg(a) $\pm$ exe(bi) $\pm$ jud(Cj) + m_1j = NI created in the Intellectual sphere (Subdivision I)

IP Division II

$\pm$ leg(a) $\pm$ exe(bi) $\pm$ jud(Cj) + C_2 + V_2i + m_2j = GDP created in the Intellectual sphere (Subdivision II)

$\pm$ leg(a) $\pm$ exe(bi) $\pm$ jud(Cj) + V_2i + m_2j = NDP created in the Intellectual sphere (Subdivision II)

$\pm$ leg(a) $\pm$ exe(bi) $\pm$ jud(Cj) + m_2j = NI created in the Intellectual sphere (Subdivision II)

IP Division III

$\pm$ leg(a) $\pm$ exe(bi) $\pm$ jud(Cj) + C_3 + V_3i + m_3j = GDP created in the Intellectual sphere (Subdivision III)

$\pm$ leg(a) $\pm$ exe(bi) $\pm$ jud(Cj) + V_3i + m_3j = NDP created in the Intellectual sphere (Subdivision III)

$\pm$ leg(a) $\pm$ exe(bi) $\pm$ jud(Cj) + m_3j = NI created in the Intellectual sphere (Subdivision III)

IP Division IV

$\pm$ leg(a) $\pm$ exe(bi) $\pm$ jud(Cj) + C_4 + V_4i + m_4j + $A_{STP}k_2$ = GDP created in the Intellectual sphere (Subdivision IV)

$\pm$ leg(a) $\pm$ exe(bi) $\pm$ jud(Cj) + V_4i + m_4j + $A_{STP}k_2$ = NDP created in the Intellectual sphere (Subdivision IV)

$\pm$ leg(a) $\pm$ exe(bi) $\pm$ jud(Cj) + m_4j + $A_{STP}k_2$ = NI created in the Intellectual sphere (Subdivision IV)

$\pm$ leg(a) $\pm$ exe(bi) $\pm$ jud(Cj) + $A_{STP}k_2$ = assimilated resource STP within Subdivision IV

IP Division V

$\pm$ leg(a) $\pm$ exe(bi) $\pm$ jud(Cj) + C_5 + V_5i + m_5j + $A_{STP}k_3$ = GDP created in the Intellectual sphere (Subdivision V)

$\pm$ leg(a) $\pm$ exe(bi) $\pm$ jud(Cj) + V_5i + m_5j + $A_{STP}k_3$ = NDP created in the Intellectual sphere (Subdivision V)

$\pm$ leg(a) $\pm$ exe(bi) $\pm$ jud(Cj) + m_5j + $A_{STP}k_3$ = NI created in the Intellectual sphere (Subdivision V)

$\pm$ leg(a) $\pm$ exe(bi) $\pm$ jud(Cj) + $A_{STP}k_3$ = assimilated resource STP within Subdivision V

IP Division VI

$\pm$ leg(a) $\pm$ exe(bi) $\pm$ jud(Cj) + C_6 + V_6i + m_6j + $A_{STP}k_4$ = GDP created in the Intellectual sphere (Subdivision VI)

$\pm$ leg(a) $\pm$ exe(bi) $\pm$ jud(Cj) + V_6i + m_6j + $A_{STP}k_4$ = NDP created in the Intellectual sphere (Subdivision VI)

$\pm$ leg(a) $\pm$ exe(bi) $\pm$ jud(Cj) + m_6j + $A_{STP}k_4$ = NI created in the Intellectual sphere (Subdivision VI)

$\pm$ leg(a) $\pm$ exe(bi) $\pm$ jud(Cj) + $A_{STP}k_4$ = assimilated resource STP within Subdivision VI

IP Division VII

$\pm$ leg(a) $\pm$ exe(bi) $\pm$ jud(Cj) + C_7 + V_7i + m_7j + $A_{STP}k_2$ = GDP created in the Intellectual sphere (Subdivision VII)

$\pm$ leg(a) $\pm$ exe(bi) $\pm$ jud(Cj) + V_7i + m_7j + $A_{STP}k_2$ = NDP created in the Intellectual sphere (Subdivision VII)

$\pm$ leg(a) $\pm$ exe(bi) $\pm$ jud(Cj) + m_7j + $A_{STP}k_2$ = NI created in the Intellectual sphere (Subdivision VII)

$\pm$ leg(a) $\pm$ exe(bi) $\pm$ jud(Cj) + $A_{STP}k_2$ = assimilated resource STP within Subdivision VII

IP Division VIII

$\pm$ leg(a) $\pm$ exe(bi) $\pm$ jud(Cj) + C_8 + V_8i + m_8j + $A_{STP}k_3$ = GDP created in the Intellectual sphere (Subdivision VIII)

$\pm$ leg(a) $\pm$ exe(bi) $\pm$ jud(Cj) + V_8i + m_8j + $A_{STP}k_3$ = NDP created in the Intellectual sphere (Subdivision VIII)

$\pm \text{leg}(a) \pm \text{exe}(bi) \pm \text{jud}(Cj) + m_8j + A_{STP}k_3 = $ NI created in the Intellectual sphere (Subdivision VIII)

$\pm \text{leg}(a) \pm \text{exe}(bi) \pm \text{jud}(Cj) + A_{STP}k_3 = $ assimilated resource STP within Subdivision VIII

IP Division IX

$\pm \text{leg}(a) \pm \text{exe}(bi) \pm \text{jud}(Cj) + C_9 + V_9i + m_9j + A_{STP}k_4 = $ GDP created in the Intellectual sphere (Subdivision IX)

$\pm \text{leg}(a) \pm \text{exe}(bi) \pm \text{jud}(Cj) + V_9i + m_9j + A_{STP}k_4 = $ NDP created in the Intellectual sphere (Subdivision IX)

$\pm \text{leg}(a) \pm \text{exe}(bi) \pm \text{jud}(Cj) + m_9j + A_{STP}k_4 = $ NI created in the Intellectual sphere (Subdivision IX)

$\pm \text{leg}(a) \pm \text{exe}(bi) \pm \text{jud}(Cj) + A_{STP}k_4 = $ assimilated resource STP within Subdivision IX

IP Division X

$\pm \text{leg}(a) \pm \text{exe}(bi) \pm \text{jud}(Cj) + C_{10} + V_{10}i + m_{10}j + A_{STP}k_2 = $ GDP created in the Intellectual sphere (Subdivision X)

$\pm \text{leg}(a) \pm \text{exe}(bi) \pm \text{jud}(Cj) + V_{10}i + m_{10}j + A_{STP}k_2 = $ NDP created in the Intellectual sphere (Subdivision X)

$\pm \text{leg}(a) \pm \text{exe}(bi) \pm \text{jud}(Cj) + m_{10}j + A_{STP}k_2 = $ NI created in the Intellectual sphere (Subdivision X)

$\pm \text{leg}(a) \pm \text{exe}(bi) \pm \text{jud}(Cj) + A_{STP}k_2 = $ assimilated resource STP within Subdivision X

IP Division XI

$\pm \text{leg}(a) \pm \text{exe}(bi) \pm \text{jud}(Cj) + C_{11} + V_{11}i + m_{11}j + A_{STP}k_3 = $ GDP created in the Intellectual sphere (Subdivision XI)

$\pm \text{leg}(a) \pm \text{exe}(bi) \pm \text{jud}(Cj) + V_{11}i + m_{11}j + A_{STP}k_3 = $ NDP created in the Intellectual sphere (Subdivision XI)

$\pm \text{leg}(a) \pm \text{exe}(bi) \pm \text{jud}(Cj) + m_{11}j + A_{STP}k_3 = $ NI created in the Intellectual sphere (Subdivision XI)

$\pm \text{leg}(a) \pm \text{exe}(bi) \pm \text{jud}(Cj) + A_{STP}k_3 = $ assimilated resource STP within Subdivision XI

IP Division XII

$\pm$ leg(a) $\pm$ exe(bi) $\pm$ jud(Cj) + C_{12} + $V_{12}i$ + $m_{12}j$ + $A_{STP}k_4$ = GDP created in the Intellectual sphere (Subdivision XII)

$\pm$ leg(a) $\pm$ exe(bi) $\pm$ jud(Cj) + $V_{12}i$ + $m_{12}j$ + $A_{STP}k_4$ = NDP created in the Intellectual sphere (Subdivision XII)

$\pm$ leg(a) $\pm$ exe(bi) $\pm$ jud(Cj) + $m_{12}j$ + $A_{STP}k_4$ = NI created in the Intellectual sphere (Subdivision XII)

$\pm$ leg(a) $\pm$ exe(bi) $\pm$ jud(Cj) + $A_{STP}k_4$ = assimilated resource STP within Subdivision XII

IP Division XIII

$\pm$ leg(a) $\pm$ exe(bi) $\pm$ jud(Cj) + C_{13} + $V_{13}i$ + $m_{13}j$ + $A_{STP}k_2$ = GDP created in the Intellectual sphere (Subdivision XIII)

$\pm$ leg(a) $\pm$ exe(bi) $\pm$ jud(Cj) + $V_{13}i$ + $m_{13}j$ + $A_{STP}k_2$ = NDP created in the Intellectual sphere (Subdivision XIII)

$\pm$ leg(a) $\pm$ exe(bi) $\pm$ jud(Cj) + $m_{13}j$ + $A_{STP}k_2$ = NI created in the Intellectual sphere (Subdivision XIII)

$\pm$ leg(a) $\pm$ exe(bi) $\pm$ jud(Cj) + $A_{STP}k_2$ = assimilated resource STP within Subdivision XIII

IP Division XIV

$\pm$ leg(a) $\pm$ exe(bi) $\pm$ jud(Cj) + C_{14} + $V_{14}i$ + $m_{14}j$ + $A_{STP}k_3$ = GDP created in the Intellectual sphere (Subdivision XIV)

$\pm$ leg(a) $\pm$ exe(bi) $\pm$ jud(Cj) + $V_{14}i$ + $m_{14}j$ + $A_{STP}k_3$ = NDP created in the Intellectual sphere (Subdivision XIV)

$\pm$ leg(a) $\pm$ exe(bi) $\pm$ jud(Cj) + $m_{14}j$ + $A_{STP}k_3$ = NI created in the Intellectual sphere (Subdivision XIV)

$\pm$ leg(a) $\pm$ exe(bi) $\pm$ jud(Cj) + $A_{STP}k_3$ = assimilated resource STP within Subdivision XIV

IP Division XV

$\pm$ leg(a) $\pm$ exe(bi) $\pm$ jud(Cj) + C_{15} + $V_{15}i$ + $m_{15}j$ + $A_{STP}k_4$ = GDP created in the Intellectual sphere (Subdivision XV)

$\pm$ leg(a) $\pm$ exe(bi) $\pm$ jud(Cj) + $V_{15}i$ + $m_{15}j$ + $A_{STP}k_4$ = NDP created in the Intellectual sphere (Subdivision XV)

$\pm$ leg(a) $\pm$ exe(bi) $\pm$ jud(Cj) + $m_{15}j$ + $A_{STP}k_4$ = NI created in the Intellectual sphere (Subdivision XV)

$\pm$ leg(a) $\pm$ exe(bi) $\pm$ jud(Cj) + $A_{STP}k_4$ = assimilated resource STP within Subdivision XV

IP Division XVI

$\pm$ leg(a) $\pm$ exe(bi) $\pm$ jud(Cj) + C_{16} + $V_{16}i$ + $m_{16}j$ + $A_{STP}k_4$ = GDP created in the Intellectual sphere (Subdivision XVI)

$\pm$ leg(a) $\pm$ exe(bi) $\pm$ jud(Cj) + $V_{16}i$ + $m_{16}j$ + $A_{STP}k_4$ = NDP created in the Intellectual sphere (Subdivision XVI)

$\pm$ leg(a) $\pm$ exe(bi) $\pm$ jud(Cj) + $m_{16}j$ + $A_{STP}k_4$ = NI created in the Intellectual sphere (Subdivision XVI)

$\pm$ leg(a) $\pm$ exe(bi) $\pm$ jud(Cj) + $A_{STP}k_4$ = assimilated resource STP within Subdivision XVI

IP Division XVII

$\pm$ leg(a) $\pm$ exe(bi) $\pm$ jud(Cj) + C_{18} + $V_{18}i$ + $m_{18}j$ + $A_{STP}k_4$ = GDP created in the Intellectual sphere (Subdivision XVII)

$\pm$ leg(a) $\pm$ exe(bi) $\pm$ jud(Cj) + $V_{17}i$ + $m_{17}j$ + $A_{STP}k_4$ = NDP created in the Intellectual sphere (Subdivision XVII)

$\pm$ leg(a) $\pm$ exe(bi) $\pm$ jud(Cj) + $m_{17}j$ + $A_{STP}k_4$ = NI created in the Intellectual sphere (Subdivision XVII)

$\pm$ leg(a) $\pm$ exe(bi) $\pm$ jud(Cj) + $A_{STP}k_4$ = assimilated resource STP within Subdivision XVII

IP Division XVIII

$\pm$ leg(a) $\pm$ exe(bi) $\pm$ jud(Cj) + C_{18} + $V_{18}i$ + $m_{18}j$ + $A_{STP}k_4$ = GDP created in the Intellectual sphere (Subdivision XVIII)

$\pm$ leg(a) $\pm$ exe(bi) $\pm$ jud(Cj) + $V_{18}i$ + $m_{18}j$ + $A_{STP}k_4$ = NDP created in the Intellectual sphere (Subdivision XVIII)

$\pm$ leg(a) $\pm$ exe(bi) $\pm$ jud(Cj) + $m_{18}j$ + $A_{STP}k_4$ = NI created in the Intellectual sphere (Subdivision XVIII)

$\pm$ leg(a) $\pm$ exe(bi) $\pm$ jud(Cj) + $A_{STP}k_4$ = assimilated resource STP within Subdivision XVIII

IP Division XIX

$\pm$ leg(a) $\pm$ exe(bi) $\pm$ jud(Cj) + C_{19} + $V_{19}i$ + $m_{19}j$ + $A_{STP}k_4$ = GDP created in the Intellectual sphere (Subdivision XIX)

$\pm$ leg(a) $\pm$ exe(bi) $\pm$ jud(Cj) + $V_{19}i$ + $m_{19}j$ + $A_{STP}k_4$ = NDP created in the Intellectual sphere (Subdivision XIX)

$\pm$ leg(a) $\pm$ exe(bi) $\pm$ jud(Cj) + $m_{19}j$ + $A_{STP}k_4$ = NI created in the Intellectual sphere (Subdivision XIX)

$\pm$ leg(a) $\pm$ exe(bi) $\pm$ jud(Cj) + $A_{STP}k_4$ = assimilated resource STP within Subdivision XIX

IP Division XX

$\pm$ leg(a) $\pm$ exe(bi) $\pm$ jud(Cj) + C_{20} + $V_{20}i$ + $m_{20}j$ + $A_{STP}k_4$ = GDP created in the Intellectual sphere (Subdivision XX)

$\pm$ leg(a) $\pm$ exe(bi) $\pm$ jud(Cj) + $V_{20}i$ + $m_{20}j$ + $A_{STP}k_4$ = NDP created in the Intellectual sphere (Subdivision XX)

$\pm$ leg(a) $\pm$ exe(bi) $\pm$ jud(Cj) + $m_{20}j$ + $A_{STP}k_4$ = NI created in the Intellectual sphere (Subdivision XX)

$\pm$ leg(a) $\pm$ exe(bi) $\pm$ jud(Cj) + $A_{STP}k_4$ = assimilated resource STP within Subdivision XX

IP Division XXI

$\pm$ leg(a) $\pm$ exe(bi) $\pm$ jud(Cj) + C_{21} + $V_{21}i$ + $m_{21}j$ + $A_{STP}k_4$ = GDP created in the Intellectual sphere (Subdivision XXI)

$\pm$ leg(a) $\pm$ exe(bi) $\pm$ jud(Cj) + $V_{21}i$ + $m_{21}j$ + $A_{STP}k_4$ = NDP created in the Intellectual sphere (Subdivision XXI)

$\pm$ leg(a) $\pm$ exe(bi) $\pm$ jud(Cj) + $m_{21}j$ + $A_{STP}k_4$ = NI created in the Intellectual sphere (Subdivision XXI)

$\pm$ leg(a) $\pm$ exe(bi) $\pm$ jud(Cj) + $A_{STP}k_4$ = assimilated resource STP within Subdivision XXI

IP Division XXII

$\pm$ leg(a) $\pm$ exe(bi) $\pm$ jud(Cj) + C_{22} + $V_{22}i$ + $m_{22}j$ + $A_{STP}k_4$ = GDP created in the Intellectual sphere (Subdivision XXII)

$\pm$ leg(a) $\pm$ exe(bi) $\pm$ jud(Cj) + $V_{22}i$ + $m_{22}j$ + $A_{STP}k_4$ = NDP created in the Intellectual sphere (Subdivision XXII)

$\pm$ leg(a) $\pm$ exe(bi) $\pm$ jud(Cj) + $m_{22}j$ + $A_{STP}k_4$ = NI created in the Intellectual sphere (Subdivision XXII)

$\pm$ leg(a) $\pm$ exe(bi) $\pm$ jud(Cj) + $A_{STP}k_4$ = assimilated resource STP within Subdivision XXII

IP Division XXIII

$\pm$ leg(a) $\pm$ exe(bi) $\pm$ jud(Cj) + C_{23} + $V_{23}i$ + $m_{23}j$ + $A_{STP}k_4$ = GDP created in the Intellectual sphere (Subdivision XXIII)

$\pm$ leg(a) $\pm$ exe(bi) $\pm$ jud(Cj) + $V_{23}i$ + $m_{23}j$ + $A_{STP}k_4$ = NDP created in the Intellectual sphere (Subdivision XXIII)

$\pm$ leg(a) $\pm$ exe(bi) $\pm$ jud(Cj) + $m_{23}j$ + $A_{STP}k_4$ = NI created in the Intellectual sphere (Subdivision XXIII)

$\pm$ leg(a) $\pm$ exe(bi) $\pm$ jud(Cj) + $A_{STP}k_4$ = assimilated resource STP within Subdivision XXIII

IP Division XXIV

$\pm$ leg(a) $\pm$ exe(bi) $\pm$ jud(Cj) + C_{24} + $V_{24}i$ + $m_{24}j$ + $A_{STP}k_4$ = GDP created in the Intellectual sphere (Subdivision XXIV)

$\pm$ leg(a) $\pm$ exe(bi) $\pm$ jud(Cj) + $V_{24}i$ + $m_{24}j$ + $A_{STP}k_4$ = NDP created in the Intellectual sphere (Subdivision XXIV)

$\pm$ leg(a) $\pm$ exe(bi) $\pm$ jud(Cj) + $m_{24}j$ + $A_{STP}k_4$ = NI created in the Intellectual sphere (Subdivision XXIV)

$\pm$ leg(a) $\pm$ exe(bi) $\pm$ jud(Cj) + $A_{STP}k_4$ = assimilated resource STP within Subdivision XXIV

IP Division XXV

$\pm$ leg(a) $\pm$ exe(bi) $\pm$ jud(Cj) + C_{25} + $V_{25}i$ + $m_{25}j$ + $A_{STP}k_4$ = GDP created in the Intellectual sphere (Subdivision XXV)

$\pm$ leg(a) $\pm$ exe(bi) $\pm$ jud(Cj) + $V_{25}i$ + $m_{25}j$ + $A_{STP}k_4$ = NDP created in the Intellectual sphere (Subdivision XXV)

$\pm$ leg(a) $\pm$ exe(bi) $\pm$ jud(Cj) + $m_{25}j$ + $A_{STP}k_4$ = NI created in the Intellectual sphere (Subdivision XXV)

$\pm$ leg(a) $\pm$ exe(bi) $\pm$ jud(Cj) + $A_{STP}k_4$ = assimilated resource STP within Subdivision XXV

IP Division XXVI

$\pm$ leg(a) $\pm$ exe(bi) $\pm$ jud(Cj) + C_{26} + $V_{26}i$ + $m_{26}j$ + $A_{STP}k_4$ = GDP created in the Intellectual sphere (Subdivision XXVI)

$\pm$ leg(a) $\pm$ exe(bi) $\pm$ jud(Cj) + $V_{26}i$ + $m_{26}j$ + $A_{STP}k_4$ = NDP created in the Intellectual sphere (Subdivision XXVI)

$\pm$ leg(a) $\pm$ exe(bi) $\pm$ jud(Cj) + $m_{26}j$ + $A_{STP}k_4$ = NI created in the Intellectual sphere (Subdivision XXVI)

$\pm$ leg(a) $\pm$ exe(bi) $\pm$ jud(Cj) + $A_{STP}k_4$ = assimilated resource STP within Subdivision XXVI

IP Division XXVII

$\pm$ leg(a) $\pm$ exe(bi) $\pm$ jud(Cj) + C_{27} + $V_{27}i$ + $m_{27}j$ + $A_{STP}k_4$ = GDP created in the Intellectual sphere (Subdivision XXVII)

$\pm$ leg(a) $\pm$ exe(bi) $\pm$ jud(Cj) + $V_{27}i$ + $m_{27}j$ + $A_{STP}k_4$ = NDP created in the Intellectual sphere (Subdivision XXVII)

$\pm$ leg(a) $\pm$ exe(bi) $\pm$ jud(Cj) + $m_{27}j$ + $A_{STP}k_4$ = NI created in the Intellectual sphere (Subdivision XXVII)

$\pm$ leg(a) $\pm$ exe(bi) $\pm$ jud(Cj) + $A_{STP}k_4$ = assimilated resource STP within Subdivision XXVII

IP Division XXVIII

$\pm$ leg(a) $\pm$ exe(bi) $\pm$ jud(Cj) + C_{28} + $V_{28}i$ + $m_{28}j$ + $A_{STP}k_4$ = GDP created in the Intellectual sphere (Subdivision XXVIII)

$\pm$ leg(a) $\pm$ exe(bi) $\pm$ jud(Cj) + $V_{28}i$ + $m_{28}j$ + $A_{STP}k_4$ = NDP created in the Intellectual sphere (Subdivision XXVIII)

$\pm$ leg(a) $\pm$ exe(bi) $\pm$ jud(Cj) + $m_{28}j$ + $A_{STP}k_4$ = NI created in the Intellectual sphere (Subdivision XXVIII)

$\pm$ leg(a) $\pm$ exe(bi) $\pm$ jud(Cj) + $A_{STP}k_4$ = assimilated resource STP within Subdivision XXVIII

Calculation of GDP with the use of complex numbers

Subdivision I	$GDP_1 = C_1 + V_1 i + m_1 j$
Subdivision II	$GDP_2 = C_2 + V_2 i + m_2 j$
Subdivision III	$GDP_3 = C_3 + V_3 i + m_3 j$
Subdivision IV	$GDP_4 = C_4 + V_4 i + m_4 j + A_{STP} k_2$
Subdivision V	$GDP_5 = C_5 + V_5 i + m_5 j + A_{STP} k_3$
Subdivision VI	$GDP_6 = C_6 + V_6 i + m_6 j + A_{STP} k_4$
Subdivision VII	$GDP_7 = C_7 + V_7 i + m_7 j + A_{STP} k_2$
Subdivision VIII	$GDP_8 = C_8 + V_8 i + m_8 j + A_{STP} k_3$
Subdivision IX	$GDP_9 = C_9 + V_9 i + m_9 j + A_{STP} k_4$
Subdivision X	$GDP_{10} = C_{10} + V_{10} i + m_{10} j + A_{STP} k_2$
Subdivision XI	$GDP_{11} = C_{11} + V_{11} i + m_{11} j + A_{STP} k_3$
Subdivision XII	$GDP_{12} = C_{12} + V_{12} i + m_{12} j + A_{STP} k_4$
Subdivision XII	$GDP_{13} = C_{13} + V_{13} i + m_{13} j + A_{STP} k_2$
Subdivision XIV	$GDP_{14} = C_{14} + V_{14} i + m_{14} j + A_{STP} k_3$
Subdivision XV	$GDP_{15} = C_{15} + V_{15} i + m_{15} j + A_{STP} k_4$
Subdivision XVI	$GDP_{16} = C_{16} + V_{16} i + m_{16} j + A_{STP} k_4$
Subdivision XVII	$GDP_{17} = C_{17} + V_{17} i + m_{17} j + A_{STP} k_2$
Subdivision XVIII	$GDP_{18} = C_{18} + V_{18} i + m_{18} j + A_{STP} k_3$
Subdivision XIX	$GDP_{19} = C_{19} + V_{19} i + m_{19} j + A_{STP} k_4$
Subdivision XX	$GDP_{20} = C_{20} + V_{20} i + m_{20} j + A_{STP} k_4$
Subdivision XXI	$GDP_{21} = C_{21} + V_{21} i + m_{21} j + A_{STP} k_4$
Subdivision XXII	$GDP_{22} = C_{22} + V_{22} i + m_{22} j + A_{STP} k_4$
Subdivision XXIII	$GDP_{23} = C_{23} + V_{23} i + m_{23} j + A_{STP} k_4$
Subdivision XXIV	$GDP_{24} = C_{24} + V_{24} i + m_{24} j + A_{STP} k_4$
Subdivision XXV	$GDP_{25} = C_{25} + V_{25} i + m_{25} j + A_{STP} k_4$
Subdivision XXVI	$GDP_{26} = C_{26} + V_{26} i + m_{26} j + A_{STP} k_4$
Subdivision XXVII	$GDP_{27} = C_{27} + V_{27} i + m_{27} j + A_{STP} k_4$
Subdivision XXVIII	$GDP_{28} = C_{28} + V_{28} i + m_{28} j + A_{STP} k_4$

$$Z_{GDP} = GDP_1 + GDP_2 + GDP_3 + GDP_4 + GDP_5 + GDP_6 + GDP_7 + GDP_8 + GDP_9 + GDP_{10} + GDP_{11} + GDP_{12} + GDP_{13} + GDP_{14} + GDP_{15} + GDP_{16}$$

Calculation of NDP with the use of complex numbers

Subdivision I	$NDP_1 = V_1 i + m_1 j$
Subdivision II	$NDP_2 = V_2 i + m_2 j$
Subdivision III	$NDP_3 = V_3 i + m_3 j$
Subdivision IV	$NDP_4 = V_4 i + m_4 j + A_{STP} k_2$
Subdivision V	$NDP_5 = V_5 i + m_5 j + A_{STP} k_3$
Subdivision VI	$NDP_6 = V_6 i + m_6 j + A_{STP} k_4$
Subdivision VII	$NDP_7 = V_7 i + m_7 j + A_{STP} k_2$
Subdivision VIII	$NDP_8 = V_8 i + m_8 j + A_{STP} k_3$
Subdivision IX	$NDP_9 = V_9 i + m_9 j + A_{STP} k_4$
Subdivision X	$NDP_{10} = V_{10} i + m_{10} j + A_{STP} k_2$
Subdivision XI	$NDP_{11} = V_{11} i + m_{11} j + A_{STP} k_3$
Subdivision XII	$NDP_{12} = V_{12} i + m_{12} j + A_{STP} k_4$
Subdivision XII	$NDP_{13} = V_{13} i + m_{13} j + A_{STP} k_2$
Subdivision XIV	$NDP_{14} = V_{14} i + m_{14} j + A_{STP} k_3$
Subdivision XV	$NDP_{15} = V_{15} i + m_{15} j + A_{STP} k_4$
Subdivision XVI	$NDP_{16} = V_{16} i + m_{16} j + A_{STP} k_4$
Subdivision XVII	$NDP_{17} = V_{17} i + m_{17} j + A_{STP} k_2$
Subdivision XVIII	$NDP_{18} = V_{18} i + m_{18} j + A_{STP} k_3$
Subdivision XIX	$NDP_{19} = V_{19} i + m_{19} j + A_{STP} k_4$
Subdivision XX	$NDP_{20} = V_{20} i + m_{20} j + A_{STP} k_4$
Subdivision XXI	$NDP_{21} = V_{21} i + m_{21} j + A_{STP} k_4$
Subdivision XXII	$NDP_{22} = V_{22} i + m_{22} j + A_{STP} k_4$
Subdivision XXIII	$NDP_{23} = V_{23} i + m_{23} j + A_{STP} k_4$
Subdivision XXIV	$NDP_{24} = V_{24} i + m_{24} j + A_{STP} k_4$
Subdivision XXV	$NDP_{25} = V_{25} i + m_{25} j + A_{STP} k_4$
Subdivision XXVI	$NDP_{26} = V_{26} i + m_{26} j + A_{STP} k_4$
Subdivision XXVII	$NDP_{27} = V_{27} i + m_{27} j + A_{STP} k_4$
Subdivision XXVIII	$NDP_{28} = V_{28} i + m_{28} j + A_{STP} k_4$

$$Z_{NDP} = NDP_1 + NDP_2 + NDP_3 + NDP_4 + NDP_5 + NDP_6 + NDP_7 + NDP_8 + NDP_9 + NDP_{10} + NDP_{11} + NDP_{12} + NDP_{13} + NDP_{14} + NDP_{15} + NDP_{16}$$

Calculation of NI

Subdivision I	$NI_1 = m_1j$
Subdivision II	$NI_2 = m_2j$
Subdivision III	$NI_3 = m_3j$
Subdivision IV	$NI_4 = m_4j + A_{STP}k_2$
Subdivision V	$NI_5 = m_5j + A_{STP}k_3$
Subdivision VI	$NI_6 = m_6j + A_{STP}k_4$
Subdivision VII	$NI_7 = m_7j + A_{STP}k_2$
Subdivision VIII	$NI_8 = m_8j + A_{STP}k_3$
Subdivision IX	$NI_9 = m_9j + A_{STP}k_4$
Subdivision X	$NI_{10} = m_{10}j + A_{STP}k_2$
Subdivision XI	$NI_{11} = m_{11}j + A_{STP}k_3$
Subdivision XII	$NI_{12} = m_{12}j + A_{STP}k_4$
Subdivision XII	$NI_{13} = m_{13}j + A_{STP}k_2$
Subdivision XIV	$NI_{14} = m_{14}j + A_{STP}k_3$
Subdivision XV	$NI_{15} = m_{15}j + A_{STP}k_4$
Subdivision XVI	$NI_{16} = m_{16}j + A_{STP}k_4$
Subdivision XVII	$NI_{17} = m_{17}j + A_{STP}k_2$
Subdivision XVIII	$NI_{18} = m_{18}j + A_{STP}k_3$
Subdivision XIX	$NI_{19} = m_{19}j + A_{STP}k_4$
Subdivision XX	$NI_{20} = m_{20}j + A_{STP}k_4$
Subdivision XXI	$NI_{21} = m_{21}j + A_{STP}k_4$
Subdivision XXII	$NI_{22} = m_{22}j + A_{STP}k_4$
Subdivision XXIII	$NI_{23} = m_{23}j + A_{STP}k_4$
Subdivision XXIV	$NI_{24} = m_{24}j + A_{STP}k_4$
Subdivision XXV	$NI_{25} = m_{25}j + A_{STP}k_4$
Subdivision XXVI	$NI_{26} = m_{26}j + A_{STP}k_4$
Subdivision XXVII	$NI_{27} = m_{27}j + A_{STP}k_4$
Subdivision XXVIII	$NI_{28} = m_{28}j + A_{STP}k_4$

$$Z_{NI} = NI_1 + NI_2 + NI_3 + NI_4 + NI_5 + NI_6 + NI_7 + NI_8 + NI_9 + NI_{10} + NI_{11} + NI_{12} + NI_{13} + NI_{14} + NI_{15} + NI_{16}$$

Calculation of A_{STP}

Subdivision IV	$NI_4 = A_{STP}k_2$
Subdivision V	$NI_5 = A_{STP}k_3$
Subdivision VI	$NI_6 = A_{STP}k_4$
Subdivision VII	$NI_7 = A_{STP}k_2$
Subdivision VIII	$NI_8 = A_{STP}k_3$
Subdivision IX	$NI_9 = A_{STP}k_4$
Subdivision X	$NI_{10} = A_{STP}k_2$
Subdivision XI	$NI_{11} = A_{STP}k_3$
Subdivision XII	$NI_{12} = A_{STP}k_4$
Subdivision XII	$NI_{13} = A_{STP}k_2$
Subdivision XIV	$NI_{14} = A_{STP}k_3$
Subdivision XV	$NI_{15} = A_{STP}k_4$
Subdivision XVI	$NI_{16} = A_{STP}k_4$
Subdivision XVII	$NI_{17} = A_{STP}k_2$
Subdivision XVIII	$NI_{18} = A_{STP}k_3$
Subdivision XIX	$NI_{19} = A_{STP}k_4$
Subdivision XX	$NI_{20} = A_{STP}k_4$
Subdivision XXI	$NI_{21} = A_{STP}k_4$
Subdivision XXII	$NI_{22} = A_{STP}k_4$
Subdivision XXIII	$NI_{23} = A_{STP}k_4$
Subdivision XXIV	$NI_{24} = A_{STP}k_4$
Subdivision XXV	$NI_{25} = A_{STP}k_4$
Subdivision XXVI	$NI_{26} = A_{STP}k_4$
Subdivision XXVII	$NI_{27} = A_{STP}k_4$
Subdivision XXVIII	$NI_{28} = A_{STP}k_4$

Total: $Ok + A^{COL}_{STP}k_2 + A^{UN}_{STP}k_3 + A^{LIB}_{STP}k_4 + A^{EX}_{STP}k_2 + A^{MU}_{STP}k_3 + A^{CIR}_{STP}k_4 + A^{TH}_{STP}k_2 + A^{CON}_{STP}k_3 + A^{SH}_{STP}k_4 + A^{CIN}_{STP}k_2 + A^{SENT}_{STP}k_3 + A^{RAD}_{STP}k_4 + A^{TV}_{STP}k_4$

Part 2

The Intellectual Sphere of the USA[13]

13   THE INTELLECTUAL SPHERE OF THE USA
     ISBN 0595-18731-5
     Publishing 2001

The author considers the intellectual sphere of the USA as an economic system in the 1980s some of the parameters of the intellectual sphere of the USA were:

Book Publishing

1,205 publishers,

50 of largest publishing houses produce 70 per cent of all books

35,469 titles per annum;

1,24 billion copies

income for book sales is $4.4 billion per annum

Newspapers

1,760 daily newspapers

61,5 million daily copies

70 per cent of income comes from advertising, $ 11 billion annually;

30 per cent of income comes from newspaper sales $ 4,7 billion annually

Magazines

2,394 publishers

37,000 titles, 50—with a circulation of over a million

total income on advertising $ 2,1 billion

Film Distribution

15,969 cinema halls

annual attendance 1,1 billion visitors

Income from ticket sale and advertising $ 1,8 billion per annum

TV Broadcasting

728 commercial stations;

256 non commercial stations;

3 TV networks;

    1 network of social (educational) broadcasting

    121 million TV sets, covering 98 per cent of the households

    total income from advertising is over $ 7,6 billion per annum

Cable TV

3,832 systems, including 8 largest companies cater for 37 per cent of the subscribers

12 million subscribers

total income is $ 900 million annually

Radio Broadcasting

4497 stations;

2837 FM stations;

839 stations of social broadcasting;

4 commercial networks;

1 network of social broadcasting

425 million radio-receivers

income from advertising is over $ 2,5 billion per annum

The system of primary and secondary education in the USA has 105,500 schools with 44 million pupils and 3,300 of various institutes with over 12 million students.

The USA produced:—44.1 million radios and 17.6 million TV sets.

This branch grew into a gigantic sphere in advanced countries long ago. Thus, the absolute size of the Gross Domestic Product of the US sport industry amounted to $ 63.1 billion dollars, including:

sport recreation and health improvement activity	$ 22.8 billion
production of sports equipment	$ 1.9 billion
ticket sales for sports contests	$ 3.2 billion
golf clubs	$ 8.0 billion
tennis, racquetball, squash and recreational clubs	$ 6.3 billion
water recreation	$ 4.7 billion
bowling and billiard clubs	$ 2.0 billion
other kinds of sports health-improvement activity	$ 1.8 billion
etc	$ 1.9 billion

From the above figures, it is clear that the US sports business supports a great number of stadiums, edifices and companies. Organization of such a branch, which annually produces various shows and other kinds of production worth over $ 60 billion is long and complex, as in its formation and development as an economic system.

CHAPTER 1

The Economic Parameters of the Branches of Intellectual Production Division I

A. Periodical Press

There is a wide range of periodicals in the USA. As regards the number of published periodicals, the country takes a leading place in the capitalist world: 20,624 publications were produced the USA in 1987, including 9,031 newspapers and 11,593 magazines or publications of magazine type.

In 1987, 1646 daily newspapers were published in English with a circulation over 62,5 million; 16 daily newspapers were also published in foreign languages. 776 Sunday editions of daily newspapers were circulated to over 58 million with 6,750 weekly newspapers (a circulation of 48 million).

The American press is private property. Newspapers and magazine publishing is monopolized, and there is a very high level of concentration and monopoly in the printing industry. There are 149 companies in the USA that own two or more then two newspapers, meaning that they control about 71 per cent of all daily newspapers and 77 per cent of all circulation. The 20 largest press monopolies control over 52 per cent of the daily newspaper circulation.

The main tendency in development during the 1970s and 1980s was acceleration and growth in the level of concentration and monopoly in the printing industry. One of the consequences of this process has been a continuous decrease in the number of towns that publish competing papers. Thus, in 1979 competing newspapers were published in 45 towns. By 1985 that had fallen to 23 towns (daily newspapers were published in 1,533 towns). The number of towns and cities increases when the different people who own newspaper possess agreements on joint publishing. Two newspapers (evening and morning ones) are published in 100 towns and cities. Newspapers owned by a press monopoly compete with so-called independent publications is only 18 towns. There are agreements on a mutual publishing in 8 towns. Competing newspapers not owned by a monopoly are published in only four towns.

There other consequence of concentration and monopoly in the printing industry process is a decrease in the number of daily newspapers. There were 2,042 daily newspapers in 1900; in 1,963; 1955 and 1,730 in 1980. By 1987 there were just 1,646 daily newspapers were only left in 1987.

Financial and industrial capital maintains a control over the press in various forms: through bank credit, by owning shares in the newspapers, through the system of managing staff, etc. Newspaper and magazine companies are closely connected with the leading industrial monopolies, banks and corporations.

Commercial advertising exerts a huge, every day control over the press industry. Advertising provides the finance for newspapers and magazines. Between 70-80 per cent of profit is obtained from an advertisements; the rest from newspaper circulation. On average, advertisements account for 60-70 per cent of newspaper and magazines lines.

Newspapers are the largest recipients of advertising profits. In 1986 they came to $ 27.5 billion: advertising profits of TV came to $ 21.5 billion in 1986, radio—$ 7 billion and magazines—$ 6,3 billion.

The concentration and monopolization of the printing industry is characteristic of a tendency to absorb separate publications and big publishing companies into huge monopolies. There are no enterprises among the leading monopolies that would limit themselves to just one type of production, newspapers in particular. As a rule, the monopolies are diversified, i.e. they are engaged with publishing various products: newspapers, magazines, books, they own radio- and TV-stations, cable TV systems, etc. They also own capital investments in different industries. The main monopolies of the natural press are massive conglomerates in the communication sector and they own practically all the leading bodies of the American Press.

The largest information propaganda monopolies in the USA are as follows. «Gannett Company» leads 90 newspapers with a circulation of over 5.7 million companies, out of the total number of dailies in America. A majority of them published in 33 states have a comparatively small circulation. But since 1982, the Cannett has published the massive national newspaper, «USA Today», with a circulation of 1.4 million. They also publish 42 weekly newspapers, own 16 radio and 9 TV stations, an advertising company and a popular questionnaire since. The list could go on. In recent years, Gannett has been considerably aggressive in the newspaper market. A number of their daily newspapers have doubled circulation in a decade. The Company purchased «Family Weekly» in 1985, (a Sunday supplement for 267 newspapers over 14 million copies), which was renamed to «US Week-End». She also bought the Evening News Association: 5 weekly newspapers, 2 radio stations and 5 TV stations.

«Night-Reader Newspapers» take second place in terms of total circulation of daily newspapers that owns 32 dailies with a circulation of over 3.6 million and 6 weekly newspapers. The company's largest newspapers are «Detroit Free Press» (over 639,000 copies), «Philadelphia Inquirer» (494,000 copies) and «Miami Herald» (over 437,000 copies). The company also publishes a daily newspaper «Journal of Commerce and Commersional» (22,000 copies) has 4 TV stations and a paper factory.

Furthermore the «News House Newspapers» monopoly supports 26 daily news-papers with a total circulation of about 3 million. Her largest newspaper is «Cleveland Plane Dealer»(454,000 thousand copies). The company also owns weekly magazine «Parade» the largest weekly magazine circulation in the country at over 32.5 million copies, distributed as a Sunday supplement to 313 newspapers and the weekly «New-Yorker» (over 500,000 copies). In addi-tion, News House owns «Conde Nast Magazines», a company that publishes woman's magazines, including «Vogue», «Mademoiselle» and «Glamour», the large publishing firm «Random House» as well as radio- and TV-stations.

The ten largest newspapers monopolies include: «Tribune Company» (7 daily newspapers with circulation of over 2.6 million, including «New York Daily News»—1.28 million copies and «Chicago Tribune»—758,000 copies); «Times Mirror» (6 daily newspapers with a circulation of over 2.6 million, including «Los Angeles Times»—over 1.1 million copies, «News Day»—624,000 copies and 5 magazines); «Dow Jones and Company» (23 daily newspapers with a circulation of over 2.5 million, including «Wall Street Journal»—the largest newspaper in the country with the highest circulation—nearly 2 million); «New York Times Company» (25 daily newspapers with a circulation of over 1.8 million including the leading «New York Times»—over 1 million cop-ies, 7 weekly newspapers, and the magazine «Family Circle»—6.2 million copies); «Thomson Newspapers» (84 daily newspapers with a circulation of over 1.4 million copies, 4 weekly publications, 23 special magazines); «Hurst Corporation» (15 daily newspapers including «San Francisco Chronicle»—557,000 copies, «Los Angeles Herald Examiner»—285,000 copies, 40 weekly newspapers and 13 magazines including «Good Housekeeping»—5 million copies, «Red Book»—4 million copies, «Cosmopolitan»—2.9 million copies).

The leading newspaper monopolies also include «Capital Cities Communications» (which purchased ABC TV-Company in 1985), «Washington Post Company», and the corporations owned by Murdock, Scrips-Howard, Hart-Hanks, Cokes, Kopley, «Media General» and others.

«Time Incorporated» occupies a leading place among magazine monopolies—a publisher of six magazines («Time», «Life», «Fortune», «Sports Illustrated», «People», «Money») with a total circulation of over 13 million. «Time Incorporated» own a publishing house, cable TV systems, paper factories, etc. «McGraw-Hill» Concern is the largest publisher of business magazines in the world (over 60). One of its leading magazines is «Business Week» (over 875,000 copies) and the company also publishes textbooks, directories and other literature.

«Readers Digest Association» publishes two magazines its monthly «Readers Digest» with a US circulation of 16.6 million and 39 foreign publications in 15 languages. Its entire, global circulation is over 28 million. Other large monopolies in magazine publishing are: «Try-Angle Publication» (2 publications including «TV Guide»—16.8 million, «Makkol Corporation» (4 magazines including a ladies' magazine «Makkols»—5.2 million copies), «Meredith» («Better Homes and Gardens»—over 8 million copies), «MCFatten» Company (ladies' magazines including «True Story»—over 1.5 million copies), etc.

The printing industry produces massive profits, and the largest newspaper-magazine monopolies possess a very solid place side by side with the leading industrial corporations of the country. Monopolies such as «Times Mirror», «Gannett Company», «Tribune Company», «Night Readers Newspapers», «Time Incorporated», «McGrew-Hill», «New York Times Company», «Washington Post Company», «Dow Jones and Company», «Capita Cities Communications», «Meredith» enter the so-called «Club 500»—a list of the nation's leading corporations published by «Fortune» magazine every year. The largest newspaper-magazine companies of Thomson, Merdock, Hurst, Gannett, «Dow Jones», «Time Incorporated», «Readers Digest Association», «McGrew-Hill», «New York Times Company», «Washington Post Company» bear an international and transnational character.

Daily newspapers occupy a leading role in country's system of newspaper printing. A majority of American daily newspapers (72 per cent) are evening ones, however, their number has decreased and there is a crisis in the evening press conditioned by competition from TV, other newspapers and other factors. Evening newspapers have closed merged with morning ones or transferred into morning ones. In the second half of the 1970s and the beginning of the 1980s huge evening newspapers such as «Chicago Today», «Washington Star», «Philadelphia Bulletin» and «Cleveland Press» shut up shop.

A specific characteristic of American newspapers is that they bear a mostly regional or local character. A majority of papers are distributed within the town or state where they are published. This is conditioned by historical development of newspaper printing in the US, the expense of supplying newspapers long distances and, mostly, by their dependence on local advertisements. Circulation figures of American newspapers are not high. The majority of the country's daily newspapers (1,417) possess a circulation of less than 50,000 copies. Only 35 newspapers have a circulation of 250,000 or more. Average circulation of a daily is 34,800 copies, and the number of newspaper copies per 1000 capita (282 copies in the USA) lags behind other leading capitalist countries.

In fact, until the late 1970s and early 1980s there weren't any national newspapers. Several such as «New York Times», «Washington Post», «Christian Science Monitor» and the financial «Wall-Street Journal» did distribute a small portion of their circulation beyond their state boundaries. Nowadays, with satellite communication in operation, a tendency towards creating a national newspaper press has developed «Wall-Street Journal» has become national (its 4 regional publications are printed in different states through satellite). «USA Today» (1.4 million copies) has been published in Washington since 1982. A national weekly edition of «Washington Post» started in 1984. «Wall-Street Journal» and «USA Today» are printed in Europe and Asia through satellite. They are becoming transnational and global newspapers, alongside the American «International Herald Tribune» published in Paris.

The concept «big press» includes large city newspapers—New York, Chicago, Los Angeles, Detroit, San Francisco, Philadelphia, Boston etc. In 1987, the largest newspaper circulations, apart from those already mentioned, were «New York Daily News» (1.28 million copies), «Los Angeles Times» (over 1.1 million), «New York Times» (over 1 million), «Chicago Tribune» (758,000 copies), «Detroit News» (678,000 copies), «Detroit Free Press» (639,000 copies), «San-Francisco Chronicle» (557,000 copies), «Boston Globe» (500,000 copies) and others.

Suburban newspapers pose serious competition to the newspapers of big cities and towns. There are over 1,000 suburban newspapers with a total circulation of 13 million published across the country. The largest suburban newspaper in the USA is «News Day» of Long Island (624,000 copies) that competes successfully with the newspapers of New York.

In recent years free newspapers have developed widely. They are entirely on revenue from advertising and sent, by free post, as advertising materials. A part of them publishes nothing but advertisements, and another part publishes a very small quantity of the information. There are over 3,000 free newspapers in the country, with a circulation of 34 million.

Experts believe the future for the newspaper industry lies in an electronic newspaper. They believed that by the end of the 20th century, 40 per cent of American families would read a newspaper on video terminal. However, the experiments carried out electronic newspaper format have revealed that it is not profitable, that the market is not yet ready for videotext, and so the arena is very limited.

In contradiction to tabloids full of entertaining information, sensation and criminal activity with loud illustrations and titles, qualitative publications distribute broad information and analysis of the politics and world affairs.

The qualitative us newspapers include the «New York Times», «Washington Post», «Wall Street Journal», «Christian Science Monitor», «Boston Globe», «Los Angeles Times». The leading popular newspapers are «USA Today», «New York Post» and «San Francisco Chronicle».

As far as their political tendency is concerned papers are conservative, and few could be described as bourgeois-liberal. The largest newspapers reflect the interests of these or those monopoly groups. Thus, «New York Times», «Washington Post» are the papers of «an eastern establishment» and the bank-industrial capital of the North as whereas «Los Angeles Times» is the mouth-piece for Californian monopolies.

Although most American newspapers are not formally connected with political parties and believe themselves «independent» their political orientation is clear during Presidential elections. Despite an increase in the number of newspapers giving no preference, there is a steady tendency amongst most American papers to support candidates from the Republican party. Among the large newspapers, Republican candidates are steadily supported by «New York Daily News», «Chicago Tribune», «New York Post» (since 1976 when it was acquired by Rupert Murdock), «San Francisco Examiner». «New York Times», «Washington Post» and «Boston Globe» support the Democratic Party.

In the 1984 elections newspapers such as «Wall Street Journal», «Los Angeles Times» and «USA Today» showed no preference to any candidate, nevertheless they have supported and continue to support a political course of the Republican Administration.

The country's information industry has achieved a high level of concentration in the sphere of supplying news to newspapers. Two information agencies Associated Press (AP) and United Press International (UPI) have become global, monopolized collection and distribution of information. It is they who practically create an informational picture of the world, in which the bourgeois press functions.

AP possesses a leading place. As for its status it is a co-operative agency, member shareholders represent 82 per cent of American newspapers—a total of 1,365 and 6,000 broadcasting stations. UPI is a commercial Agency. 800 newspapers and 3,300 broadcasting stations subscribe to it. In the last decade the Agency has beard losses, under a changing ownership. Owned by Scripps (95 per cent) and Hurst (5 per cent), in 1982 it was sold to «Media News Corporation» Company. In 1986 «New UPI» Corporation and 1988 it was sold to «World News Wire» Company purchased it.

Press-syndicates exert considerable influence upon the activities of newspapers, especially local ones. There are private agencies specialized to supply various production needs to newspapers—such as articles, studies, comments, illustrations, full lines, women's pages, etc. There are over 350 press-syndicates in the country, and the largest ones distribute over 100 types of press production: The syndicated materials are published in hundreds of US and Canadian newspapers simultaneously. For instance, the words of J. Anderson, a political observer, are published by nearly 800 newspapers, advice by Ann Launders and Abby (Abigail Van Burin) are published in nearly 1,000 newspapers and the comics «Peanuts» and «Blonde»—in nearly 2,000 newspapers in the USA and Canada.

A large number of press-syndicates are owned by the largest information-propaganda monopolies, newspapers. The leading press-syndicates of the country are «King Features Syndicated» owned by Hurst Monopoly. The syndicate's services are used by nearly 2,000 newspapers in the US and Canada (observer—J. Kingsberry Smith); the other big company is «United Features Syndicated» owned by a publishing company of Scripps-Howard (leading observers—J. Anderson, U. Rasher).

«North America Syndicated», owned by Hurst from 1987 (R. Evens, R. Novak, A. Landers, N. Podgoretz); «Universal Press Syndicated» (W. Buckley, M. Mackgrory); «Los-Angeles Times Syndicated» (A. Boohvald, J. Krickpatrick); «Washington Post Writers Group» (J. Will, D. Browder); «New York Times Syndication Sales Corporation» (J. Raston, D. Middleton, T. Weeker, Y. Sefire, R. Baker).

The country possesses a very strong and broad magazine press. The magazine reading audience is more differentiated than the newspaper one. This is connected to the fact that the majority of newspapers are general political press, and magazines (those of a general nature excluded) are various in characters and so are instead for specific readers.

The 11,500 American magazines and journals have a total circulation that exceeds 350 million. Monthly publications prevail in the country's magazine press (they were 4,031 in 1987). In the same year there were 1,984 quarterly publications, 1,400 weekly publications and 1,402 issued once every two months.

A specific character of magazines is that, in a contradiction to a more local and regional newspaper press of the majority the magazines are distributed across the nation. This conditions a large circulation of magazines than newspapers over 50 magazines have a circulation exceeding 1 million; six magazines boast a circulation that exceeds 10 million.

In the 1960s and 1970s magazines suffered to a greater extent than newspapers from the development of TV, and the re-distribution of advertising to benefit the latter. Several large magazines with a big circulation were closed. As for as profits from advertising are concerned (over $ 6 billion in 1986), magazines take fourth place behind newspapers, TV and Radio. A struggle for advertisers and readers has conditioned a specialization in magazine publishing. *A tendency towards specialization is one of the leading developments in the branch.*

The American magazine market is characterized by a great number of various types of publications. A social differentiation conditions an availability of publications for the elite as and for the masses.

The most influential magazines are political weekly publications, so-called «magazines of news»—such as «Time» (4.8 million copies, with four main foreign editions—nearly 6 million copies), «News Week» (over 3 million copies, with three foreign editions—3.5 million copies) and «US News and World Report» (2.2 million copies). The purpose of weekly publications is to sum up and interpret the news of the previous week for the interests of a «business-like» person. This «explanation» of the news is presented in the tendentious position of «information» magazines that in reality deal with news propaganda and interpretation according to its policy. Among the magazine-digests, «Readers Digest» stands out. It is a monthly publication of pocket size, re-printing articles from other publications and publishing its own as well. A giant of the information propaganda industry, circulation of the domestic edition is 16.6 million, which the 39 foreign editions make over 28 million copies. The magazine maintains a very skilful balance of propaganda politics, diluting political articles with informative and entertaining articles.

Magazines have a large circulation Sunday newspaper supplements contain mostly entertaining pieces («Parade»—32,5 million copies, «USA Week-end»—over 14 million copies), women's and housekeeping magazines («Woman's Day», «Family Circle», «Better Homes and Gardens», «Good Housekeeping», «Lady's Home Journal»). Magazines for men, which, together with all materials of a bourgeois «mass culture» naturally relish sex, publish serious articles on political questions and works of literature («Playboy», «Penthouse»). Entertaining, cheap magazines and comics also have a great circulation.

Among small publications, the most influential are the literary-political and the political-economic magazines («Business Week», «Fortune», «Forbes»), magazines («Atlantic», «Harpers», «New Yorker») and the magazines concerned with foreign policy («Foreign Affairs», «Foreign Policy»).

The magazines represent a wider range of political orientation within a bourgeois ideology that newspapers, from left liberal to ultra-right. The viewpoints of different political groups are reflected in magazines of different opinions. As a rule, their circulation is not large, but their influence is on political processes is high. There is a small group of liberal magazines—«Nation», «Progressive», «New Republic», «Mother Jones». There is a wider group of right using magazines that includes «traditional» conservative editions («National Review», «Human Events»), new conservatives («Commentary», «Public Interest»), «new right» («Conservative Digest») and the ultra-right («New American», ex—«American Opinion»).

Specialized periodicals are a very important component of the USA information-propaganda set. The largest of them are business (industrial), religious, for ethnic groups, military and trade union press. An association of the USA business press unites over 2,800 publications with a total circulation of nearly 65 million. Pentagon publishes over 1,000 newspapers, nearly 400 magazines and different reports and statistics with a total circulation of over 12 million. The Catholic Church publishes over 400 editions and different Protestant Churches, over 1,500. 43 ethnic groups publish nearly 900 magazines with a total circulation of over 8 million.

The private character of the bourgeois press does not exclude state influence. The government uses its monopoly on informing about its activities, with the means of official press conferences, briefings and the publication of propaganda literature. The government is interested in the press's support of its political course, and press criticism leads to stronger Government pressure on the mass media. Critical articles and comments, etc. in the press are conditioned by the tactics and political motivations of competitive groups in the ruling class to defend their own interests. As a whole, the press supports the policy of official Washington.

B. Film Production in the USA[14]

American cinematography during the 1970s and the 1980s is very complicated and contradictory. Only 173 films out of the 511 made in the USA in 1987 were made by large companies, both old and new: «Warner Brothers», «Buena Vista», «XX Century Fox», «De Laurenthis Group», «Columbia», «Cannon», «Metro-Goldwin-Mayer», «Orion», «Paramount», «Three star», «United Artists» and «Universal». More than 100 independent producers and small companies made the other 338 films. They are all united in a central organization of the American film industry—the American Film Association. Its main function is to protect the interests of its film companies, export and import films and to participate in international film festivals. 10 film shows are made in the USA annually. The largest of them take place in New York, San Francisco, Los Angeles and Chicago.

The American Academy of Cinematography Art And Science unites over 4,000 filmmakers. It is a social organization that deals with the problems of increasing the educational, professional and technical level of American cinematography. With secret balloting, the organization awards «Oscars» to the American films for achievement in 26 separate areas of cinematography annually. An «Oscar» is also given to the best foreign film of the year shows in the USA. The Academy gives lectures, helps young filmmakers and publishes various directories.

Articles and reviews about cinema are published in editions such as «American Film»—a magazine of the American Institute of Cinema—a research and an educational center; «Film Quarterly»—a quarterly publication made by Californian University (Berkley); «Film Comment»—the magazine of Lincoln's Cinema Center (New York); «American cinematography»—a magazine of operators; the weekly «Variety» (New York). In addition articles on film art and articles devoted to separate films are regularly published in magazines such as «News Week», «New Yorker», «Time», «New Republic» and in newspapers like the «New York Times», «Washington Post», «People's Daily World», etc.

Cinema critics and filmmaker personnel are prepared in over 600 educational institutions in the USA with lecture courses on cinema and TV. The largest

---

14   The United States of America. Encyclopaedia Guide. M.

of them are: Columbia University in New York, New York University, Californian University (Berkley), Temple University in Philadelphia and the school of Art in Chicago.

Huge work achievements of American and world cinematography has been done by film archives: such as the J. Washington in Washington, Museum of Modern Art in New-York, Pacific Ocean Archive in Berkley, the cinema archive at the Californian University in Los Angeles and the cinema archive «Cinema Anthology» in New York, etc.

Hollywood[15]

It is most probable that the notorious area in Los Angeles intended for living buildings and called «Hollywood» in 1887 would have been limited to city and suburbs, but the first film studio appeared there several decades later. Later on the Center of American Cinematography strong with its main features: a system of stars, standardization of cinema drama and conveyer-belt production of films oriented to cheap, popular taste. All that, together with the high technical provision and availability of a qualified staff, turns helped Hollywood into a «factory of dreams» that conquered almost all cinema markets in the world. Thus, the name of a region of a city—Hollywood—has become a part of «the American dream», as being contradictory and many-sided as America itself. It is no surprise that the century celebrations of Hollywood automatically turned into a jubilee of American cinematography associated with its name.

«Hollywood» is something much bigger than just a geographical reference. In our mind we immediate it associated with a picture of open sky, projector rays and a stream of white limousines going to infinity. The 20-meter high letters on the hill confirm the reality of Hollywood, a small part of Los Angeles. And still Hollywood remains a fairy tale kingdom, as unreachable as the lamp of Aladdin, which throws down a challenge to those willing to conquer it.

The first one who wanted to make it was a man from Kansas, Harvey Wilkocks, a real estate broker. On 1st of February, 1887 he divided a 120-acres into small allotments just at the center of the place now named Hollywood, which has already celebrated its official branch. Wilkocks David named a piece Hollywood (i.e. a holly wood forest) taking the name from the country house of her Chicago friends. There is no holly growing in Southern California, and such absurdity befits the name of a place that has become «a factory of dreams».

A century of this trumpery town has been nothing but tricks and falsification.

---

15 Biyan D. Johnson, «Mackleanse», Toronto. «Abroad» 41.

The first film studio only appeared there in 1911. And the myths take over reality in the town, putting its prosperity down to its own eulogy.

From the very beginning the town was a magnet to foreigners. The pioneers of cinema industry were immigrants such as Charlie Chaplain, an Englishman, and Adolph Sucker, a Hungarian. In the 1920s one third of Hollywood producers were people from other countries.

An introductory subtitle of the 1928 film, «The Last Crew» has in some way summed up the idea of an immortal town: Hollywood is an Empire of miracles of the 20th Century! It is the Mecca of mankind!

And owners of studios used to rule the film industry as kings. Darryl F. Zanuk, an owner of «Twentieth Century Fox» studio, surrounded himself with phones. The microphones were put everywhere: in the bedroom, in the dining room and in his office to give instructions to people 24 hours a day.

David O. Selznik forced his staff to work 24 hours a day and in 1939 he hired a group of 14 writers to make the film «Gone With The Wind». Great novelists such as Scott Fitzerald and Folkner William were simple screws in the screen conveyer; they were «crackers in under-woods», as Jack Warner studio owner once called the writers working for him. It was an industrial revolution in the arena of fantasy.

A Hollywood «factory of dreams» has made the world in its own image. Producing miracles, tastes and feelings, it has caused a kind of mass mental illness. When people saw the film «The Ten Commandments», made in1923, with as Red Sea opening, they got so excited that the producer had to explain that not a single horse was injured during the making of the film. And when Clark Gable threw away his shirt, flashing his torso, in the film «It Happened Once at Night», made in 1934, sale of men's vests dropped by half.

After the war, Hollywood overcame several bad periods. In the late 1940s it was subject to anti-communist attacks. «The black lists» of liberal actors, producers and other staff ruined the careers of many people. In the 1950s attendance of cinema-halls fell sharply and film production suffered due to the development of TV. The studios tried their best to compete by augmenting film meters and expanding the size of the screen, while simultaneously struggling for their own place in TV. In the 1980s Hollywood struggled again to put away the threat from home VCRs. It has now arranged a new market for its production, based upon video releases of films.

The owners of companies never create or kill film stars with one throw of their cigar. The stars and their lawyers have become businessmen themselves. However, in terms of the monopolizing administration of corporations such as «Coca-Cola» («Columbia») and «Gulf and Western Incorporated» («Paramount»), the leading studios turned into «full-scale entertainment enterprises», as Frank Mankusso, president of «Paramount», said. Mankusso adds that the support given to studios by these corporations «provides a financial stability that was not before».

«Paramount» is the only leading film studio left within the municipal boundaries of Hollywood. And there, beyond the walls surrounding its 55-acres, Mankusso sits in his study behind a marble executive desk at which Sucker and de Mill sat at before him. Given his experience, he is more of an expert in production sales than an organizer of film production. In 70s he worked in a Canadian department of «Paramount» in Toronto. He became a head of the studio in 1984, and the following year the studio took first place in cash collection, making four of the ten best films of that year, collecting over a billion dollars. Net profit came to around $ 150 million. Mankusso admits that he has increased «an increase in the authority of the studio system» by signing long-term contracts with successful producers and stars of the Eddie Murphy type.

«Universal Pictures» is the oldest and largest company owned by «MKA Incorporated»—a particularly popular monopoly in picture manufacturing. «Universal» has made some of the most expensive blockbusters, including «Jaws» and «ET». The TV using of «Universal», responsible for «Sin of May», is believed to be the greatest TV production company in America MKA also possesses capital invested into the music business, book publishing, toy production and sales, retail cutlets and mail order sales. The company owns 48 per cent of the shares in the biggest network of American cinema-halls—«Cineplex» of Drabinsky.

Film industry businessmen call MKA «an octopus», and tentacles of the octopus have penetrated the White House. In his book, «Dark Victory: Regain, MKA and People», Dan Moldea, with documentary accuracy, describes an FBI investigation into the predatory practice of MKA and discloses close connections between the monopoly and President Ronald Reagan. When Reagan headed the Guild of Actors in the 1950s, he gave MKA an unlimited right to employ actors which the film studios did just as the unions represented their rights. As Moldea says, MKA also helped Reagan to become a multi-millionaire, allowing him to secure profitable land deals and in 1965 the company helped him enter the Californian political scene (Reagan became Governor of California). It was a current joke at that time: «MKA has got their own governor», Moldea writes.

The chief of MKA administrative building is called «Black Tower», precise building of steel and glass in the center of «Universal City» that eats up 420 acres. The «City» consists of 36 closed film studios, two hotels, administrative buildings, open air decorations imaging everything from towns in the Far West to streets of European cities, a bridge with 8-lines of traffic over the Hollywood Freeway, and a lake.

Sydney Sheinberg, President of MKA, rules his Empire from his big study on the top floor of the «Black Tower». His small, very old, oak desk is always free from unnecessary clutter. The desk looks familiar to MKA—an inheritance from company founder Julice Stein. Stein's collection of English antiques from the XVIII century and pictures that depict fox hunting, do not quite correspond to the modern time and spirit of the «Black Tower».

Sheinberg, a 52-old lawyer from Texas, admits that he has never handled any of the rare books in his study. His passion is for business.

«MKA is a typical impresario company, he says, impresario. I repeat the word so frequently that people smile at me. And this is not just a modern word. I really believe it».

The studio impresarios try to make their fortune as if to find a cup of Holy Grail for Sheinberg: a «blockbuster» is something bigger than just an entertaining.

«The behavior of people during a first viewing of «ET» is something like a massive religious-dramatic action», he says.

Nevertheless, the increasing expenses of creating a paradise on Hollywood earth are a constant cause for anxiety. Every «mega-success» is accompanied by «mega-failure». And the people responsible for film production very rarely keep their places long enough to pay for a failure in full. Norman Dwison, a Canadian producer, says that large film studios «are headed by honest, ambitious and serious directors. They are transferred from one studio to another and constitute a group of professionals in constant movement».

Agency lawyers have become brokers in Hollywood and they have real power. While negotiating on the films made especially for their superstar clients, they frequently conquer the traditional role of signing general studio contracts that hire producers, scriptwriters and actors. Michele Litvak, author of the book «Power of Cinema», considers that Mike Obits, a lawyer heading an agency of art employees, is the most powerful person in Hollywood. «And although Obits does not deserve any praise as a film creator, everybody involved in the film industry knows his price», he writes.

The fees earned by film stars negotiated for by Obits and his colleagues considerably increase expenses of film production. And even MKA, a master of «mega-successes», is anxious about Hollywood wastefulness.

«Our society has obtained a lot, a lot of bad habits. I am seriously afraid that our business would finally leave abroad. Should we see a volume of the film production in Toronto», Sheinberg says.

On average, 22 million people go to American cinemas every week. The largest number of viewers was 90 million in 1946, but nevertheless, <u>cinema business remains as profitable as ever before.</u>

Garth Drabynsky, president of Cineplex Odeon Corporation, with its head office in Toronto, predicted that cash collection from 1987 would exceed a record cash collection of $ 5,5 billion received in 1984. Now the majority of producers get the same profit from TV programs and videocassette sale as they do cinema showings of their films.

«The industry is in a very good condition. It has easily overcome a period of bad predictions. Development of video equipment helps to expand production. The secret of Hollywood life lies in its capability to master new technologies and new talents», Drabynsky says.

«Creators of film pictures throughout the world are intrigued by the «factory of dreams». The factory is full of people making business deals and their cases bulging with new film scripts», Denis Arkand, a producer from Montreal, notes.

But the old Hollywood magnificence has fallen into decline. At the very beginning several dozen owners ruled the «silver screen». Later on, large corporations took over the main studios, and the despot with a cigar changed to a lawyer in striped trousers. While continuing to invest in films intended for well-known film stars the new generation of film company directors do not want to take any risks in search of new talent.

They adopt the role of bankers for independent and producers who are bolder. And in turn, independent producers constantly challenge the wisdom of Hollywood, showing that it is not always necessary to invest huge capital into a film, equal to Gross Domestic Product of a small country, to make a successful film. An independent producer spent $ 8 million on making the film «Platoon» that won an «Oscar» and made a profit of $ 180 million.

It is only thanks to their financial strength that studios such as «Universal», «Paramount», «Columbia», «Warner Brothers», «Orion» and «Fox» keep their leading positions as «super-powers» in cinema production. Backing onto a developing network of TV, they still remain the most influential force in the formation of Western culture. The ideals of Hollywood conquer large and small screens from the Arctic to the Amazon because of the efforts of the companies above.

CHAPTER 2

The Economic Parameters of the Branches of Intellectual Production in the USA Divisions II & III

State and Private Education System in the USA[16]

The education system in the USA includes both state and a private sectors. In 1986 the expenses of state educational institutions came to $ 211.6 billion, and those of the private sector came to $ 48.6 billion.

The state sector has its biggest grip in the field of a primary and secondary education: over 90 per cent of school age children go to state schools. The role of the private sector is more considerable in the field of higher education. Over half of all higher education institutions—1,800 of about 3,300—are private. Even so only 21 per cent of all students in the USA are educated in them.

The expansion of the private sector in higher education that took place in the 1960's-1970's was connected to the rapid growth of a network of the two-year, so-called junior colleges. Their growth was meant to absorb a fast growing stream of working class entrants to the universities and four-year colleges. The majority of the newly created educational institutions were, as a matter of fact, special secondary educational institutions that provided a professional-technical education. As the result, a structure of the state higher school changed considerably: in the 1980's only one third of its educational institutions were higher education institutions of full value (universities and colleges); two thirds of it are «truncated» higher education institutions—junior colleges,—which nearly half the state sector students are educated.

The Reagan administration expressed the traditional conservative party line by fully increasing the private sector and trying its best to limit the development

---

16 The United States of America. Encyclopedia Guide.

of education's state sector. With regard to primary and secondary education, giving tax credits to parents who chose a private school for their children was proposed.

However, congress did not approve it. In the field of higher education, the policy of reducing state assistance to students, hitting students from poor families hard, has led to a reduction in the number of entrants, mostly in the higher education institutions in the state sector.

Primary and Secondary Education

The USA's primary and secondary education system is one of the most developed in the world. There were 105,500 schools in 1985 educating 44 million school-age children (27.2 million in primary schools, 16.8 million in secondary schools). The state budget accounted for 91 per cent, or $ 145.5 billion out of the entire $ 159 billion spent on primary and secondary education in 1986. A free-of-charge state school, giving general education, is the basis of the primary and secondary education system.

A peculiar feature of the US system of education is a de-centralization of its administration and financing. Despite a foundation from the Ministry of Education in 1979, states and local authorities continue to play a leading role in the field. In 1986 state and the local authorities paid 93 per cent of the state budget on primary and secondary education, coming to $ 135.6 billion, where as the federal government paid 6.2 per cent of the expenses of school education ($ 9,9 billion). All school legislation and administration of school activities is regulated and maintained by the education departments of local authorities and by some 16,000 bodies of local self-government—school districts.

The length of general education is 12 years, beginning, when a child is aged 6. However, there is no unique school structure in the USA. State laws on periods of obligatory education only define the age until which a child must be at school, and not the obligatory years of education. A majority of states have obligatory education with the age of 16 years and four of them until 18. The dominating type of primary school is a school with a six-year course of education. A preparatory class is attended by three quarters of all children aged five.

Secondary schools in most states are divided into a junior secondary school (7-9 classes) and a senior secondary school (10-12 classes). The main principle of education in American secondary schools is that the pupils, in the senior classes especially, can choose a set of subjects according to their will, depending on their wishes and abilities.

In the ninth class already several programs of education are differentiated for girls and boys aged 16 to 18. There are three profiles of education built into the teaching programs: an academic one directed to preparation for college; a professional one giving practical knowledge for work and a general one that gives no specialized training.

Computers are rapidly implemented into the educational process, taught in the primary classes more and more. According to the data of a private investigation company in Denver, which investigated 51,400 primary schools in the autumn 1983 30,350 of the above schools used at least one computer, used by only 14,000 schools in 1982 and 6,500 schools in 1981. According to the data of 1985, state schools used approximately 5,790,000 computers, while 215,000 were used in primary schools. They were used in aural and practical classes (19 per cent), programmed education (21 per cent), classes for pupils with «above average abilities» (12 per cent) and those considered "below average" (15 per cent).

Gives that school education is free-of-charge and its democratic organization as a whole, the wide drawing of young people into a system of secondary education makes the American system more progressive than the school systems in a number of other countries.

American pedagogy proceeds to nurture and is based on a child's maturity. Intellectual testing is widely spread in the USA on the basis of the above principle. In accordance with the test results, pupils are selected into groups, and educational profiles are compiled in secondary schools.

There is a big gap in the level and quality of education not only between private schools and a number of the state schools, but also between state schools located in the inner cities, which poor children attend and status schools is a wealthy district. Hence, a shortage of financial means caused by low tax (a main resource for a state school financing is a tax on real estate levied by the local authorities) conditions an extremely low level of education in the schools of the inner cities. The level of a student's knowledge also depends upon the profile at which senior pupils are educated.

A serious problem in the USA is pupil dropout rates. Private schools do not actually have a dropout problem, whereas the problem is very stark in state schools. Nearly 25 per cent of children do not finish secondary school; a proportion that rises to 40 per cent among the black population. Sociological investigations and questionnaires reveal that the cause of dropping out lies in the social class of pupils. The biggest proportion of pupils who stop their education come from poor families with rather limited material capabilities to provide for the children up to the age of 18. The dropout rate is obvious at the age of 14 and reaches its peak in the tenth class at the age of 16. The direct reasons of leaving school are the impossibility of continuing one's education after secondary school; a negative attitude towards school and the subjects being taught (nearly 20 per cent of those interviewed in 1978). Only 6.3 per cent of dropout the pupils that pointed out a poor progress in the studies as a reason to stop their education, and only 6.2 per cent were excluded from school.

A problem in the quality of education has become one of the sharpest social problems of the 1980's. In 1981 a National Commission was founded to increase the quality of education. It pointed towards «a growing tendency towards mediocrity that threatens the future of the country and the people», in its April, 1983report. It estimated that nearly 23 million adult Americans were illiterate. According to the Commission's data, the schools discharged 13-20 per cent functionally illiterate people.

Law on education for National Defence became a turning point in federal government policy. The Law stipulated a number of very important measures to be taken to improve the quality of education quality in secondary and higher schools. Physical and natural sciences took first place. Determining policy in the field of education has become one of the most important directions of the activities of federal government. The federal government in the field of education expanded further in the mid 1960's under the influence of mass democratic movements. The ruling circles were forced to extend representation of racial-ethnic groups and women in education. A Law drawn up in 1964 stipulated a whole number of different measures to increase the level of education available to the poor (programs to fight illiteracy, assistance to young people at work to obtain a higher education, educational programs for adults, etc.). It was then that other laws were approved, which still remain the judicial basis of federal intervention in the sphere of education: A 1965 Law on primary and secondary education was the most important one, in which the government provided $ 1 billion for education of children from poor families.

In the last 20 years, the education system, particularly secondary education, has been severely influenced by a principle of «egalitarism». In their opinion, the well-known rapprochement in the level of knowledge, white and non-white pupils has only become possible due to a decline in the whole level of progress made in studies. The Reagan administration decreased federal assignations to primary and secondary education that were intended to help children from

Indian and Negro background and children with physical and intellectual disabilities. Federal expenses in this field fully by 20.6 per cent in 1985 compared to what they were 1980 (accounting for the inflation rates).

The questions connected to education reform, a first applied to secondary education became most significant in the USA in the 1980's. The new demands, put into practice have intensified and argumentated effectiveness of the secondary education. Special attention in reforming secondary schools is paid to training the most capable pupils, to increasing the significance of an academic education and a more intensive implementation of computer education. Increasing a competence of schoolteachers is also at the center of reform.

Higher Education

At present the US system of higher education includes nearly 3,300 various institutes with 12 million students in them. The number of people with a higher education in the USA increased by 126 per cent at the beginning of the 1980s compared to 1970. Every year', four times the number of students graduate from the US universities and colleges, compared to countries in the EU.

The US system of higher education supports a variety of different institutions:

- junior, or local, two-year colleges, where education is financed by the local authorities and meant to meet local needs in expertise. The junior colleges award so-called degrees of a junior expert. The degree is a professional one and has become more and more widespread due to the growth in the number of local colleges and due to the comparatively they price the education on offer. At present, nearly 40 per cent of all American students attend junior or local, colleges.

- technical institutes and professional schools that award bachelor degrees. Graduates obtain a technical qualification after a two-year or three-year course.

- four-year educational institutions—universities and independent colleges award a bachelor degree (a master's degree is available after an additional one or two years).

The above institutions can be both state and private. The private sector possesses 72 per cent and the state sector only 28 per cent of the 1,900 four-year educational institutions. And at the same time only 21 per cent of students are educated in the private institutions of higher education.

There are 146 universities in the USA. A very important component of expert training in the universities is scientific research, which both post-graduates and under-graduate are enlisted to. At present nearly 60 per cent of fundamental US investigations are carried out in institutions of the higher education. The main role in executing scientific research belongs to the largest, so-called multi-universities, both private and state, that carry out, in addition to fundamental ones, a great number of applied investigations.

Since the 19th Century, the US higher education system has been supported by the state. Federal government assistance expanded considerably in the second half of the 20th Century, when there was a sharp increase in the number of students due to a growth in population and because of the financial assistance given to Second World War veterans who wished to get an education. The next peak in the state programs to assisting higher education came to the 1960's. But federal assistance to higher education institutions has been limited since the mid 1970s. By the end of the 1970s, the beginning of the 1980s, the routine of assistance from federal government stopped growing. Nevertheless, the aggregate value of federal expenses on higher education remains high. Nearly 3 per cent of GDP is spent is this field.

Although the volume of state assistance to US higher education institutions considerable exceeds the scale of state financing of higher education in a majority of other developed countries, its decline has a negative impact on the financial situation of American colleges and universities, reducing the base of their further activities in future. In 1973 the federal government covered 15.7 per cent of all expenses of higher education institutions. In 1982 the figure stood at—14,1 per cent. The other expenses were covered by states (27.4 per cent in 1973, 31.1 per cent in 1982) and from other sources. State financial support does not correspond to the real needs of higher education institutions especially if we consider that must of the equipment being used by universities for research investigations has become obsolete.

A considerable source of income for higher education institutions comes from high student fees. Education in private universities and colleges is more expensive than that in state institutions. In 1985/1986 student fees in a private institution came to $ 12,000 per annum, in the most "prestigious" ones it came to $ 14,000–17,000. In state institutions it came to between $ 2,000–5,000 per annum, and in the so-called junior colleges, about $ 800 per annum. The high cost of higher education is partially compensated for assistance programs for students and post-graduates paid for at the expense of state and private funds. The Reagan administration brought with it a sharp reduction in federal programs of financial assistance; consequently, student expenses have increased.

In the late 1970's and early 1980's there was a higher growth in the number of people obtaining master and doctorate degrees than the number of people obtaining a bachelor's degree. This was the case in some of the leading US universities (Stanford, Californian, etc.). The most qualified scientific staff we trained by a number of leading, mostly private, higher education institutions, including Harvard, Stanford, Columbia, Californian universities (Berkley) and Massachusetts Technological Institute.

Sport in the USA[17]

The USA is a leading sports power. American sport first developed in the second half of the 19th Century. Both amateur and professional sport spread widely over the country.

Morill's Law of 1862, putting military instructors into educational institutions made the physical training classes in schools, universities and colleges very active. The first sports organization was founded in 1879—the National Association of amateur sport.

The basis of *amateur sport* is the sport in schools and higher education institutions. In the mid-1980s nearly 18 million pupils and 3 million students have participated in sport programs and competitions.

There are no official statistics for the number of people participating sporting activities across the USA as a whole, but it is estimated that nearly 10 per cent of Americans do some sort on a regular basis. At the beginning of the 1980s, according to the Nelson Service data, there were 1.02 billion people swimming, 72.2 million cycling, 62.6 million taking active holidays, 34.3 million jogging, 25.5 million playing tennis, 14 million basketball, 13.6 million baseball and 8 million playing soccer (European football).

There exist a number of «privileged» sports—bowling, golf, tennis, fencing, figure skating, horse riding, sailing and auto-sport, etc. Participating in these sports requires some definite higher social status, possession of a high level of income and admittance to special sports' facilities. There are over 13,000 private sports clubs in the USA with first-class sports facilities (swimming-pools, golf courses, tennis courts, etc.)

In the 1950s, the role of the state in the development of physical culture and sports was much debated. When compulsory military service was introduced in 1951, it was discovered during the war in Korea that young people enlisted for the army had a very low level of physical fitness, also confirmed by a

---

17   The United States of America. Encyclopaedia Guide.

sociological survey in 1950-1953. The federal government then started to pay serious attention to youth physical training. In 1956 Eisenhower founded a President's Council on to consider measures to improve the physical fitness of young people. The functions of the Council were expanded in 1963, and in 1968 the Council became the President's Council for physical training and sport that is still in existence and acts as the regulating body for the development of popular sport in the country.

Many different organizations are involved in the management of amateur sport in the USA. The most important are: the Olympic Committee of the USA (founded in 1896), the Amateur Sport Union (founded in 1879, but up to 1888 known as the National Association of amateur sport) the American Union of health, physical training, rest and dance (1885), the National Association of student sport (1905), the National sport association of junior colleges (1937), the National federation of the sport associations of secondary schools (1920), the National Council of young Christians' associations (1923). There also exist over 30 national federations for different kinds of sport.

The activities of the above organizations were de-centralized in character until the mid-1970s, when it was recognized that this situation led to competition between different organizations that had a negative effect on physical culture and sports development. A President's Commission on Olympic sports was founded in 1975 to scrutinize the state of affairs in amateur sport. The Commission reported that it was necessary to centralize sports management over the whole country. In 1978 Congress passed a law on amateur sport in the USA that made the Olympic Committee of the USA the only co-coordinating organ for amateur sport.

The main sources of finance for amateur sport are membership fees of the sport clubs and teams, profits from ticket sales and the sale of rights for TV broadcasting of sporting competitions, donations from individuals and corporations, grants from federal government and local authorities. Legislation was passed exempting amateur sport organizations from income tax. The amateur sport organizations spent over US $3 billion in the second half of the 1980s. The budget of the USA Olympic Committee came to US $136 million for the four-year period, 1985-1988, and totaled US $6 million for 1965-1968. Two Olympic educational training centers were founded, one in Colorado-Springs for summer sports, the other in Lake-Placid for winter sports. Starting from 1977, an Olympic Festival of the USA has taken place annually with 35 kinds of sport.

USA sportsmen were dominant at the Olympic Games until 1952, but overall the championship went to the USSR sportsmen at the Olympic Games of 1956, 1960, 1964 and 1972, and to the East German sportsmen in 1976. American sportsman have won 1,656 medals—692 gold, 526 silver and 438 bronze—in summer Olympic Games (the USA has participated in all the Olympic Games except for the one of 1980) and at winter Olympic Games they have won 127 medals—44 gold, 47 silver and 36 bronze.

Professional sport in the USA has developed in parallel with amateur sport. The first professional sports were horse racing and boxing, followed by baseball, American football, basketball, hockey, golf, tennis, bowling, auto-racing, volleyball, soccer, mountain skiing and figure skating. The organizational structure of professional sport is not identical for team and individual events. In certain sports there are team leagues; sportsmen competing in individual events have relevant professional associations. The most profitable kinds of professional sport are American football, baseball, basketball and hockey. By the beginning of 1988 the National Football League had 28 teams, and another 12 teams played in the USA's Football League. There were 26 teams in the Main Baseball League, 25 in the National Basketball Association and 21 in the National Hockey League. There are other teams in the lower leagues in baseball and hockey.

Professional sport in the USA has been developing at an unprecedented rate over the last 25 years and it has turned into one of the most prosperous branches of show business. Professional sport gets its main profits from the sale of tickets and of broadcasting rights. The total income of professional sport came to over US $3 billion in 1987, of which that of the National Football League was US $750 million, the Main Baseball League US $630 million, the National Basketball Association US $250 million and the National Hockey League US $210 million. The average payments to sportsmen under contracts in the above four leagues varied from US $160 thousand to US $450 thousand per annum. Over 100 professional sportsmen came had incomes of over US $1 million per annum.

Maximum annual audience figures for each sport (amateur and professional) are as follows: baseball—78 million people; horse racing—76 million; car racing—55 million; American football—54 million; basketball—42 million; hockey—20 million; soccer—8 million; boxing—7 million and tennis—4 million. Americans spend over US $3 billion annually on tickets alone. According to Associated Press, in 1986 the country as a whole spent US $48 billion on physical culture and sport, including expenditure on sport goods and services.

According to an opinion poll, in the first half of the 1980s 54 per cent of Americans listened to sports news on radio and TV every day, 39 per cent read sports pages in the newspapers and 17 per cent watched sport on TV. The National TV Companies ABC, NBC and CBS each give over 500 hours to sports news annually, and including the 24-hour sports broadcasting of the «Entertainment and Sports Programming Network» TV Station and that of other TV stations, the total volume of sports broadcasting exceeds 16 thousand hours per annum.

There is no National sports newspaper in the USA. However, nearly all the daily newspapers have sports sections. Over 1000 books and over 300 magazines on sports news are published in the country every year, including «Sports Illustrated», «Sport», «Sporting News», «Inside Sports», etc.

Theatre in the USA[18]

The organizational structure of American theatre, functioning mostly on the basis of a shareholder system, took shape at the turn of the 20th century. New theatre buildings were constructed mainly in Broadway and adjacent streets in New York. A «Broadway theatre» concept has sprung up, i.e. a large commercial enterprise, where, for every performance, a building was rented, a new company employed, with an obligatory quota of «stars», and a daily show performed—for several years if successful. The very expensive musical shows (reviews, vaudevilles, comedies, and subsequently musicals) poised for big success, filled up the theatres of Broadway. This is the way the existing type of Broadway commercial theatre has developed.

At the beginning of the 20th Century some attempts were already made to balance the repertoire groups with more serious dramatic and classical art. The most serious and progressive form of protest against Broadway commercial theatre was a movement of the so-called «small theatres» of Boston, Chicago, New York and other cities in the first decade of the 20th Century. These half-amateur groups tried their best to create a popular repertoire theatre, to develop and improve national dramatic art and scenery, to popularize classical art, to encourage ensemble acting, to invent new art forms and to combine different arts. Vitally important in the development of American stage art were two groups in the van of the «small theatres» movement—the «Washington-Square Players» (reformed as the «Gild Theatre» in 1919) and the «Province Town Players». These two groups set in train a new movement in theatre life

---

18   The United States of America. Encyclopaedia Guide.

in America, encouraging new actors, producers, playwrights and set design-
ers. A leading playwright was Y. O'Nill, whose creative work started with the
«Province Town Players» group directed by J. K. Cook.

The «Gild Theatre» had a great impact until the 1930s. Its repertoire included
the works of Western European and Russian writers such as L. Tolstoy, L.
Andreev, A. Stindberg, P. Klodell, E. Toller, B. Shaw, K. Chapek, and of
American playwrights such as Y. O'Nill, R. Sherwood, S. Bermann, F. Barry,
M. Anderson, S. Howard, etc.

MHAT (Russian Theatre) greatly influenced American Theatre when it visited the
USA in 1923-1924. The creative principles of MHAT, Stanislavsky's system,
were of great significance for many American theatre people. And even today
there are so many versions and interpretations of Stanislavsky's system in the
USA, the system is called the «Method» (with a capital letter). In 1926 E. Le
Galjenne, an actress of the «Gild Theatre», made an attempt to form a group
under the creative principles of MHAT. Her «Popular Repertoire Theatre»
only survived to 1932, but became a notable landmark in American theatre
history.

In 1931 a small group of progressive young people left the «Gild Theatre». This
group was led by G. Klerman, C. Croford and L. Strasbourg. They organized
the close knit «Group-Theatre», with a repertoire consisting mainly of plays
highlighting acute social problems written by the progressive playwrights of
1930s America, J. G. Lowson, P. Green, S. Kingsley and W. Saroyan. While
the «Province Town Players» is associated with the name of O'Nill, it is K.
Odets who became the soul of the «Group-Theatre». The greatest success of
the latter is connected with the plays of the above author, which met with a
huge social response. Most of those who set up the «Group-Theatre» became
leading actors, producers and teachers, who have shaped the face of American
Theatre. Its creators assimilated and spread the ideas of Stanislavsky. The group
included such famous actors as S. Adler, L. Adler, R. Louis, E. Kazan, M.
Karnovski, L. Cob and others. Their theatre activities were directly connected
with the increased social activity in the country in the 1930s, named «the red
ten years». A «Group-Theatre» school was founded to train producers and
actors for working-class amateur and semi-professional theatre groups. The
«Group-Theatre» ceased to exist in 1941, but there can be no doubt that its
influence upon the American Theatre was profound. The influence of this
theatre group was felt in all progressive developments in American theatre of
that time.

A proletarian theatre—principally a new phenomenon for the country—grew
up after the First World War and especially in the period of the 1929-1933

economic crisis. During strikes and meetings the actors used to show short plays, so-called «leaflets» or «alive newspapers», with hot political content. There were also stationary working theatres such as «Union», «Artef» and others, staging the plays of A. Maltz, M. Gold, F. Wolf, E. Rythe, M. Gorky.

The 1929-1933 economic crisis had an impact on the professional theatres as well: most of them closed owing to financial difficulties. Many actors became unemployed. The very poor resulting condition of the theatre forced the government to begin subsidizing it. The measures were taken within the framework of the «new course» policy of F. Roosevelt and it was called a Federal Theatre Project (1935-1939). And 158 federal theatres grew up as a result. It was the most significant financial assistance given to the theatre by the federal government.

The 1940s and the beginning of the 1950s marked a crisis in theatre life in the USA for a number of international and national reasons. The conformists grabbed the theatre scene. The form of entertainment prevailing at Broadway became the center of the country's theatre life. The situation was not remedied despite the very different work of L. Helman, A. Miller, T. William, playwrights who became classics of American and World theatre and concentrated on the individual and his/her social and psychological problems.

Meanwhile, a new movement appeared outside Broadway, a movement of the «small theatres». Many theatre groups sprang up in disadvantageous surroundings: in small halls, cellars and attics. They were united with a desire to meet creative and artistic, rather than commercial aims. They were named «off-Broadway». The movement appeared in an earlier form in the first ten years of the century. However, the real birth of the «off-Broadway» dates from the staging of a play by T. William, «Summer and Smog», by H. Kintero in the theatre «Circle in the Square» in 1952). People still use the name, although it has lost its primary meaning. At the very beginning, the off-Broadway groups were formed as a principal alternative to Broadway. They did not agree with its aesthetic laws and they gravitated towards serious dramatic art. The theatres staged both classical and modern plays, including A. Miller, T. Williams, and later E. Olby. But meanwhile there was a merging of the «off-Broadway» theatres with Broadway itself. On the one hand, it assisted the flow of new, fresh force into the Broadway theatres, and, on the other hand, it limited the excesses of those, who, in the search for new scenery forms, were losing artistic independence. The most famous «off-Broadway» groups are «Phiniks», «Sheridan Square Playhouse», «Circle in the Square».

In the 1960s there appeared a new concept in a structure of American «off-Broadway theatre», which is still associated with the most controversial and risky stage experiments. The theatres like «Experimental Theatre Club La Mama» founded by E. Stuart, «Judson Poets Theatre» directed by E. Carmins, «Caf Chino» organized by J. Chino, and others were a stage for the American vanguard, a stage where young playwrights and producers used to try their powers, and their names became very famous by the 1980s.

It was at that very period that a process of de-centralization in USA theatre life was notably increased. If it was located mainly in New York before, then, from the later 1950s the so-called «regional theatres» came to life. The permanent professional theatres founded in many large cities began to play a significant role in the cultural life of America. The activities of these theatres, as a rule, were connected with the names of the well-known leading producers. The Washington theatre «Arena Stage» was for many years led by Z. Phichandler; «Gary Theatre» in Minneapolis was founded by a famous English producer T. Gatry; «Alley Theatre» in Houston was headed by H. Vans, followed by P. Brawn. «American Conservatory Theatre» in San-Francisco was very famous under the leadership of Y. Boll for many years; famous too were «Trinity Square Repertory Theatre» in Providence headed by A. Hall, «Center Theatre Group» located together with its head G. Davidson in the building «Mark Taper Forum» in Los Angeles Musical Center, and others. Different from Broadway with its every-day plays, the above theatres made up their repertoire for 9-10 months of a season with classical works and the works of young modern playwrights. They did not have permanent companies. The basic source of their financing was made up of voluntary donations and season tickets.

The American theatre of the 1980s continued to bear the marks of the artistic ideas born two decades earlier during a period of unprecedented theatrical boom in the country that never was before. And although the social-political atmosphere of the USA has completely changed, the ideas and strivings of those years still tell on the scenery creations nowadays. In the 1960s, which were marked with an increase of the democratic movement, with meetings and strikes, with a protest against the war in Vietnam, with a struggle for the civil rights of the black Americans, the so-called «theatres of protest» played a great role in relation to the questions of social and political life then current. «The theatres of protest», or «the radical theatres» as they are sometimes called, included groups of different aesthetic and social aims. They were also related with the off-Broadway experimental groups like «Living Theatre» (J. Beck and J. Malina as heads), «Open Theatre» (J. Chaikin as a head), «Performance Group» (R. Shehner as a head). Their activities were very much debated and assisted the new theatrical ideas to come such groups as «Bread and Puppet»,

«San-Francisco Mayam Group», «El Theatre Campesino», that later on became popular themselves; and semi-amateur street «partisan» groups initially set up for propaganda activity. The 1960s were also marked with an appearance of a large number of Negro theatres that is undoubtedly connected with a growth of the national self-consciousness of black Americans. The most well-known groups that have been in existence some decades are «Negro Ensemble» and «New Lafayette Theatre» staging the plays of L. Hansberry, Larroy Jones, E. Bullins, and others. Such actors as J. E. Jones, O. Davis, R. Dee, S. Puttee, and producers D. T. Word, D. Makbeth, D. O'Nill can be named in the same breath as the names of the most famous theatrical figures of the country.

A lot of theatres that appeared on the wave of the social movement of the 1960s ceased to exist in the 1970s, when the movement waned. However, their creative work enriched the creative colors of modern stage art, bringing new themes and ideas, making the beginning of any spectacle very active. The influence is sometimes not felt directly, but indirectly, and it tells on different aspects of modern theatrical life. And the expressive language of the latest dramatic art has also changed. The plays staged in the 1970s and 1980s of S. Shepherd, D. Mamet, D. Rabe, A. Coupit, J. Guarre, P. Jones, L. Wilson, A. Innuarato analyze American phenomena that influenced the formation of a generation. Many things were not expressed in the words and can be read apart from the dialogues. Such a tendency has found its extreme expression in the representatives of the American post-vanguard. In their plays, R. Foreman and R. Wilson, each of them functioning as text author, producer and designer at the same time, use a synthesis of different arts while avoiding traditional story-telling and dialogue on the stage, giving preference to the creation of artistically enciphered pictures and moving objects.

The actors and the producers of America work both in the Broadway theatres and in the «non-commercial» theatres. The face of the American theatre of the recent decade is determined with such producers as M. Nickels, J. Papp, A. Shnaider, E. Rabb, G. Prince, G. Davidson, A. Sherban, P. Cellars. The modern scene is rich with individual actors such as J. Scott, H. Kronin, A. Pachino, D. Hoffman, M. Patinkin, J. Malkovich, A. Bankroft, J. Page, J. Tandy, K. Dueherst, and others. In the 1980s Broadway continued to play an important role in a stage art of the country although it lost the dominating place that belonged to it before. The most popular plays were the comedies of N. Simon—a master of the so-called «well done» play. Flexible and mobile in essence, the «Broadway Theatre» adjusted and made commercial a number of the ideas, methods and tricks of experimental theatre. And from time to time it staged work devoted to socially significant problems.

Changes also occurred with such a specific Broadway genre as the musical. With rare exceptions a traditional musical constituted a huge magnificent show with easily remembered music, with beautiful dances and a very simple, rather primitive story. The musical is a very American theatrical genre. The best samples of it are «Oklahoma» (1943), «My beautiful lady» (1956), «Westside Story» (1957), «Hello, Dolly» (1964), «Fiddler on the roof» (1964). Over the last two decades new, uncharacteristic themes have frequently been brought into this «light» genre. At the end of the 1960s Broadway staged the musical «Hair» (1968, producer T. O'Horgan) a striking example of the assimilation of youth sub-culture by commercial art. The tragic faith of Negro women was described in the poetic spectacle «For the colored girls thinking of the suicide, when a rainbow ended» (1977, producer O. Scott). It was rather characteristic when there came a political musical «Evita» (1979, producer G. Prince). All records of the duration and cash taking were over taken by «Cordeballet» staged from 1975 (producer M. Bennett) where for the first time after «Westside Story» social problems were sharply highlighted with the example of the hard labor of an actor. The 1980s were rather different with the prevailing English drawing-room plays and a renewal of old shows, «retro-musicals». However, some hopes that the genre would be renovated were raised by the new musical «Great River» (1985, producer D. Mak-Enouff) based on the works of Mark Twain. As a whole these ten years did not bring any really new artistic ideas to the USA theatres.

Finance for the development of the USA theatre comes mainly from the donation organizations, in particular from Ford's Fund, Rockfeller's Fund, from the National Fund of Art, and from various corporations as well. However, the American theatres continue to suffer permanent financial difficulties.

In the USA stage education can be got at some special university faculties and also in the private studios. The Actors' Studio founded by the followers of Stanislavsky's system, E. Kazan, R. Louis and L. Strasberg, in 1947 takes a special place in the theatrical pedagogy of the USA. Over the years the Actors' Studio headed by L. Strasbourg has obtained a reputation as the most influential professional school nurturing «stars» for the American theatre and cinema.

The most popular theatre magazines are «American theatre», «Drama Review» and «Performing Arts Journal».

Religion in the USA[19]

There has never been a state church in the USA. Religion, according to the USA Constitution, is a private affair of the citizen. However, the principle is constantly violated—the government keeps chaplains in the Congress, in the army, in the navy, in prisons; church property is not taxed; the President swears on the Bible; the National motto is: «In God We Trust».

These constant violations of the principle of church separate from state are connected with the fact that in reality there is no mass atheism in the USA, as in most Western Europe countries. A poll reveals that 98 per cent of the Americans permanently say «Yes» to the question: «Do you believe in God?» Nearly 40 per cent of the population attends the church or synagogue every week; 68 per cent of Americans are formal member of Church communities, and 91 per cent identify themselves with this or that religious denomination. However, this rather high institutional religiosity mostly bears a formal character. The polls show a very low level of the knowledge about religion.

The USA characteristically displays a very high degree of religious pluralism. Whereas in the early phase of the United States existence this was a pluralism of various brands of Protestantism, now, after immigration by members of different religious traditions from all over the world and from different missionaries' activities, almost all religions are available in the USA. There are nearly 2,000 different religious organisations in the country.

Protestantism continues to be the main religious denomination in the USA. The Protestants comprise 57 per cent of the country's population, 74 per cent in the Southern states, 63 per cent in the mid-west. A preponderant majority of black Americans (82 per cent) are Protestants. Protestantism is divided into several different branches with a number of the churches belonging to each. The basis for their differences can be theological, organizational, religious, racial or in the ethnic composition of the flock.

One of the largest branches of American Protestantism (20 per cent of the population) is the Baptists, especially widespread in the South states both among whites and blacks. In second place, by number of followers (9 per cent) is Methodism. Baptists and Methodists are democratic in their composition; they were the basic religious affiliations of American farmers in the last Century. The Lutherans (7 per cent of the population) are mainly descendants of German and Scandinavian immigrants. Not so numerous, but more elite in social standing are the oldest denominations of American Protestantism:

---

19 The United States of America. Encyclopaedia Guide.

the Episcopalian Church—3 per cent (an American variant of Anglicanism), Presbyterians—2 per cent (Presbyterianism is the state church of Scotland), United Church of Christ—2 per cent (the church is a direct descendant of the churches of «fathers-pilgrims»—the founders of New England colonies in America). Orthodox Church—2 per cent. The others, less numerous denominations of Protestantism, nevertheless play an important role in American religious life—Mennonites, Pentecostalists, and others.

No less important for American Protestantism, than division by denomination is the difference between the Liberal churches that accept Biblical criticism and Evangelical and Fundamental Churches, which endorse literal reading of the Bible. The first have their followers in the higher social classes, and the second in the lower. The main Liberal Protestant Churches of different denominations together with a number of Orthodox Churches are members of the largest religious organization of the USA—the National Council of the Churches of Christ.

Catholicism is followed by 28 per cent of the USA population. They are mainly descendants of immigrants from the catholic countries of Europe in the North East of the country (44 per cent of the Northern-East population are Catholics). A considerable proportion of the workers in the largest industrial centers are Catholics. In recent years immigration of Spanish speaking Catholics from the Latin American countries has increased.

Judaism is followed by nearly 2 per cent of the population living mainly in the large cities, almost half in New York. A peculiar feature of American Judaism is the prevalence of the non-Orthodox, modern forms of Judaism—«Reformism», «Conservatism» and «Reconstructionism». The Jewish community is the richest and the most educated when compared with the other large communities. A very high social composition is characteristic of the non-Orthodox Jewish organizations. The Conformists are the poorest and the least educated ones.

Protestantism, Catholicism and Judaism are three basic religious directions, but *Orthodoxy,* also plays a notable role in the USA. There are 26 separate independent Orthodox Churches with different ethnic composition in the USA.

A number of religious tendencies have appeared first in America earth and can be attached to some aspect of Christianity; *Mormons*, for instance, who comprise a majority of the population in the state of Utah.

Various Eastern religions have established a strong presence in the USA over recent decades. *Islam* has been brought by immigrants and is widespread among the black population of the USA. Also available are immigrant communities of different branches of *Buddhism, Hinduism* and the *Sikh* religion. Buddhism and Hinduism are rather notably disseminated among the American professional classes. The political positions of the American churches are very various. Nevertheless, American clergy take left-liberal positions to a greater extent than the population as a whole.

Film Distribution in the USA[20]

Commercial distribution of films belongs to the large companies. The income from the distribution industry amounted to US $4.25 billion in 1987, (US $2,8 billion in 1979). The sharp growth in profits is connected with doubling the ticket price and an increase in the number of commercial hits that attract a young audience (80 per cent of the tickets sold are purchased by 20 per cent of the population only—by young people of 12-14 years old).

There were over 20,000 cinema halls in the USA by the mid 1980s. They are mostly the cinema halls of a usual type, however, there exist open cinema halls, where films can be watched without leaving the car, and cinema halls in large supermarkets, where shoppers can rest while watching a new film.

Film watching with videotapes increased sharply at the end of the 1970s, early 1980s. Twenty companies provide the stock of videotapes. The most popular videotapes can be bought in the large supermarkets, in drug stores and at newsagents. The repertoire of videotapes reached 14,000 names by the mid 1980s; nearly 400 new films are added every year. There were about 24 million VCRs in a personal use in the USA in the mid 1980s.

Not to loose out to this competition, the cinema exhibits films that secure the maximum financial return when shown in the cinemas. The films, especially thrillers and fantasies, employ very expensive techniques—computerized shooting, operator's tricks, electronic imprinting, unusual methods of the film development. More frequently and more openly we can now see scenes of violence and sex since the Hays Rules of decency were revised. The Rules now permit the showing of different sexual perversions and the most sadistic killings, etc. However, it is necessary to differentiate between shows of cruelty required to reveal the ideas and theme and its use to attract audiences and excite their nerves and feelings.

---

20 The United States of America. Encyclopaedia Guide.

TV Broadcasting in the USA[21]

TV Broadcasting in the USA is divided into commercial broadcasting playing the main role in the country's life and abroad, and non-commercial social TV. There were about 1200 TV stations in the USA in the mid 1980s, including over 860 commercial ones.

Experimental work in the field of TV was started in the USA in the 1920s. The 1930s saw the appearance of the first TV stations. In 1940 the Federal Commission on USA communication (FKC) approved a plan for the commercial development of TV with a standard scanning of 525 lines. And the first TV stations started regular programs for several hours daily in July 1941.

The Second World War hampered TV development. It was unprofitable in the first years after the War, when American TV was still in the making, but starting from 1951 it began to be profitable becoming a giant commercial enterprise.

While being founded, TV benefited from the commercial capabilities of American radio whose main companies provided financial and production backing for TV, accelerating its development. Three radio broadcasting corporations played a leading role in the development of American TV—the «National Broadcasting Company» (NBC), the «Columbia Broadcasting System» (CBS) and the later «American Broadcasting Company» (ABC), which united with the company «Capital Cities Communications» in 1985. These corporations formed the three main TV networks in the country and their productions fill up a main portion of the broadcasting time of the majority of TV stations in the USA.

American TV has developed and is developing under severe competition between the different forms of mass media and within TV itself; the struggle for profits augments year by year. Thus, at the beginning of the 1970s American TV as a whole had an annual income of US $3.5 billion, in the mid 1980s CBS alone obtained US $5 billion per annum. A main source of the profits of the TV corporations is advertising. The cost of this has accelerated very rapidly. One minute of advertising time costs US $500,000 in most of the popular programs. The 30-second «advertisement» has become the popular and widespread type. Combined advertising in which advertisements are owned by several customers is widespread as well and the general population constantly protest about the amount of advertising on TV.

---

21   The United States of America. Encyclopaedia Guide.

While obtaining great profits from advertising, the TV corporations make big profits from their other business activities namely, film and videotape production, publishing books and magazines, maintaining sport teams and also participating in the military production of the USA, in particular in the field of a missile manufacture.

Each of the leading corporations has its own stations—mostly in such cities as New York, Los Angeles, Chicago, San Francisco, Philadelphia, Saint Louis and Detroit. They are currently allowed to have 12 stations. Moreover, each of the corporations has got nearly 200 affiliates.

The financial interests of the three leading TV Networks are threatened by the existence and growing power of the so-called «independent» stations (i.e. not owned by any of the above TV networks). Their number has been constantly increasing and exceeded 200 by the mid 1980s. They cover over 80 per cent of USA territory with their broadcasting, making an income of over US $2 billion annually.

A fourth TV network opened in the USA in 1987—«Fox Broadcasting Company» (FBC) owned by R. Murdoch, a press magnate. However, it was initially at an experimental stage and only broadcasted for a few hours a week. Its full capacity was only put into operation at the beginning of the 1990s.

American TV is constantly in touch with its audience, investigating opinion after each successful program. There are special services for this, the most popular being Nelson's service and «Trendex». Each of the services has its own method of audience survey and of analyzing the statistical data. Nelson's service works best: every morning it informs the networks of the audience figures for this or that TV program. The program is deemed successful if it is watched by not less than one third of the total audience. If the figure falls below this, it is taken off the screen, advertisers would not be prepared to finance it.

American TV Broadcasting has the strongest technical basis of all TV organizations in the world, in particular, it has the biggest number of the channels, totaling 28 in large cities. However, all parts of the country usually receive up to four to five programs simultaneously. Broadcasting goes out practically 24 hours a day in the large cities. Nearly all the programs are in color (with the American system, NTSC). In 1987 87.4 million of American homes possessed TV sets, 82.7 million of these color. According to the Nelson service data, at the beginning of 1988 59 per cent of the homes received 15 programs and above, and 31 per cent received over 30 broadcast and cable programs.

Side by side with commercial TV there also exists a non-commercial, social TV. In 1952 the Federal Commission on USA communication gave 242 channels to the educational stations owned by universities, colleges and the social organizations of large cities. Their financial situation was very difficult, as they had to survive on the donations and support of charitable funds. In 1967 a decision of Congress combined all the stations into one organization named the «Public Broadcasting Service» (PBS), which was then given a specific grant from the government (the amount of the donation is regularly changed). However, the financial basis of the non-commercial TV still remains very weak as compared to a commercial one.

In its programs PBS lays special stress on films of a cultural-educational content and on classical works, particularly English films.

PBS had nearly 300 stations in the mid 1980s.

The second direction of American TV development is cable TV (CATV). It operates on the principle of a co-operative antenna and a coaxial network.

The first cable systems came into being in Pennsylvania and Oregon in 1949 as a technical device for improving TV reception in the mountains. The development of cable TV was very rapid in the 1960s, and in the 1970s cable TV entered the large cities.

Among the cable systems responsible for the technical side, «TelePrompTer» (founded in 1967) and «American Television and Communications» (ATV, founded in 1968) took a leading role. Each of them has over a million clients. Another four systems—«General Electric Cable», «Telecommunications», «Warner AMEX» and «Times Mirror»—have taken third, fourth, fifth and sixth places.

In the sphere of program production there are two large companies in the lead—«Home Box Office» (HBO, founded in 1972) and «Show Time» (founded in 1978). The first has over 9 million subscribers, the second nearly 4 million.

Initially a main source of income for cable TV was a subscription payment. This meant that the programs could be shown without any advertising and this was very popular with the audience. But in the process of its development Cable TV went over to commercial principles and advertising was put in. Viewers eager to watch the programs without any advertising had to make an additional payment. Hence, paid TV was born. The first paid stations appeared in 1971. They functioned as follows: every month a subscriber paid US $8-10 above the usual payment, and for this amount of money he/she was shown several films, sports games, etc. But meanwhile a new form sprang up, where a payment was not made monthly, but for every separate program watched. A small counter was attached to every subscriber's TV set to count the programs watched. A bill then followed. And the «menu» included the programs requested by viewers.

The success of cable TV has upset the commercial networks who began a severe struggle against it. CATV can give an audience advantages not available from commercial TV: a high quality picture and a wide selection of programs—and these are not the only advantages of cable TV. Theatre, sports and cinema are reluctant to give commercial TV addressed to and its popular audience rights to show films, shows, etc., that normally attract large numbers of people to stadiums and theatres. The limited audience of CATV is of no serious danger for them, and thus the cable TV and show-businessmen have close contacts.

One more advantage of CATV is that it is able to create the programs meant for a narrow, specialized audience. Specialized channels have come into being for sports, music, health, etc.

A lot of changes occurred in the sphere of information, as well: On the 1 June, 1980 a cable information channel «Cables News Network» (CNN) started its operation in Atlanta, and channel CNN-II was started on the 31 December, 1981; it was re-named «Headline News» later. They are both owned by millionaire businessman, T. Turner, and they aim to provide TV information of all types, 24 hours a day.

Pornography takes a prominent place in the CATV specialization. So-called «adult» films are shown on CATV under the names of «the Blue Night» and others. In the 1980s, specialized services have come into being—«Intimate viewing» and «Playboy»—a creation of the magazine of the same name.

A peculiar feature of CATV is the establishment of a two-side connection between the viewer and the transmitting station. This circumstance causes a lot of Americans much anxiety: the cable TV could become the means of «an electronic shadowing» by FBI and CIA.

At present cable TV offers over 30 channels. Equipment capable of receiving up to 100 channels is in process of elaboration. 52 per cent of American houses received cable TV by the beginning of the 1980s.

Active development of cable TV became possible due to the use of satellite communication. Programs transmitted on air by satellite through cable and commercial networks can be received by personal TV sets, provided a special antenna is installed.

The USA TV is the largest in the world. It produces many times more TV production than any other countries in Western Europe, Asia, Africa and Latin America. A peculiar feature of the American TV programs is the preference given to entertainment programs: 70-80 per cent of the whole volume of the transmitted programs. The proportion of social-political broadcasting amounts to a mere 10-20 per cent of the time.

Every-day TV programs can be provisionally divided into three time slots: morning-daytime (from 6.00 till 19.30), evening (from 19.30 till 23.30) and night (from 23.30 till 6.00). Such a division is based upon the character of the programs. The morning-daytime block is filled up with programs for women and children—serials, games and competitions, cartoon films.

The evening block is mainly filled up with serial films like westerns, detectives and domestic comedies. Apart from serial programs with a steady place in the programs for months, the evening block entertaining shows and provides feature films. As a whole, the evening block program consists mainly of the shows and pictures of previous years. Its programs are meant for a mixed audience. The number of programs meant for children (sports, education and scientific) increase their output on Saturdays and Sundays. A necessary ingredient of the Sunday programs is religion.

As a rule the news programs last 30 minutes on TV. The main evening news are named after the network—«News CBS», «News NBC», etc. They are made by qualified personnel and by political commentators, whose opinions are respected by the audience. Apart from the evening news, every network has its own morning news appearing on the screen at 7 am. A number of other informational programs exist and news that give national and international news to the audience all day long and in the evening while giving preference to sensationalism.

The dependence of American TV on large capital investment inevitably has implications for the content of the programs transmitted: they are determined by the position of the American ruling circles. They propagandize «an American way of life» and stereotype «popular culture».

GDP of the USA Underestimated by US$ 1500 Billion
Spare Time of Population as a Resource

Some years ago I looked through the works of two American professors CAMPBELL R. McCONNELL & STANLEY L. BRUE "Economics, principles, problems, and policies." I was interested in how they have solved the problem of spare time in the frame of the American economic theory. They declared that the "increased volume of spare time, naturally, has had a very positive effect on our well-being.

However, a social accounting system of the USA doesn't reflect complete well being for it doesn't consider the circumstances".[22]

This is the most expensive resource of a society as it constitutes the spare time that we can spend as to our consideration and will. The resource of spare time of an individual comes to 125000—130000 hours for a period of 60 years.

For instance, as per the preliminary calculations, the USA adult population spare time resource came to 900 billion man-hours and if accounting for the children as well a total resource is estimated at 1500 billion man-hours per annum. It should be noted that the borders of the resource are considerably expanded in terms of mass unemployment due to reduction in working time.

A resource of the population spare time is a social wealth. The assertion has strongly entered our mind, and not only as a saying. Really the spare time of the population is a wealth of a society and it should compose its result, i.e. a Gross Domestic Product (GDP). However, so far its inclusion into an aggregate result of the activities of the people of a region, a town is missing. Lack of the intellectual services in the Gross Domestic Product creates many problems in an entire set of the social-economic targets of development. For instance, it is not clear what portion of the population's spare time constitutes a society wealth and what portion of the same does not?

What direction should we take while improving a structure of the population spare time being a society wealth? We will not succeed in considerable improvements of effectiveness to the planning, organizing and administrating of the intellectual sphere branches without well-defined replies to the questions above.

An analysis of the literature reveals that economists have not reached any single opinion as to what makes up a purposeful guide-line for the branches as "Education", "Enlightenment", "Culture", "Art", Sport-entertainment", "Church", "Film distribution", "TV" and "Radio Broadcasting". The branches above utilize such indices as "man-visit", "man-service", "man-place", "man-lecture", "man-show", "TV-viewer", "Radio-listener" as a unit of measurement to estimate the results of their activities. Should a "man-visit" index and the same be used as a social guide-line, it reflects a fact of the involvement of an individual and population into a process of the intellectual servicing only. And nothing else. Meanwhile, lack of an adequate social index of functioning of the institutions under consideration leads to inaccuracies in the statistics. For instance, "a man-visit" can be a 30-minutes or two-hours. The statistics

---

22 "Economics: Principles, Problems, and Policies" Campbell R. McConnell, Stanley L. Brue (p. 142)

treats these two different values as identical and equal. Such an inadequate reflection of the development results of the non-material-intellectual sphere enterprises leads to negative economic and social consequences.

Moreover, they distort an entire industrial economic mechanism. And the most wistful is that they divert the researchers' attention from an estimation of the actual economic tendencies taking place in them. A conclusion is possible, that "a man-visit" index and the rest of this kind can not serve as an economic guide-line of development for the economic branches under consideration and thus, they are to be related to "intermediate estimations".

Assimilated Resourse of Spare Time of Population as a Purposeful Social Indicator

I propose "time of intellectual servicing of the population" or duration of the intellectual services consumption by population to be used as a natural measure and an absolute indicator of the intellectual sphere enterprises' activities. This unit of measure of the activities of the servicing branches is the only one possible and natural measure.

The intellectual services are not possible to be measured with metres, kilograms or other indices but only with the time of consumption of the intellectual services by individuals. The services are discrete and continuous. Their amount depends upon a number of persons involved into a process of the intellectual servicing, upon the quality of its production technology, a state of the capital assets, labor resources and preparedness of the visitors-listeners to consume the services. Moreover, activities of the intellectual sphere enterprises are directed to generalize activities of the population different groups at their spare time. As to my opinion, it is just the above stated that makes up "a measure of a society wealth".

The assimilated resource of the population spare time comes out as the target that the intellectual sphere branches should implement hourly, daily and annually expanding a level of generalizing the population activities at its spare time. Utilisation of a time indicator while estimating activities of the said branches enterprises softens different quality of the services to the population, their specific character, and it leads to a unique and single measurability. I am sure to be opposed that my suggestion to use a time parameter to determine an absolute volume of the intellectual production services is open to question.

From the very beginning I would like to draw your attention that the economics treat working time of the population as a resource being constantly calculated and analysed. However, at the same time, spare time of an individual and of the population has not so far been considered as a resource constantly present which is, as any other resource, to be assimilated using special means and instruments of labour, different from those of the material sphere of production. A speech, a song, a dance and a musical show constitute a special technology of the population spare time assimilation. I propose the resource ASTP to be assimilated and mastered as any other resource, i.e. oil, gas, coal, gold, and it should be mastered with its own special instruments of labour such as musical instruments and others.

Assimilation and mastering of the resources is not something farfetched; for instance, a coal industry determines an annual volume of the resource explored with open, closed and other methods, resource deposits and its non-mastered portion are found out. The same occurs in the oil industry. Thus, for example, an oil resource of the Caspian region is estimated at 20 bln. In other words, every resource has got its geological maps of deposits, its potential reserves are evaluated, etc.

Consideration of the resource takes an important significance in terms of sex, age, education and other population factors. It is deemed to be necessary to make up the "topographic maps" of the potential resource of the population spare time of an area, a region, a town, on one hand, and, on the other one, to set up the borders of its assimilation, i.e. which portion of STP is assimilated and which one is not mastered yet. The above stated is a very important social-economic problem.

In terms of an economic crisis potential borders of the population spare time resource can reach their critical values. If the resource is in plenty in a society, its non-utilisation and non-assimilation could lead to unpredictable consequences. On one hand, a volume of STP resource, both its assimilated and non-assimilated portions, comes out as a social indicator of a society well-being, and, on the other one, it comes out as an indicator reflecting a social crisis. A deliberate formation of the borders between an assimilated portion and nonassimilated one of the resource in a society meets a lot of economic problems; first and foremost, a problem with establishing priorities and volumes of capital investments into "Enlightenment", "Education" branches targeting to increase an educational level of the population and capital investments into "show-sphere" branches to entertain the population. Solution of the problems needs a theoretical basis that assists to maintain arithmetic calculations (composition and subtraction of the indices, setting up absolute and relative economic characteristic features linked with the assimilation of the population spare time resource). It's an elaboration of the economic structure of an intellectual service to be started with, elaboration of its components, and elaboration of the economic foundation for a cost of an intellectual product created by a society per annum.

Insertion of the assimilated resource of STP (or an absolute volume of the intellectual services) as one of the components of an aggregate result of activities of a region, a town completely corresponds to an elementary economic logic. It should be noted that another portion of the population spare time that remains out of a socially arranged process of the intellectual sphere enterprises' activities does not come out as "Wealth of a society".

There are more than enough reasons to insert a spare time resource into the cost of an intellectual service:—first, the production of an intellectual service is not possible without assimilation of the resource of population spare time, otherwise the service would not be implemented;—second, the consumption of an intellectual service takes place while in process of its creation;—third, phases of starting and ending of the intellectual service production coincide with the same phases of consumption;—fourth, exclusion of A_{STP} out of the cost evaluation of the services is a big theoretical mistake, which considerably reduces intellectual and entire level of the population welfare. And it is quite natural the mistake is to be corrected.

Cost Evaluation of the Population Spare Time Resource

A resource of spare time of population (STP) assimilated by the intellectual sphere branches is a wealth of a society as any other resource (oil, gas, coal mastered by the material production branches). And as any wealth, STP has got its cost. What is the cost? It is not an easy task to determine a cost of STP resource. Spare time has got an inner structure as in terms of age, sex, education, etc.:

1) spare time of children of pre-school and school age;

2) spare time of students;

3) spare time of the working part of population, etc.

Each of the above is to be evaluated and their own special ratios to be set up to transfer time parameters into the cost ones. Cost of the resource is naturally decreased in terms of mass unemployment, and a cost of the population spare time hour considerably increases in terms of complete maximum employment. While evaluating an assimilated resource of the population spare time, the circumstance is to be accounted that "Education" branch masters spare time of population aiming to give professional training required for a person to be involved in a socially arranged production process of values and services. Another portion of the population spare time resource is assimilated by enterprises of the "show-sphere" consisting of "Sport-Entertaining", "Culture", "Art", "Film distribution", "Church", "TV and Radio Broadcasting".

Cost Evaluation of the Intellectual Services in the USA

The volumes of the assimilated resource of the USA population spare time are as follows as per each group:

- children pre-school institutions 20 bln. man-hours;
- secondary schools 39 bln. man-hours;
- universities 9,2 bln. man-hours;
- TV and Radio Broadcasting 170 bln. man-hours;

Total: 238,2 bln. man-hours

Should one suppose a film distribution and a system of the church institutions to master 10-12 billion man-hours per annum, a whole volume of the spare time resource assimilated in the USA came to 250 billion man-hours in 1990. The minimum salary was USD 3,35 per a working hour that year. The cost evaluation of the assimilated spare time resource is calculated as below:

250 billion man-hours X USD 3.35 = USD 837,5 billion.

The value is to be added with the past labour expenses and wages of the employees producing the intellectual services. In 1990 the expenses on education came to about USD 250 billion plus the expenses of the branches of "Culture", "Art", "Sport-entertainment", "Church", "Film Distribution", "TV Broadcasting" and "Radio Broadcasting", which are approximately estimated at USD 150 billion.

Summing up a cost of the resource of the USA population spare time assimilated by the branches producing the intellectual services and the expenses at amount of USD 400 billion, a total cost of an immaterial product of the intellectual sphere is estimated at USD 1237,5 billion in 1990 and USD 1462.5 billion in 1999. The same comes to 15—20% of the USA GDP. Thus, the conception proposed by myself to measure the show services makes it possible:

First: to calculate an immaterial portion of the Gross Domestic Product (GDP) produced in the intellectual sphere;

Second: to eliminate a considerable gap in calculations of GDP for the USA and many a country including.

Attachment 1

On Liberty
by John Stuart Mill

From the Publisher

Published in 1859, John Stuart Mill's On Liberty presented one of the most eloquent defenses of individual freedom in nineteenth-century social and political philosophy and is today perhaps the most widely-read liberal argument in support of the value of liberty. Mill's passionate advocacy of spontaneity, individuality, and diversity, along with his contempt for compulsory uniformity and the despotism of popular opinion, has attracted both admiration and condemnation.

About the Author:

John Stuart Mill was born in a suburb of London on May 20, 1806. By the age of ten he was reading classical authors in the original Greek and Latin, was proficient in history, algebra, and geometry, and soon after began to study logic, political economy, and law. He was elected to Parliament in 1865 and held the Radical seat for Westminster for the next three years. Mill died in Avignon, France, on May 7, 1873.

The Debates of Liberty: An Overview of Individualist Anarchism, 1881-1908
by Wendy McElroy

From the Publisher

Wendy McElroy provides a comprehensive examination of one of the most remarkable and influential political phenomenons in America: the anarchist periodical Liberty and the circle of radicals who surrounded it.

Synopsis

Having published an index of American journalist Benjamin Tuckers' periodical Liberty in 1982, McElroy here explores its expression of the political philosophy that inspired it. She looks at Tucker's background, the state and politics, violence, egoism versus natural rights, children's rights, intellectual property, trial by jury, and the money debate. Annotation (c)2003 Book News, Inc., Portland, OR

The Ethics of Liberty
by Murray N. Rothbard, Hans-Hermann Hoppe, Hans-Hermann Hoppe (Introduction)

From the Publisher

In recent years, libertarian impulses have increasingly influenced national and economic debates, from welfare reform to efforts to curtail affirmative action. Long out of print, Murray N. Rothbard's classic The Ethics of Liberty stands as one of the most rigorous and philosophically sophisticated expositions of the libertarian political position. What distinguishes Rothbard's book is the manner in which it roots the case for freedom in the concept of natural rights and applies it to a host of practical problems. An economist by profession, Rothbard here proves himself equally at home with philosophy. And while his conclusions are radical—that a social order that strictly adheres to the rights of private property must exclude the institutionalized violence inherent in the state—his applications of libertarian principles prove surprisingly practical for a host of social dilemmas, solutions to which have eluded alternative traditions. The Ethics of Liberty authoritatively established the anarcho-capitalist economic system as the most viable and the only principled option for a social order based on freedom. The current edition is newly indexed and includes a new introduction that takes special note of the Robert Nozick-Rothbard controversies.

Author Biography: The author of numerous books, the late Murray N. Rothbard (1926-1995) was the S. J. Hall Distinguished Professor of Economics at the University of Nevada, Las Vegas, and Academic Vice President of the Ludwig von Mises Institute. Hans-Hermann Hoppe is Professor of Economics at the University of Nevada, Las Vegas.

From The Critics

Booknews

In his new introduction to this current edition of this classic in the field originally published in 1982 (Humanities Press), Hoppe (economics, U. of Nevada, Las Vegas<—>as was the late author) extols Rothbard's marriage of the "value-free" science of economics with the normative enterprise of ethics and their offspring: libertarianism. Discussion areas are: natural law, a theory of liberty, the state vs. liberty, modern alternative theories of liberty, and toward a theory of strategy for liberty. Annotation c. by Book News, Inc., Portland, Or.

Active Liberty: Interpreting Our Democratic Constitution
by Stephen Breyer

From the Publisher

This book, based on the Tanner lectures on Human Values that Justice Stephen Breyer delivered at Harvard University in November 2004, defines the term "active liberty" as a sharing of the nation's sovereign authority with its citizens. Regarding the Constitution as a guide for the application of basic American principles to a living and changing society rather than as an arsenal of rigid legal means for binding and restricting it, Justice Breyer argues that the genius of the Constitution rests not in any static meaning it might have had in a world that is dead and gone, but in the adaptability of its great principles to cope with current problems.

Giving us examples of this approach in the areas of free speech, federalism, privacy, affirmative action, statutory interpretation, and administrative law, Justice Breyer states that courts should take greater account of the Constitution's democratic nature when they interpret constitutional and statutory texts. He also insists that the people, through participation in community life, can and must develop the experience necessary to govern their own affairs. His distinctive contribution to the federalism debate is his claim that deference to congressional power can actually promote democratic participation rather than thwart it. He argues convincingly that although Congress is not perfect, it has done a better job than either the executive or judicial branches at balancing the conflicting views of citizens across the nation, especially during times of national crisis. With a fine appreciation for complexity, Breyer reminds all Americans that Congress, rather than the courts, is the place to resolve policy disputes.

Active Liberty is a declaration of the first importance, made by a judge often regarded as one of the court's most brilliant members.

Three Pillars of Liberty
by Francesca Klug, Keir Starmer (Editor), Stuart Weir (Editor)

From the Publisher

The Three Pillars of Liberty is a landmark study on the state of democracy in the UK. The book identifies 44 violations and 19 near violations of human rights laws. It provides an up-to-date description of law and practice with respect of freedom of information, freedom of expression, freedom of assembly and public protest, freedom of association and trade unionism, state surveillance, the right to life and liberty, and the right to vote and stand in elections. It measures political freedom against the "Human Rights Index," an important tool for monitoring human rights around the world.

The first-ever analysis of both the political and legal systems for securing political freedom in the UK as a whole, it is the most rigorous and systematic review of those systems yet published, and it finds them lacking. It strikes at the heart of the historic traditions of government and the rule of law in the UK. It will be essential reading for all those interested in their rights and the rights of others.

The Subject of Liberty: Toward a Feminist Theory of Freedom
by Nancy J. Hirschmann

From the Publisher

This book reconsiders the dominant Western understandings of freedom through the lens of women's real-life experiences of domestic violence, welfare, and Islamic veiling. Nancy Hirschmann argues that the typical approach to freedom found in political philosophy severely reduces the concept's complexity, which is more fully revealed by taking such practical issues into account.

Hirschmann begins by arguing that the dominant Western understanding of freedom does not provide a conceptual vocabulary for accurately characterizing women's experiences. Often, free choice is assumed when women are in fact coerced—as when a battered woman who stays with her abuser out of fear or economic necessity is said to make this choice because it must not be so bad—and coercion is assumed when free choices are made—such as when Westerners assume that all veiled women are oppressed, even though many Islamic women view veiling as an important symbol of cultural identity.

Understanding the contexts in which choices arise and are made is central to understanding that freedom is socially constructed through systems of power such as patriarchy, capitalism, and race privilege. Social norms, practices, and language set the conditions within which choices are made, determine what options are available, and shape our individual subjectivity, desires, and self-understandings. Attending to the ways in which contexts construct us as "subjects" of liberty, Hirschmann argues, provides a firmer empirical and theoretical footing for understanding what freedom means and entails politically, intellectually, and socially.

Liberty & Liberalism: A Protest Against The Growing Tendency Toward Undue Interference By The State, With Individual Liberty, Private Enterprise, And

by Bruce Smith

Product Details
ISBN: 160206038X
ISBN-13: 9781602060388
Format: Paperback, 460pp
Publisher: Cosimo Classics

Fundamental Liberties and Rights: A 50-State Index
by Barbara Faith Sachs

Product Details
ISBN: 0379204134
ISBN-13: 9780379204131
Format: Ringbound, 1pp
Publisher: Oceana Publications

About the Author

S. S. Khrystenko was born on May 28, 1954. He graduated from the economic faculty of The Politechnic Institute in 1976. He finished his postgraduate studies specializing in political economy. He published his first book in 1989. Today, he has published ten monographs and prepared for publishing a new book: *A Periodic Table of Economic Elements vol. 1, vol. 2.*

978-0-595-43412-1
0-595-43412-6

www.ingramcontent.com/pod-product-compliance
Lightning Source LLC
Chambersburg PA
CBHW022245290526
45785CB00015B/245